Praise for *Expanding Your Power*

"This is the book I wish I had in every executive transition. Marsha offers not just wisdom, but a powerful toolkit—one that helps leaders expand their influence while staying grounded in authenticity and inclusion. A must-read for anyone serious about transformational leadership."

—**Jeff Bettinger,** 3x CHRO and founder of myjobjump.com

"Jam-packed with rich and practical information. Marsha Clark provides a roadmap for aspiring female leaders. That is enough to make this a must-read, but even more important, her experience, wisdom, and warmth shine through as personal support from someone who has been there and who cares deeply."

—**Ethan Schutz,** president and CEO, The Schutz Company

"Reading this felt like a trusted conversation with a brilliant friend who's been in the trenches and knows exactly how to help you rise. Marsha offers real tools, honest stories, and the kind of insight every woman in leadership deserves. If you're ready to grow your influence, own your voice, and expand your power . . . start right here."

—**Judy Hoberman,** executive coach and Mastermind facilitator for women

"Marsha Clark has crafted an engaging book that invites leaders to actively participate in their own growth while reading. She offers thoughtful prompts and reflection points, encouraging readers to examine their personal experiences/trauma that may affect team dynamics. This powerful approach not only deepens self-awareness but also provides a practical roadmap for evolving and enhancing one's leadership journey."

—**Lisa Tran,** Ed.D., managing director of Corporate Engagement & Strategic Partnerships, SMU Cox School of Business

"She's done it again! Marsha has written another book that doesn't just empower—it ignites. One of the best quotes in the book is this one: 'What is the difference between therapy and coaching? Therapy is looking back and asking why; coaching is looking ahead and asking how.' Another must-read for anyone ready to reclaim their power and step fully into their potential."

—Chris Arnold, Dallas Mavericks emcee and inclusion ambassador, Texas Radio Hall of Fame 2020

"For decades, Marsha Clark has helped women step fully into their power, not with theory but with tools that work. Every chapter in this book is a coaching session, a workshop, and a mirror. If you lead a team or aspire to, you won't just read this book. You'll return to it again and again."

—Eugina Jordan, CEO and cofounder of YOUnifiedAI

A Woman's Opportunity to Inspire Teams
& Influence Organizations

EXPANDING *Your* POWER

MARSHA L. CLARK

GREENLEAF
BOOK GROUP PRESS

Published by Greenleaf Book Group Press
Austin, Texas
www.gbgpress.com

Distributed by Greenleaf Book Group

For ordering information or special discounts for bulk purchases, please contact Greenleaf Book Group at PO Box 91869, Austin, TX 78709, 512.891.6100.

Design and composition by Greenleaf Book Group and Teresa Muñiz
Cover design by Greenleaf Book Group and Teresa Muñiz
Image 4.2 used under license from © Adobe Stock/jesadaphorn
Figure 6.1 image used under license from © Adobe Stock/istry

Publisher's Cataloging-in-Publication data is available.

Print ISBN: 979-8-88645-190-0

eBook ISBN:979-8-88645-191-7

To offset the number of trees consumed in the printing of our books, Greenleaf donates a portion of the proceeds from each printing to the Arbor Day Foundation. Greenleaf Book Group has replaced over 50,000 trees since 2007.

Printed in the United States of America on acid-free paper

25 26 27 28 29 30 31 32 10 9 8 7 6 5 4 3 2 1

First Edition

Grateful acknowledgement is made to the following for permission to use copyrighted material:

- **Michelle Bogan:** "The Many Dimensions of Diversity Wheel." All rights reserved.
- **Juliet Bourke and Bernadette Dillon:** From "The Six Signature Traits of Inclusive Leadership." Copyright © 2016 by Juliet Bourke and Bernadette Dillon.
- **Chris Drew, PhD:** From "The 9 Types of Stereotypes (A Guide for Students)." https://helpfulprofessor.com/wp-content/uploads/2021/10/The-9-Types-of-Stereotypes-A-Guide-for-Students-Helpful-Professor-Answers.pdf.
- **Sue Hammond and the ELI Group:** Group Trust Model. www.theeligroup.com.
- **Becky Hemsley:** "Handle with Care" from *Letters from Life: Words to Feed Your Heart and Soul.* Copyright (c) 2023 by Becky Hemsley. All rights reserved.
- **Oriah "Mountain Dreamer" House:** From "The Invitation" from Oriah "Mountain Dreamer" House's book *THE INVITATION* © 1999. Published by HarperONE. All rights reserved. Presented with permission of the author. www.oriah.org.
- **The Organization Workshop Leaders Guide:** Material from chapters 8 and 9. Copyright © by Power + Systems Inc., Boston, MA 2009.
- **Clare Rolquin, MSW, LCSW-A:** From "Unhealed Trauma: Signs, Impacts, & How to Heal," https://www.choosingtherapy.com/unhealed-trauma/. Copyright (c) 2004.
- **Ethan Schutz:** For material from chapter 5. Copyright © 2024 Business Consultants, Inc. Japan. For more information on The Human Element®, go to thehumanelement.com. Thank you to Ethan Schutz and TSC for their assistance in editing and updating these materials. *The Human Element®* and Element B® are copyrighted by Business Consultants, Inc. FIRO-B is copyrighted by The Myers-Briggs Company. The Human Element® is copyright © 1994 by Will Schutz under International, Pan American, and Universal Copyright Conventions. All rights reserved.

Dedicated to Every Woman who aspires to be a great leader and make the world a better place for girls and women.

CONTENTS

INTRODUCTION

And the story continues. Here I am, writing a second book that reflects the leadership needed to inspire teams and influence organizations. In my first book, *Embracing Your Power: A Woman's Path to Authentic Leadership & Meaningful Relationships*, I focused on greater self-awareness to maximize authentic leadership as well as behaviors and tools that lead to meaningful relationships. This book will guide you to expand upon what you learned in that book. As my teaching continues to evolve and I enter my seventh decade of life, I have designed an offering that will keep my teaching available and accessible. I invite you to think about my two books as companion books for a comprehensive approach to powerful and authentic leadership development. The first book focuses on self-awareness and interpersonal relationships, and this second book focuses on team dynamics and organizational systems. In addition, I am launching a self-study training program that links my books to my podcasts and to my videos. If interested, you can learn more about that on my website: marshaclarkandassociates.com.

For those who have read the first book, you know that my writing is an outcome of having delivered a nineteen-day leadership program for women for more than twenty years, entitled the Power of Self. I have delivered variations of this program to thousands of women around the world. I have learned so much from the women who have put themselves out there, being vulnerable and exploring their capabilities as authentic and powerful female leaders. A clear message in my writing, teaching, and coaching is to support women in defining success on their own terms. I have learned that you first have to acknowledge you have power and understand that power before you can embrace it.

Now, I'm going to take you beyond embracing your power to expanding your power. This book is for all the women who are leading teams—across different professions, functions, and many industries, and both small and large teams. It is also for the women who have a "seat at the table" or aspire to have a seat at the table. Remember, once you have a seat, scoot over and pull up a chair for another woman. Here's to women supporting women!

PART 1

EMBRACING YOUR POWER

CHAPTER 1

EMBRACING YOUR POWER

I want to start this book by sharing the ending of my last book—with a poem.

"Embrace Your Own Greatness"

Live your life through your own eyes
Hold close your grandest vision of yourself
Do not compromise your greatness for another's vision
Express your own soul
You owe nothing to another
Only to yourself
Be honest with yourself and your desires
Speak of your highest thoughts
Be all you held in your childhood dreams
No one can take away your power
Unless you are the one to give it away
Walk with your head held high

So you can see everything clearly
Decide daily who you wish to be
Create your own moments with wisdom
Carve out your future with clarity
Become your desires
Expand your horizons
Leave yesterdays behind
Run toward tomorrow
Change your mind often
Learn how to flow with the river
Close your eyes and let life take you
Go where your heart leads
Never give up
Don't believe that mistakes are destroyers of life
See them as gifts for future success
Dance on rainbows
Meet fairies
Sing with angels
And always give thanks
For the treasure that is life

—Lynette Ann Lane

I can't begin to tell you how much I love this poem. I read it at the graduation of the Power of Self program, classes two through twenty. A program participant from class two gave me this poem, which is why I didn't read it at the graduation of class one.

As women, we get so many messages that we are not enough and, at other times, that we are too much. Living our lives through our own eyes—defining success on our own terms—is central to being our best, most authentic selves. We will never be enough trying to please everyone else. In order to live our best lives, we create our grand vision based on living out our dreams. We are enough. *You* are enough.

An especially important part of this poem that speaks so loudly to me is "No one can take away your power . . . unless you are the one to give it away." This is one of the first lessons I teach in every program. It isn't about positional or hierarchical power based on a job title or a box on an organization chart. Someone gives you that power and, therefore, can also take it away. It is not about relational power where you choose to partner with someone to accomplish something neither of you could achieve on your own. It is about your personal power—that inside-out power. It comes from within you. You hold on to that power by being clear, thoughtful, and intentional. You know and live your grand vision. You live fully and learn.

In that spirit of learning, here are my favorite learning agility questions:

1. What did I do?
2. What did I learn?
3. How will this help me going forward?

We all know that life brings us many ups and downs. I believe that one of the most important life and leadership competencies is perspective. By being clear on who you are and what you want to accomplish, by being thoughtful and intentional in your actions, by learning and growing, and by reflecting and asking yourself these learning agility questions, you gain perspective. You don't sweat the small stuff. You give yourself time and respond with thoughtfulness and clarity. You hold on to your power. Your true power comes from not letting someone else define you. You are the author of your own story. You are not perfect. You are human. That includes being vulnerable, admitting mistakes, and giving yourself and others grace and space for being human.

In order to embrace your power, you have to acknowledge that you have power. You then have to understand what that power is for you. This starts with self-awareness, which is the will and the skill to understand yourself and how others see you.

Self-aware people possess the following insights:

- The values and principles that guide their lives
- Their passions—those things that bring them joy and help them live a purposeful life
- Their goals and aspirations to live a fulfilling life
- A clear view of the best place for them—an environment or culture
- Clarity of their patterns, defaults, and strengths
- Clarity on how they want to show up and the impact they have on others

REFLECTION

- How well do you know these things about yourself?

- How do you think others see you?

- What work do you want to do to better align how others see you and how you see yourself?

When I am working with coaching clients, I almost always ask them about their self-awareness. Many tell me they are pretty self-aware. They may know their patterns and defaults. Some can articulate their values and aspirations. Some are still trying to discover their passions or find that best-fit culture or environment. I encourage you to get clear. The clearer you are, the more intentional you can be in living the best version of yourself.

I also want to emphasize that the point about being very aware of our impact on others is one of the big gaps. As the English translation of the great eighteenth-century Scottish poet and songwriter Robert Burns's famous line goes, "Oh would some Power the gift give us, to see ourselves as others see us." Solicit feedback and take it in, ask questions, explore new and different people and situations, and notice. That last item—*notice*—elicits one of my one-liners (often referred to as "Marsha-isms"): "Notice what you notice."

SELF-AWARENESS

Here are some questions to ponder.

ACTIVITY

- How much airtime do you occupy in conversations?

____

- How much of your conversations are focused on your story?

____

- How often in your conversations do you ask questions or invite the other person(s) to share their story?

____

____

continued

- How adept are you at "reading the room" or interpreting nonverbal signals or body language (e.g., rolling of the eyes, crossed arms, disengagement)?

- What can you do to help yourself recognize when you are blind to or not paying attention to how others are experiencing you?

I hope you will indulge me in sharing my thoughts regarding living your best life. For me, it is living a purposeful life. It has been my journey to live and discover the answer to this question: What is my purposeful life?

I call myself a social justice warrior. I can clearly recognize that there were two main life experiences that led to this moniker. I had a special needs sister, Erin, who wasn't like the rest of us. She wore diapers and drank from a bottle until she died at the age of eighteen. She taught me so much. The most important lesson was unconditional love. She didn't have the ability to speak her thoughts and feelings, yet I always knew she appreciated my love and care. Many people made fun of Erin because of her special needs. I became a fierce protector—a warrior for her safety.

I also grew up at a time in history when women's rights left much to be desired. The opportunities to live my best life were not as available, and I was often a "first" or one of the few to achieve certain outcomes as a woman. And that's where the "social justice" part of my moniker was learned. I want to be and strive to be a compassionate supporter and leader. I learned some years ago that my name, *Marsha*, means "warlike, or dedicated to Mars, the Roman god of war."[1] I suppose I am living out my name, and I'm okay with that.

I also want to share my thoughts about being compassionate. I recently read a *Harvard Business Review* article entitled "Connect with Empathy but Lead with Compassion." The authors described four levels along two axes: "willingness to act to support" (the vertical axis) and the "understanding of the other's experience" (the horizontal axis).[2] At the lowest level, we pity or *feel sorry for* the other person. At the next higher level, we have sympathy or *feel for* the other person. At the next higher level, we have empathy or *feel with* the other person. And at the highest level, we have compassion or the highest level of *understanding* and the *willingness* to act, show our support, and *help* the other person.

I can't know what it was like to be my sister Erin. Pity and sympathy weren't enough. I wanted to act to help her. The same is true in other areas. I can't know what it is like to walk in the shoes of a woman of color, a woman who has experienced spousal abuse, or a woman who has been raped. What I can do is support and help those women with unconditional love and compassion. Each of us has a story, and we can't know another person's story if we don't know our own and acknowledge others' stories as well. It isn't a contest to see whose story is more dramatic or heartbreaking. It's about how our story has shaped our life and how other people's stories have shaped their lives.

Knowing this has helped me to better understand my purpose—to be a social justice warrior for women and girls. I offer this book, my podcast (*Your Authentic Path to Powerful Leadership*), my teaching, and my coaching as a reflection of my purpose. I hope I can help you find your purpose too—to fully embrace and then expand your own power!

REFLECTION

- What does embracing your power mean to you?

- What work do you have to do to fully embrace your power?

- What does expanding your power mean to you?

- What work do you have to do to fully expand your power?

- How will you stand in your power to live your best life?

CHAPTER 2

TRAUMA AND PSYCHOLOGICAL SAFETY

"After all, when a stone is dropped into a pond,
the water continues quivering even
after the stone has sunk to the bottom."

—Arthur Golden, Memoirs of a Geisha

Being effective at inspiring teams and influencing organizations requires you to understand the residual impact of the traumas that have occurred in your life. (How's that for an opening chapter statement!) In more recent leadership programs that I've designed and delivered, I've added the topic of trauma and explored how it has impacted one's life. It's been fascinating to hear clients' responses to both the topic and what they consider trauma in their lives. Some even declare that they have had no trauma in their life. I have two reactions to that. First, I want your life. It's hard for me to imagine getting twenty-five years into my professional life or even twenty-five years of living without experiencing any trauma. The second reaction is that you need to pay more attention. (Notice what you notice.) Then I remind myself not to project my "stuff" on to others. Their truth is their truth, and my truth is my truth.

As you continue reading this chapter, my wish is that you will better understand how trauma has or may be impacting you in the context of authentic, powerful leadership, as well as supporting you in your leadership journey to create conditions in your teams, organizations, and family to recognize, acknowledge, and reduce trauma-inducing conditions.

WHAT IS TRAUMA?

Before we go any further, let me define trauma. According to Nicole Lewis-Keeber's (MSW, LCSW) article, "Big T Trauma vs. little t trauma," Bruce Perry MD, PhD, defines *trauma* as "any pattern activating your stress response system that leads to an alteration of how the system functions."[1] Much like betrayal being defined in the eyes of the betrayed (rather than the betrayer), trauma is in the eyes of the traumatized. Only *you* get to define whether or not an event or situation or behavior is traumatizing.

TRAUMA VS. TRAUMA

We are all products of our life experiences and have had things happen that we may or may not classify as traumatic. Maybe we declare it as "no big deal" or "that's life." All the same, it may have been a traumatic experience . . . Lewis-Keeber makes the distinction this way: Big-T Trauma and small-t trauma. Big-T Traumas are major events that most would agree are traumatic. This could be losing a loved one; sexual abuse; or being physically, emotionally, or verbally abused. Small-t traumas accumulate over time. It is reflective of the "death by a thousand cuts" metaphor and, over time, can build to be a Big-T Trauma. It can include bullying; being the parent of a child who is struggling; not feeling seen, heard, or valued; or consistently being marginalized—as a woman, as a person of color, by practicing a certain religion or doctrine, and even through the lens of generational or ethnicity bias.

Lewis-Keeber states, "Whichever classification you would give to your trauma—because it's your interpretation that matters—it has the same effect on your brain."[2]

As I write this book, the world has continued to emerge from a global pandemic. We have lost loved ones to a deadly virus. We have also witnessed racial strife, political upheaval, devastating wars in Ukraine and Israel, and horrendous climate events. One of my clients described it as a time of "once-in-a-generation events" happening on a routine basis. On a very personal level, we may have been confined to our homes, many have lost and changed jobs, feared evictions, and even experienced significant food insecurity. Research warns of long-term health impacts for those who had COVID-19 and the long-term impacts for our children relating to their intellectual, emotional, and social development. We also know we are seeing higher rates of suicide, mental health outbursts, and domestic abuse. These events have reflected a life experience of trauma and more trauma, and our sense of safety and security has most certainly been undermined. We are suffering!

Yes, recent events have been horrific, *and* these traumas were often piled on top of the traumas of our lives pre-COVID-19, pre-2020. I want to specifically focus on the experience of women, people of color, and any marginalized groups. As many reading this will know, I have spent the last twenty-plus years delivering programs targeted specifically to women. It is through that work that the following thoughts are offered. As I continue to research and study trauma, lots of light bulbs have gone off for me as I made new connections and then declared, "No wonder!" I invite you to consider and apply this information to your own life experience. I believe it is applicable to each of us in a myriad of ways.

A review of history will show again and again that women have predominantly been in a "less than" position. Of course, there are exceptions; research is typically reflected in a bell-shaped curve. Women have been quieted, ridiculed, criticized, disrespected, and diminished. We are born into this experience around the globe merely by being a female.

As women go through life, we develop our own coping mechanisms. It might be "stuffing it" to repress the awful memories. It might be addictions—drugs, alcohol, food, exercise, even work. Your armor or protection may be a hard surface intended to protect you, yet it also prevents you from letting in the good things of life. What a loss! Our families of origin play such an important role in how we experience and manage trauma. If we grew up in a loving, nurturing, and supportive environment, we tend to be much more resilient. I envision it as being cloaked in love. That love is warm, certain, consistent, and deep. As a result, you can likely handle trauma in a healthier way. For those who didn't experience this loving early life in our families of origin, it can be a very different result. In this case, I envision a thin veil of protection—a veil that doesn't protect you well at all. Almost everything and everyone can penetrate this thin veil. You are much more vulnerable. As with most things, this is a continuum, and there are many kinds of layers of protection all along that continuum.

I invite you to think about your own means of protection.

REFLECTION

- What are some of your Big-T traumatic experiences or events?

- What are some of your small-t traumatic experiences or events?

- What did your family of origin teach you or model for you about how to handle traumatic experiences or events?

- How have you handled, managed, or responded to those adult experiences or events?

- What connections or similarities might you see in how your family of origin handled trauma and how you are handling trauma as an adult?

- What parts of your responses were almost automatic or by default?

- What parts of your responses were thoughtful and intentional?

UNHEALED TRAUMA

As leaders, it is our role to inspire strong performance. I think about this from both a personal and professional basis. You want your child to be a good student, to develop healthy habits, to forge meaningful relationships, be an all-around good person, grow up to be a responsible adult, and to be a good citizen of the world. In our professional lives, we want to lead high-performing teams, delight customers, work productively, achieve our goals, and "make our numbers." And oh so many things seem to get in the way. As I think about this topic, I remind myself that everybody has a story, and everybody is working on something. Everybody. The traumas we experience as a child can follow us into our adult lives if we don't get support and work through them. Certainly, your response to traumas can vary from person to person.

SIGNS OF LINGERING TRAUMA IN ADULTS

In her article entitled "Childhood Trauma: Types, Causes, Signs, & Treatments," Dr. Dakota King-White offers the following signs of childhood trauma in adults:[3]

- "Poor, unfulfilling, or chaotic relationships
- Lack of trust in others
- Mood changes and emotional instability
- Problems with focus, attention, and concentration
- Problematic substance abuse
- Anger and aggression"

With time, maturity, or professional treatment, you may be able to process and recover from your childhood trauma(s). Others may continue being influenced by the unwanted events from childhood and carry these feelings into adulthood.

I share this information so that you can better understand what may be driving these behaviors. It may explain someone's performance or relationship challenges. It is a tricky place to navigate as a leader. As a coach, I am often asked, "What is the difference between therapy and coaching?" I explain it this way: Therapy is looking back and asking why; coaching is looking ahead and asking how. As a leader, make sure you know the difference. Someone gave me wise counsel early in my leadership life: "Never take someone to a place where you can't take care of them when you get there." Trauma can be quite emotional. Leave trauma healing to the professionals.

Clare Rolquin, MSW, LCSW-A, outlines in her article "Unhealed Trauma: Signs, Impacts, & How To Heal" how some of these signs of trauma can manifest in individuals:[4]

- **Codependency**—Rolquin states, "In codependent relationships, you will find the couple are enmeshed with one another." This is characterized by excessive emotional or psychological reliance on a partner. "Foundationally, it is due to poor concept of self or poor boundaries, including an inability to have an opinion or say no," says Dr. Mark Mayfield, a licensed professional counselor (LPC).[5]
- **People-Pleasing Tendencies**—"Those struggling with unprocessed trauma may adopt people-pleasing tendencies. For many, this is how they can avoid conflict and keep the peace. However, this is a trauma response brought on by feeling they need to compensate as though they themselves are the problem."[6]

  This may also involve doing everything for everyone else. It is being afraid to have the hard conversations on behalf of yourself for fear of displeasing another person or damaging the relationship. Many of us have grown up with the "good-girl rules" that often suppress or discount our own thoughts, feelings, or wants. I recently saw this quote from Cheryl Richardson, and I think it reflects this sentiment: "If you avoid conflict to keep the peace, you start a war inside yourself."[7] I felt as though this quote spoke to my childhood experience.

Probably the lament I have heard most often from the women in my programs relates to deprioritizing my or their own needs in order to please others. You would never want to inconvenience others, though you have no problem inconveniencing yourself again and again. You feel that your to-do lists, along with everyone and everything else, must take the highest priority—family, work, school, community, and friends. Where are you on the list? Nowhere to be found. In my earlier book, *Choose! The Role That Choice Plays in Shaping Women's Lives*, co-authored with another dear friend and colleague, Dottie Gandy, one of our key messages is, "Don't confuse self with selfishness." Self-care, refueling, and replenishing aren't selfish. They are smart and necessary if we want to do all the things we want to do for others. Self-care helps us avoid health-related issues, burnout, and damaged relationships.

- **Increased Anger and Aggression**—"Those with unhealed trauma are at an increased risk of experiencing irritability or angry outbursts. Although some may use anger to cope with symptoms, for others it is simply a reaction."[8]
- **Trust Issues**—"Often, trust is damaged or lost after an individual experiences a traumatic event. Whether it is a loss of trust in an individual, family, a higher power, or systems that were meant to protect you . . . it is [often] difficult for those who have experienced trauma to regain that trust."[9]

I also want to share with you some anecdotal signs of unhealed trauma as told to me by many women I have taught and coached and led over the last forty-five years. I offer them to you, as you may relate to them in yourself or in others, both personally and professionally.

- **Fixing Others**—This one screams the "should" language. You tell others what they should or shouldn't do. And we "should" ourselves all the time. *I should have started on this project earlier. I shouldn't have eaten that dessert. I should have spoken up. I shouldn't have said anything.* Sound familiar? Someone shared the following perspective with me many years ago: "Should is could with shame on it." I have been very conscious of my use of the word *should* ever since. I encourage you: Don't should on yourself or others.
- **Needing to Prove Myself**—Throughout my life, I have heard and lived the adage, "Women have to work twice as hard to get half as far." And I have seen and heard many stories that reflect this adage. It often takes the form of perfectionism. My dear friend and colleague Susie Vaughan gave me a great coaching tip on this: "Strive for grace, not perfection."
- **Living on High Alert**—This is often diagnosed as ADHD. You can't focus, as you have your antennae up to ensure that you are ready for the next traumatic event. Another facet of this is constantly waiting for the next inevitable bad thing to happen. It often prevents you from enjoying and really taking in the good things.
- **Requiring External Validation**—*How do I look? Do you have any feedback for me? Wouldn't you agree?* This is the language of this sign of unhealed trauma. (Note that there is a difference between asking these questions on occasion and asking these questions frequently in order to feel a sense of security in oneself.)
- **Fearing Abandonment**—Often a person will sabotage a relationship if it is going well. In other words, you will unconsciously come up with a reason to abandon someone else so you can either create or reinforce the self-fulfilling prophecy or justify the abandonment rather than relive the trauma of abandonment.

REFLECTION

- Do any of these signs resonate with you? Which ones?

- How do they show up for you?

I encourage you to talk with someone about this. It could be a good friend, a mentor, a coach, or a therapist, depending on the severity. Two of my frequent coaching questions are, "How is that working *for* you?" and "How is that working *against* you?" Your very personal situation and answers may help guide you to the kind of person you want to talk to about your unhealed trauma.

EVERYBODY HAS A STORY

Someone sent this to me recently, and I want to share it with you in the context of this chapter. It is from Becky Hemsley in 2022. Again, it reminds me that "everybody has a story."

"Handle with Care"

Every woman I know has, at one point or another,
sobbed in the shower, cried in the car, swallowed
down tears in the supermarket, and broken down in the
bathroom.

And then she has dried her eyes, lifted her head, taken a deep breath and carried on.
She has walked into work or in through the front door or into the store or the coffee shop or the hair salon. And she has smiled and chatted to people so that no one would know she'd been crying.

And I'm not reminding us of this to say "look how strong we are to pull ourselves together when we are falling apart." Although that still stands.
I'm reminding us how easy it is to paint a brave face so that other people are none the wiser.

So whilst it might not have been you sitting in the car this morning, it might have been that woman who sits three desks down from you.
Whilst it might not have been you sobbing in the shower before getting the kids ready for school this morning, it might have been their teacher. Or another parent on the school run.

Whilst you might have gotten round the supermarket without being on the verge of tears today, it might not be the same for the person working the till. Or the person behind you in the queue.

Everyone wears their brave face in public.
And we'll never really know just how many people around us have pulled themselves together with the thinnest of threads each morning. How many people are ready to fall apart again at any point.

But compassion strengthens those threads.
Compassion is powerful. Because even when no one can see it, even when no one can hear it . . .

They can feel it.

HOW WE RESPOND TO STRESS

THE FOUR F'S: FIGHT, FLIGHT, FREEZE, AND FLOCK

We have all likely heard about the fight-or-flight response to stress, anxiety, or trauma. This goes all the way back to prehistoric days of fighting or fleeing saber-toothed tigers. Most of the early research on the stress response was done on men. Relatively recent research has added the *freeze* response. This is when we can either feel paralyzed because we are so caught off guard and don't know what to do, or we go completely still and quiet getting ready for our next move. When a recent group of women were discussing the fight response, they rarely meant literally fighting. Instead, they shared stories describing fighting for what they believe in, standing up for their values or vital issues, and fighting to finish or get through something no matter how intellectually, emotionally, or physically challenging. This provides a much broader perspective on the fight response through a woman's experience.

As women were included in the research (because we experience stress too!), two new behaviors were developed by Dr. Shelley E. Taylor and her research team at the University of California, Los Angeles, and were first published in a *Psychological Review* article in 2000.[10] She found that the "tend-and-befriend" response is a behavior exhibited in response to threat. *Tending* ranges from protecting our offspring to organizing our desks or consolidating our to-do lists—both aimed at getting things back to a nonthreatening and in-control condition.

One woman recently shared that when she began to work from home due to the pandemic, the first thing she did was deep-clean her house from top to bottom. Other women chimed in with similar stories. This is a clear example of tending. Another form of tending (and one of my favorites) is immediately going into problem-solving mode. That's my way of tending to a traumatic or stressful experience. This tending response also enables us to get back a feeling of being in control. Research tells us that when you feel out of control, you often "overcontrol" in other parts of your life. This typically happens at an unconscious level. By recognizing and acknowledging that you are responding this way, you may be making a move to regain a sense of control.

Befriending is seeking out your social group for mutual defense. This closely resembles the last *F*, *flock*. Another woman shared that she was recently "warned" that seeking out others for solace or for talking things over wasn't a good idea. The psychology might suggest otherwise. If you go back to the signs of unhealed trauma, only you can answer the question of whether you are seeking others out for the purpose of external validation or mutual defense.

In evolutionary psychology, "tend-and-befriend" is theorized to have evolved as the typical female response to stress. In my mind, it relates to Dr. Patricia Heim's research on "invisible rules" around gender. She describes the feminine framework around power as a flat structure where we are all in this together—befriending or flocking.[11]

REFLECTION

- What is your typical response when facing traumatic experiences or events?

- If it is different based on the situation, what are the nuances (e.g., work versus family, friends versus professional colleagues)?

Think of examples when you have used any one of these responses:

- Fight:
- Flight:
- Freeze:
- Flock/Befriend:
- Tend:

SAFE SPACES

In my book *Embracing Your Power: A Woman's Path to Authentic Leadership & Meaningful Relationships*, I shared a group trust model developed by Sue Hammond. I also refer to it as the flower petal model (see Image 2.1).

Image 2.1: Courtesy of Sue Hammond and the ELI Group, www.theeligroup.com

You can see that the center of the flower reflects psychological safety. In Hammond's model, psychological safety represents the environment created by the team that makes group members feel safe enough to be vulnerable and take interpersonal risks with one another in order to achieve group goals.

As a leader of a group or team, you are responsible for creating safe spaces. In the context of trauma, psychological safety is the absence of trauma. You want to create the conditions for your team, your family, and your friends to feel psychologically safe. Read that sentence again. As a leader, the last thing you want to do is create a traumatic environment.

CREATING SAFE SPACES

- Suspend judgment while inviting input from others.
- Share what is true for you and invite others to do the same.
- Ask yourself if your thoughts and actions are about being right.
- Understand that just because it is not your truth doesn't mean it isn't someone else's truth.
- Be a model for vulnerability, openness, and honesty.
- Listen—with your ears, your head, and your heart.
- Invite and encourage others to contribute their thoughts and ideas.
- Default to believing that others are doing their best (positive intent).
- Let go of old stories.
- Encourage authenticity.

Let's discuss each of these.

- **Suspend Judgment While Inviting Input from Others.** This is hard! We are so quick to judge, criticize, blame, or refute what others have to say, especially when what they are saying is different from what we are thinking or saying. When you find yourself moving to judgment, retrain your brain to give you a cue. My favorite judgment diversion is to say to myself, "Isn't that fascinating!" That diverting phrase moves me to reengage more thoughtfully and deliberately. I get curious and often say, "Tell me more," or I ask clarifying questions to actually learn. This often yields thoughts and experiences that expand my horizons and broaden my perspective. Try it.
- **Share What Is True for You and Invite Others to Do the Same.** Can you share your thoughts, ideas, recommendations,

and perspectives without fear of being criticized, judged, embarrassed, ridiculed, or even ignored? This is being on the other side of suspending judgment mentioned in the previous paragraph. When striving to suspend judgment, you are the listener. When sharing your truth, you are the speaker. Harmful consequences include others seeing you as "less than" or that such responses might damage your reputation. It can also include second-guessing or questioning yourself. Such harmful consequences can also prevent you from speaking your truth in the future. It can certainly contribute to a loss of confidence. And, in a world in which we want everyone's best thinking and ideas, your loss of confidence and the quieting of your voice serves no one.

- **Ask Yourself If Your Thoughts and Actions Are About Being Right.** We spend our school years being taught, told, and tested against a right or wrong answer. You didn't make good grades if you didn't get the right answer. When you move into your adult professional life, you often discover there are multiple "right" answers. One of the best questions offered in this scenario of needing to be right is, "Do you want to be right, or do you want to be effective?" If being right is a subjective determination or damages a relationship, is it really best to keep fighting to be right? Now, don't get me wrong, there are times when being right is of the utmost importance. If you are an engineer constructing a high-rise building or a doctor performing surgery, you want to get it right. This is a classic case of "knowing what tool to use when" (from the Foundational Elements shared in *Embracing Your Power*). Be thoughtful. Be intentional. As my friend and colleague Mia would say, "Take that dog a-hunting" to explore where that need to always be right comes from.
- **Understand That Just Because It Is Not Your Truth Doesn't Mean It Isn't Someone Else's Truth.** My best personal example of this principle happened many years ago in my corporate career

when I led a pilot program for our high-performing, high-potential employees. It was a holistic program supporting learning and development in both the participants' personal and professional lives. After we completed the pilot program, the participants shared their experience with their respective executive teams. I sat in on these so I could continue to learn and potentially modify the program for greater impact.

In one executive team meeting, one of the participants declared that the program had been a "life-changing" experience. As you might imagine, I was very happy with that kind of comment. My smile quickly evaporated when one of the men on the executive team said, "I've had a gun held to my head in Vietnam. *That's* a life-changing experience. No training program can be life changing."

Simply stated, that was his truth. After a moment of panic, I responded by saying I wouldn't wish that experience on anyone and was so sorry he'd had such a traumatic experience. I then went on to share that I had given birth and, of course, *that* was a life-changing experience too—and one he couldn't have. And that was my truth. I offered that none of us gets to tell another person that what they describe as a life-changing experience isn't one. If you believe this principle, you have to be open to others seeing something and experiencing something differently than you. That will create "safety" for everyone to share their stories.

- **Be a Model for Vulnerability, Openness, and Honesty.** Being vulnerable by sharing our fears, concerns, or challenges can be scary. Many of us may have been taught that being vulnerable is a sign of weakness. I offer a very different viewpoint. To have fears, concerns, or challenges doesn't make us weak; it makes us human. Brené Brown says, "Vulnerability is not winning or losing; it's having the courage to show up and be seen when we have no control over the outcome. Vulnerability is not weakness, it's our greatest measure of courage."[12] I would further add that if, as a leader, you are courageous enough to be open, honest, and vulnerable, you are modeling effective leadership for others.

- **Listen—with Your Ears, Your Head, and Your Heart.** I have been working on this for decades, and I still find myself periodically falling short. ("Strive for grace and not perfection!") I encourage you to stop multitasking, be present, and listen with a learner's mindset. Remember, we all want to be seen, heard, and valued. Listening is a great gift. Listen with your ears, your head, and your heart. Ask probing and clarifying questions (these often start with "what" or "how").
- **Invite and Encourage Others to Contribute Their Thoughts and Ideas.** In my first book, *Embracing Your Power*, I offer a tool called "check-in." At the beginning of longer meetings, high-stakes meetings, or collaborative meetings, consider starting with a check-in question. This gets everyone's voice in the room. And research shows that once you have spoken in a group, you are more likely to speak again when you have something to offer. Using what is called "round robin" facilitation, you pose a question or seek input you want to hear from everyone. You may need to give the introverts time to think deeply and formulate their responses. Pay attention to this and make time for it when planning your agenda.
- **Default to Believing That Others Are Doing Their Best (Positive Intent).** The Kansas Hospital Association describes *positive intent* as choosing to assume that our coworkers are working to the best of their ability with the resources and information they currently have.[13] At its core, positive intent is believing that we are all doing the best we can.
- **Let Go of Old Stories.** This is important for families; sometimes we may still see a sibling as a "little" brother or sister even

though they are now grown and married with children. Another situation to watch out for is when you join an organization in your early adult life and, years later, coworkers might still see you as "that intern," "that rookie," or "that junior player." It's incumbent upon each of us to be on the lookout if we are doing this to others. Prevent yourself from bringing up old stories that are no longer relevant. We were all young and inexperienced once. Goodness knows, I hope I am smarter now than way back when!

- **Encourage Authenticity.** This statement represents being authentic, being the best you that you can be. There's a difference between fitting in and belonging. Fitting in is about you choosing to act a certain way to make others feel comfortable. You might dress or talk a certain way as a means of going along to get along. You end up conforming to someone else's definition of what you *should* be, do, or say. (Beware of "shoulding"!) On the flip side, belonging is about feeling comfortable being your authentic self. The amount of energy required to fit in is enormous, and you lose a bit of yourself every time you choose to fit in and, dare I say, forego your authenticity.

As I share these ways of creating safe spaces, I think about my wish for a world that values women and girls equally with men and boys. It's creating these kinds of safe spaces where our voices are heard, where what we have to say and contribute is considered and valued. It will go a long way toward changing the almost automatic condition of girls being born into an environment of trauma just because they are girls. If these views seem extreme, I invite and encourage you to practice safe behaviors. This embodies "understanding that just because it's not your truth doesn't mean it isn't someone else's truth." This requires compassion. You may not be able to empathize or put yourself into someone else's shoes, but you *can* have compassion for the pain and trauma of another

REFLECTION

- Which of these behaviors for creating safe spaces do you do well?

- Which of these behaviors do you want to work on?

- How will you go about working on them?

- How will you solicit feedback on your efforts and results?

- How will you share this list with your team or your family?

human being. And remember, what is trauma to another person may not be trauma to you and vice versa. Also keep in mind that some traumas are single events or experiences. In other cases, it is a steady dose of trauma-inducing behavior that accumulates to become unreconciled trauma. Remember the saying: "Death by a thousand cuts."

When you create these safe spaces, you can change your ways of thinking and feeling and even your beliefs, as well as the thinking, feeling, and beliefs of others. The neuroplasticity of our brains allows us to lay down new neural pathways. *The psychological safety must be equal to or greater than the experienced trauma.* Read that last sentence again. With new thinking, feelings, and beliefs, you have a fresh story to tell yourself that will now influence your future thinking, feelings, behaviors, responses, and choices.

One final thought: Strive for well-being, and create spaces for others to do the same. In this case, I define *well-being* as the state of being comfortable, healthy, and consistently capable of feeling an internal joy unprompted by mandatory external stimulus. Those who experience high levels of well-being are often described as flourishing. And, again, in this case, *flourishing* is described as "the product of the pursuit and engagement of an authentic life that brings inner joy and happiness through meeting goals, being connected with life passions, and relishing in accomplishments through the peaks and valleys of life."[14] It is as if you have peace in every direction. Your life is not free of conflict or hardships or drama. You see those things for what they are, work your way through them, and help others do the same.

As I wrap up this chapter, I hope the information provides insights regarding your own traumas and how they might be showing up in your life. Maybe it gives you the language to name them—the events, your experiences, and the impact on you. I also hope it provides some guidance on how to prevent unintentional trauma situations. Each and every one of us has experienced trauma. My focus on women and girls is based on my work with women around the world and hearing their stories. Those stories are reflected in the information shared in this chapter. To everyone reading this, my heart goes out to you. I hope you are able to find effective support from someone trained in trauma. I also hope you find a loving environment that helps you to heal from whatever traumas you have experienced.

PART 1

DISCUSSION QUESTIONS

Some of you will be reading this book on your own. Others may be reading and reviewing the book as a book club or a women's group. At the end of each section, I've included some reflection questions that focus on what you've learned from the section and how you plan to apply it in your life.

If you are reading the book as a group, I encourage you to answer the questions individually before discussing them as a group. You want to do your own personal work. Once you hear others' responses, you can add, change, or even delete items in your own responses. Remember, women learn through stories. Share yours freely and deeply, and listen as others do the same.

PART 1 REFLECTION QUESTIONS

- What did you learn about yourself while reading this section?

- What stands out to you about further embracing and expanding your power and creating an environment for psychological safety and managing trauma?

- What are three things you'll do differently going forward based on what you've learned?

PART 2

INSPIRING YOUR TEAMS

CHAPTER 3

LEADING NEW TEAMS

"Alone we can do so little;
together we can do so much."

—Helen Keller

The opportunity to join a new team can be very exciting. If you read much about team development or have been a part of team-building exercises, you may have heard about the Bruce Tuckman model first proposed in 1965: forming, storming, norming, performing.[1] In the forming stage, the team meets and learns about opportunities and challenges and then agrees on team norms and goals and begins to tackle the tasks. In the storming phase, the group starts to sort itself out and gain one another's trust. In the norming stage, the team members take responsibility for and have the ambition to work for the success of the team's goals. And, in the performing stage, team members are motivated and knowledgeable; they are now competent, autonomous, and able to handle the decision-making process.

In 1977, Tuckman, along with Mary Ann Jensen, added a fifth stage: adjourning. In the adjourning phase, the team completes the tasks or achieves the goals and breaks up the team. An effective leader is aware of each of these phases or stages and is thoughtful and intentional about moving through them. This chapter can help you to be thoughtful and intentional about moving through forming and storming in a more efficient way to then operate in the norming and performing stages.

BUILD IT EXERCISE

When I teach women skills for building a new team, I start with an exercise. These are often groups of women who have been part of a learning team for several days, weeks, or months (depending on the program design), but who have not been asked to produce deliverables as a team. In that sense, the exercise simulates a new team coming together.

BUILD IT: EXERCISE SETUP

- **Room Setup**–Depending on the number of participants, set up two or three separate tables with identical supplies on each table.
- **Supply List**–Poster board (one per team), construction paper (exact number/color per team), markers (exact number/color per team), four cups, ten paper clips, twelve pipe cleaners, glue sticks (one per team), four pairs of scissors, scoring sheets (for judges)
- **Team Size**–There are generally six to eight people on each team.
- **Designating Teams**–The participants line up facing the facilitator in birthday order (month and day) from left to right. The facilitator then divides up the teams with six to eight members on each team. Example: There are twenty-four participants. Divide twenty-four by eight and you have three teams.
- **Table Designation**–Each team is then assigned to one of the tables with identical supplies.

The facilitator then reads the following instructions:

WOMEN LEADING TEAMS . . . BUILD IT

Building the Marsha Clark & Associates Resort and Conference Center

Marsha Clark & Associates is seeking a design for a resort and conference center to host corporate meetings and events in a family-friendly environment. It will be a freestanding facility with conference rooms, sleeping rooms, and all other necessary amenities to cater to business professionals as well as their families.

It must be a high-rise building and can be located anywhere in the world. It must add beauty to the local skyline, operate as a "green" facility, and also be sturdy enough to withstand extreme weather conditions on a year-round basis.

The firm is requesting that all interested design groups gather to simultaneously design and build a prototype resort and conference center, each meeting the same basic requirements and using materials provided by MC&A. At the end of the time-limited construction, each team will present their design, elaborating on its major features and explaining how it will serve the needs of Marsha Clark & Associates and reflect the vision of being a global leadership development organization.

A prize will be awarded to the team with the best-designed facility according to the following criteria:

- Building height (the higher the better) and aesthetics, with enhancement to the local skyline
- Quality of construction to be determined by a "blow/drop" test
- Appropriate amenities that attract business professionals and their families
- Naming of the facility
- Recommended global location
- Suitability in reflecting Marsha Clark & Associates' vision, including an initial marketing approach
- Marketing presentation

continued

Construction

Each group will have thirty minutes to build their structure. They are to begin when the facilitator says, "Begin production" and end when the facilitator says, "Stop production." A warning will be issued five minutes before production must stop.

Delivery

At the end of construction, each team will have thirty seconds to deliver their completed structure to the judges. Prototypes received after thirty seconds will be eliminated from the judging. No team members are allowed to remain with the prototype after it is delivered.

Presentation

Each team will have ten minutes to present their prototype to the panel of judges. Judges will select the winning team based on the above criteria. The decision of the judges is final.

The facilitator then asks everyone if they have any questions before their thirty minutes of construction begins.

Typical questions might include–

- Can we use our phones as a resource?
- Are the criteria weighted?
- Can we work together as one team rather than three teams?

You can choose to respond to the first question with a yes or no. I now say yes because I believe it is more representative of our real-world practicality. For the second question, I choose not to weight the criteria, as it complicates a relatively short exercise and doesn't have a major learning point attached to it. My answer to the last question is no. The exercise is designed to resemble a more competitive marketplace scenario as a way of raising the stakes on the outcome.

CONDUCTING THE BLOW/DROP TEST

Let me describe how to execute the blow/drop test. The facilitator will demonstrate the technique prior to the teams starting the construction phase. To conduct the blow/drop test, the facilitator holds up a small notebook or binder horizontally and from waist-high drops it on the table. The small notebook or binder is intended to represent each team's prototype. During live judging, a team's prototype passes the test if it stays generally intact (not damaged or impaired). To conduct the blow/drop test, the facilitator holds the same small notebook or binder in a horizontal position and vigorously moves it up and down ten times to simulate high winds or related storms that would negatively impact the structure. Given the judging criteria of building height—"the higher the better"—some teams may be out of balance. In other words, their prototype might be tall but may not withstand the blow/drop test. This is yet another fun moment for the teams.

CONSTRUCTION AND DELIVERY

After the blow/drop test demonstration is completed and all questions are answered, the facilitator starts the times for the construction phase. Note that this phase also includes planning as well as construction. A five-minute warning is issued at the twenty-five-minute point.

At the end of thirty minutes, each team has thirty seconds to deliver their prototype to the designated judges table. You can expect a flurry of excitement, high energy, and considerable laughter.

PRESENTATION AND JUDGING

The room setup changes at this point. Instead of eight chairs at each of the tables, the facilitator lines up three rows of chairs with eight chairs in each row. Team 1 sits in row 1, Team 2 sits in row 2, and Team 3 sits in row 3. There are three chairs set aside for the judges. I encourage facilitators to have three judges to avoid potential ties in the judges' scoring.

The facilitator will have a method for determining which team presents first. I always write down the numbers one, two, and three on small pieces of paper. I fold them up so the numbers are not visible, and a member from each team picks one. The team that gets number one goes first and so on.

I have included scoring sheets for the judges. The judges will have a scoring sheet for each team and can make notes as the respective teams are delivering their "presentation." One of the judges is designated as the timekeeper.

Building the MC&A Resort and Conference Center

Judges Scoring Sheet Team: __________

Criteria	Notes
Building Height	
Facility Name	
Blow/Drop (yes/no)	
Amenities	
Reflecting the Vision	
Financial	
Presentation	
Other	
TOTAL SCORE	

Ideally, the judges will have discussed who will ask what questions.

Questions may include–

- How many sleeping rooms are there?
- How many conference rooms are there?
- How many people in total can attend a conference there?
- Is childcare available?
- Is there easy travel or airport access?
- Where will you hire staff to run the facility?
- As a global facility, are there multiple restaurants for global food selections?

Then, there is a whole set of financial questions. You will notice that financial considerations were not listed as criteria in the instructions. And I have to say, it is a question rarely asked during the question-and-answer time frame before teams start the construction phase. (Remember, this is a leadership program. I'm not trying to trick anyone; I'm trying to make a teaching point. You will read more about that later in this chapter.)

Here are some financially related questions you might ask:

- What is the capital investment for building this resort and conference center?
- What is the payback period (the number of years before you start making a profit)?
- What are the annual operating expenses?

You can imagine that the nervous laughter volume gets louder at this point. Some teams say they want to get approval on design and will come back with a financial plan at the next meeting. Some teams make it up on the spot and could be reasonable or wildly inaccurate (too high or too low). Some teams refer to someone on their team who is not presenting to offer a response. Typically, they refer to the most senior person (hierarchically in her day job) or a person whose day job involves financials. Admittedly, the teams that present second and third have an advantage. The facilitator will want to quiet them regarding planning for their responses to this question during their presentation.

Each team presents, and at the end of the presentations, the facilitator gives all participants a fifteen-minute break while the judges confer and determine the winner. The judges discuss how they viewed each presentation and arrive at the consensus winner.

Once the break is over, the facilitator announces the winning team and discusses why they were chosen. Don't be surprised if the scoring is close. As an aside, I am always impressed with both the creativity and the variety of prototypes.

At this point, you have spent about ninety minutes of program delivery time:

1. Fifteen-minute setup
2. Thirty-minute construction and prototype delivery phase
3. Thirty-minute presentation phase (ten minutes for each team for three teams)
4. Fifteen minutes for judging and announcing the winner

TEAM DEBRIEF

The facilitator now directs the participants to go back to their teams (typically around the tables where they constructed their prototypes) and discuss the following questions:

TEAM DEBRIEF—HOW NEW TEAMS DEVELOP

- What behaviors enabled strong team performance?
- What behaviors disabled strong team performance?
- What impact did the following have on achieving strong team performance?
  - Defined outcome
  - Judging criteria—knowing how your performance would be measured
  - Timeline for deliverable
- How would you define trust in your team—High? Low?
  - How was it built?
  - How was it broken?
  - If broken, was there an effort to rebuild it? If so, how?
- Was there any conflict? How did you manage it?

continued

- How did decisions get made?

- How was work divided up? Assigned?

- How did you manage your resources?

- How does this experience compare to your day-to-day team experience?

- What can you take from this exercise and apply to your day-to-day responsibilities?

NEW TEAM CHECKLIST

Now, it has surprised me a bit that it has taken all these pages to describe what happens in about an hour and a half. *And* that the time was spent to make the teaching points from the questions I have outlined. So now I offer you the practical tool: a checklist for when you are forming a new team to help you lead your new team more efficiently and effectively through the forming and storming phases. I'm sure you will recognize that the answers to some of these questions describe the norms for the team in support of the norming phase. The simulation is a short way to drive the learning points home.

Here are my recommendations for how to use these questions. Pull your new team together and think ahead about the answers to these questions. I've included the checklist tool for your tool kit. As the leader of your new team, you will capture your team's responses to these questions. You will then distribute the consolidated lists to every new team member. The lists may also inform your summary of expectations, which we discuss in chapter 4 regarding Building High-Performance Teams.

TOOL: NEW TEAM CHECKLIST

1. What behaviors do we want to display in order to achieve strong team performance (examples—clarity of communication, gathering input from everyone)?

2. What behaviors do we think will disable strong team performance (examples—not checking out assumptions, lack of clarity on desired outcomes)?

3. What information do we want to be clear about in order to be successful? What else goes on this list?

    a. Defined requirements, deliverables, or outcomes

    b. Knowing how our performance will be measured, success factors

    c. Timelines with milestones

    d. Knowing all of our stakeholders

    e. Determining how decisions will be made

    f. Clarity of roles and responsibilities

    g. Clarity of what and when to escalate

    h. Understanding how and to whom work or tasks will be assigned

continued

i. Knowing what resources are needed and available to us (e.g., budget, team members—both full time and part time, as well as internal or external technology support)

4. How will we build trust in each other and as a team? (I highly recommend using the information shared in chapters 5 and 8 in my first book, *Embracing Your Power.*)

5. How will we handle conflict or disagreements? (Again, I recommend using the information shared in chapter 9 of *Embracing Your Power.*)

6. What feedback loops do we want to ensure that we stay aligned on (e.g., cadence of one-on-one meetings between team leader and individual team members, cadence of team meetings, cadence of stakeholder meetings)?

There are some additional thoughts and tools as you consider this checklist.

I am a strong proponent of not making stuff up. If you don't know the answer (remember the financial questions in the exercise), admit it, let your team know when you will have the answer, and get back to them. This contributes to building trust.

Two trust-building behaviors are[2]–

1. Telling the truth
2. Admitting mistakes

By modeling these two behaviors, you encourage your team to do the same, and you will be better informed regarding the accurate status of team performance. You can't give the "I don't know" answer all of the time, so work on your planning and preparation, and always follow through to provide the committed-to answers.

In allocating tasks and assignments, there are several tools that can help you. One such tool is called the **RASIN** chart.

TOOL: RESPONSIBILITY CHARTING: ESTABLISHING RASIN

Overview

Responsibility charting, a tool developed by Richard Beckhard (and expanded by many others), a noted organizational development expert, is a process that helps assign roles, key decisions, and actions. The tool focuses on ensuring that all players are clear on their responsibilities and decision-making scope. It helps reduce ambiguity, wasted energy, and adverse emotional reactions between individuals or groups whose interrelationship is affected by change.

The usefulness of responsibility charting lies not only in the end product of an agreed-upon chart but also in the new understanding and appreciation of people's roles and required behavior that grow out of the charting process.

Responsibility charting can be used in the following interdependent contexts:

- Change and transition management
- Project management
- Cross-organization integration efforts
- Team development and role clarification

continued

Methodology

The responsibility chart organizes specific activities (projects, task forces, committees, etc.) to be implemented by a particular group of people and then arrays them against the people (senior management, managers, other organization members) responsible for making the change happen. For each activity, specific roles and responsibilities are assigned.

Responsibility charting uses the **RASIN** method for allocating responsibilities. Each player (person or group) is assigned one of several behaviors for each activity. A person will not always play the same role; it will be dependent on the specific needs of each activity. A person might have to provide active support or resources for a certain action, while on another activity they may simply need to be informed or consulted before the action is taken.

- **R** = Responsible to Make It Happen
- **A** = Authority to Approve or Veto
- **S** = Support (Involved for Resources, Information, Time, People, or Money)
- **I** = Informed (Need to Be Informed; Involvement Not Needed)
- **N** = No Involvement

RESPONSIBILITY CHARTING: UNDERLYING PRINCIPLES

R = Responsible to Make It Happen

For each and every action, there must always be a clearly identified player who is responsible to make it happen. This does not necessarily mean the person responsible has authority. The central purpose of the process is assigning responsibility or deciding who has the **R**. There can be only one person responsible. Often, for someone to adequately assign the **R**, the decision must be broken down into component parts.

Consistent with organization effectiveness principles, there is value in pushing the **R** down.

A = Authority to Approve or Veto

The concept of **A** (approve/veto) needs to be wrestled with occasionally. This is often the confusing concept of responsibility but not authority. While ultimate authority may rest at another level, this does not in any way diminish an individual's responsibility. In most instances, **A** is a sign-off function often required for management control, budget, policy, or audit reasons.

S = Support

The concept of **S** (support) is important to explore because the degree of support varies from situation to situation. **S** suggests being involved or helping with required resources, information, time, people, or money. It may also suggest consultation or expertise shared. It is important to clarify what type of support is required specifically.

I = Informed

The concept of **I** focuses on involvement that is not needed but must be informed before the action is taken. This is largely due to the interdependencies between functions or work units. Careful identification of the **I** is important to avoid slowing down decision-making and effective implementation. This does not mean, however, that those players with an **I** role can stop or veto the activity. The **I** represents an obligation to inform key individuals and does not imply any attempt to limit information flow to others.

N = No Involvement

At first glance, **N** (no involvement) may seem redundant. If there is no other designation, surely this implies no involvement. While this is true, **N** is used to ensure that duplication of effort is avoided and to signify a change in the way the activity or task may have been done in the past.

RESPONSIBILITY CHARTING: MAKING A RESPONSIBILITY CHART

Two or more people (leaders) whose roles interrelate or who manage interdependent groups formulate a list of activities, actions, or decisions that affect their relationship, and they record the list along a vertical axis. They then identify the people involved in each activity—a list of players—on the horizontal axis of the table. Players can include:

- Individuals directly involved in a decision
- Bosses of those involved
- Groups (direct reports, project team members, etc.)
- External people (suppliers, customers, etc.)

The following tool can be developed by leadership and given to others for discussion or developed by subordinates and checked out with bosses. In any case, participants of the process should develop their chart according to the work to be done, not according to the status or authority of the players on the chart.

The group that develops the chart should test it out with any of the players *not present* during its production. Preferably, no major player should be absent. The participants can also use the chart to check expected behavior and hold one another accountable, calling attention to others when their actual behavior falls out of line with the consensus noted on the responsibility chart.

THE TOOL

Ground Rules for Responsibility Charting

1. No box may contain more than one letter.
2. Assign all the **R**'s first. Assigning the **R** first will help to balance out workloads.
3. No more than one **R** can exist for an activity. Agreeing on where the **R** resides is the first step. If agreement can't be reached on who has the **R**, there are three options to follow:
   - Break the problem into subparts.
   - Move the **R** up one level in the organization.
   - Move the *decision* about the location of the **R** up one level.
4. Once the **R** is placed, other letters can be agreed upon, with the ground rule that no box can contain more than one letter.
5. Avoid assigning too many **A**'s; it leads to great difficulty in obtaining a decision. Renegotiate to change some **A**'s into **S**'s or **I**'s.

Common Pitfalls

1. If an activity has several **A**'s—say one **R**, six **A**'s, one **S**, and one **I**—it will undoubtedly be very difficult to accomplish the task. Too many **A**'s will slow down the process in implementation and make the person with the **R**'s role very difficult.
2. If a second-rank manager fills out the chart, one might find a skewing of **A**'s under the senior executive. Subordinate managers tend to give their bosses more **A**'s than the bosses want.

The decision about who assigns a letter to a role can be tricky. Ensure that players who are not present in the chart development have input to it; lack of buy-in to assign roles can significantly impact effective implementation.

References

- Richard Beckhard and Reuben T. Harris, *Organizational Transitions: Managing Complex Change* (Addison-Wesley, 1987).
- Christopher G. Worley, David E. Hitchin, and Walter L. Ross, *Integrated Strategic Change: How OD Builds Competitive Advantage* (FT Press, 1995).

SUMMARY

I want to be clear: It takes a lot of thought, focus, energy, and work to start and develop a strong team. This chapter and the chapters that follow can help you navigate the many variables to consider. You and I both have learned a lot through trial and error. I offer these thoughts to help reduce the number of trials and errors experienced along your way to building and leading successful teams.

REFLECTION

- What is your experience in building or starting up a new team?

- What are lessons you've learned through trial and error?

- How can you use the New Team Checklist? (With a new team in the future? With your current team?)

- How can what you have learned in this chapter help you lead and inspire teams?

CHAPTER 4

BUILDING HIGH-PERFORMANCE TEAMS

"Never doubt that a small group of thoughtful, committed people can change the world. Indeed, it is the only thing that ever has."

—Margaret Mead

In your lifetime, you will be part of many teams—work teams, family teams, community teams, sports teams, and so on. I'll bet you can name those teams that were extra special. Everyone got along well, followed through on their commitments, trusted and respected one another, delighted their customers, delivered great results, and had fun doing it. In this chapter, we explore how to more frequently develop those teams. Admittedly, if you are in a management role, you have more latitude to create the environment that I'm going to share with you. And if you are a member or individual contributor on the team, you can still have influence in creating a high-performing team. The framework I am going to share is adapted from Gallup's work in this area. In addition, my dear friend and colleague Jerry Magar has taught me so much on this topic.

Image 4.1 shows the framework:

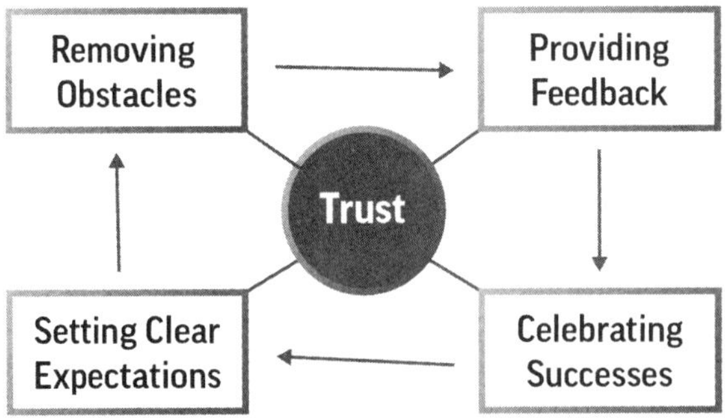

Image 4.1: Building High-Performing Teams Framework

You may be asking, "How do you know this framework produces a high-performance team?"

Gallup's research reflects positive results year after year for companies that give focus and attention to employee engagement using this framework. This includes improvements in profitability, employee productivity, safety incidents, inventory shrinkage, absenteeism, and quality.[1] What organization would not want this improvement? You can check out these results in Gallup's meta-analysis reports that they publish annually as part of their employee engagement survey section.

TRUST

I must start with the center circle entitled *Trust*. I spent a considerable amount of time in my first book sharing the behaviors that build trust.

The material I shared is from the decades of work done by Dr. Dennis Reina and Dr. Michelle Reina in their book, *Trust and Betrayal in the Workplace.*[2] I strongly recommend that you spend time building your knowledge and skills to build mutually trusting relationships. This is vital to your interpersonal relationships as well as your participation in and leadership of teams or groups. One further note—the more you practice and experience the four steps of building high-performance teams, the more trust will be sustained and deepened. And remember, trust is built, sustained, or broken in every interaction—every conversation, every email, every meeting, and even every nonverbal cue we may or may not recognize we are sending. It's back to "slow down to speed up." Get clear. Be thoughtful. Be intentional.

EXPECTATIONS

Expectations are a great segue from trust to the first step in building a high-performance team. Managing expectations is one of sixteen trust-building behaviors identified in the Reina Trust Model. Before you can manage expectations, you have to develop, communicate, and align them with everyone on your team. If you are the leader of the team, you want to manage expectations with several parties:

- Your expectations of your team members (both direct and indirect, if applicable)
- Your team members' expectations of you
- Your expectations of your boss
- Your boss's expectations of you
- Team members' expectations of one another
- Your expectations of customers or stakeholders
- Your customers' or stakeholders' expectations of you

Note that you can also use this framework with family members, book club members, sports team members, and so on. I can tell you from firsthand experience, it works.

This list may seem daunting, overwhelming, and even bureaucratic to some. In retrospect, I saw these things evident and working with some of the best teams I was a part of. My wish for you and all leaders is that you know and understand this framework and be able to use it with greater ease and greater results.

Before we review the high-performance team framework, let's back up a bit. Let me offer a slightly different yet closely related lens through which to view expectations: the lens of performance management. In this process of managing individual performance, there are four major inputs: job description, annual performance goals or objectives, quantitative metrics, and expectations.

JOB DESCRIPTION

Let's start with the job description. I'm going to bet you haven't thought about your job description in a long time, especially if you have been in your current role or at your current organization for a while. Generally speaking, it's when a job gets posted to be filled that we think about or read a job description. Well, it's time to go find that job description and determine if your team members are fulfilling the roles and responsibilities they were hired to do and are being paid to do. And while you're at it, be sure to review your own (wink, wink).

ANNUAL PERFORMANCE GOALS

Next, let's look at annual performance goals or objectives. Most people and organizations that I work with have annual planning cycles. The cycle might align with the fiscal or calendar year, and it's often tied to the annual budget cycle. Maybe these are projects or initiatives you and your team members are expected to complete in the upcoming year. Perhaps they are tied to larger departmental or business unit performance objectives. They may even be tied to personal development goals. Write them down, communicate and align on them, and track progress against them.

QUANTITATIVE METRICS

Next are quantitative metrics. These may be percentages that reflect acceptable or outstanding performance. For example, the percentage of problem tickets resolved within twenty-four hours, the percentage of sales closed in the quarter or year, the monetary amount of revenue generated, or the percentage of reduced turnover. The list goes on and on and varies by role, company, and even industry. Quantitative metrics might also reflect whether you are managing within your budget or hitting deliverable or milestone dates.

Each of these three—job description, performance goals, and quantitative metrics—constitute *what* you need to do to manage your performance in an optimum way. The fourth input, expectations, is about *how* you are going to do the first three. In other words, how you will work together as a team, with other departments, with stakeholders, or with customers.

EXPECTATIONS

Now, let's do a deep dive on this topic of expectations. First, let's look at the different kinds of expectations. The first kind is the expectations you know you have; you have communicated them, and you are aligned on what you really mean. Remember, the best way to ensure alignment is to walk through examples. We can be using the very same words yet meaning very different things. You likely have communicated your expectations periodically and in real time when leading your team.

When you communicate your expectations in these ways, others may or may not remember them or see them in bigger terms. In other words, they understood these expectations on project ABC or in situation XYZ but not in broader terms. To transfer experience or expectations across broader projects or day-to-day situations, you need to be very clear and specific. Remember that third learning agility question, "How will this help me going forward?" Don't assume your team member will understand this; state your broader expectation clearly.

A second kind of expectation is one you have but have not communicated. Since you haven't communicated it, you can't have alignment on it. These expectations often fall into the category called "common sense." If you have been in the workplace for a while, led global teams, or led multigenerational teams, you likely have discovered that common sense is not very common. Don't hesitate to state what is obvious to you. I encourage you to be transparent in offering your reasons for communicating these expectations *and* to be open to considering other ways to work together. Maybe there is new technology, new research, or marketplace conditions that require new thinking or new ways of working. I will now state the obvious: Others can't read your mind. If you haven't shared your expectations with those you work with, for, and around, it makes it much harder to provide feedback, and there will likely be a greater number of breakdowns, gaps, and more rework.

A third kind of expectation is the one you don't know you have until it is not met. I often refer to this one as the unconscious expectation. If you are early in your professional career, there may be more of these that you discover along the way. As you become conscious of these expectations, write them down. That leads to the next step of the process of developing: communicating and aligning your expectations. I have a tool that can help you get started. I call it the Expectations Menu. I have developed this tool by collecting many expectations documents from my coaching clients and leadership program participants. I have updated it from the one I offered in my first book; it now includes expectations when interaction occurs on a virtual platform. As most of us know, virtual platform interactions are more frequently used since the COVID-19 global pandemic of 2020–2021. I offer this tool to help you get started. Feel free to add, change, and delete those things that don't reflect your own expectations.

TOOL: EXPECTATIONS MENU

General Communications

- Speak up when you are not clear or when you don't understand.
- Don't just bring me problems or ideas. Identify the business problem you're trying to solve. Ideally, bring options and their pros and cons along with your recommendation for the best option.
- If there are obstacles, tell me what they are, what you've done to overcome the obstacle, and what you need from me.
- Your time and energy, as well as your priorities, should always focus on creating value for our stakeholders.

One-on-One Meetings

- Come prepared. Always have an agenda or a list of topics you want to discuss. Use the Checks and Balances tool (discussed later in this chapter) for consistent communication.
- Reach out in between meetings if you have questions or need direction.

Emails/Texts

- Respond within forty-eight hours unless a shorter time is requested.
- Clearly state your "ask" if there is one. If you need me to do something, email is the most reliable way for me to remember. I keep my inbox small and use it as my "to-do" list.
- If I am copied on an email, please include me on your reply so I know you have responded and no further follow-up is needed.

continued

- Provide context for a situation if you are asking for my advice, opinion, or decision.
- I will send emails after hours and on weekends. That is my choice. It does not mean I expect you to respond at that time.
- Emails should be short and concise and laid out in a logical manner (what, so what, now what). Bullet points are preferred.
- I prefer a text if you need me urgently.

Meetings

- State or know the objective of every meeting. Develop or ask for an agenda.
- Send agendas out at least twenty-four hours in advance.
- Be on time for meetings. Respect everyone's time as well as your own.
- End meetings at the scheduled time. Ensure that objectives were met. Recap at end of meeting.
- Be present in and contribute to meetings. Provide comments and insights. Ask questions.
- If we are using virtual platform technology to conduct our meetings, have your camera turned on. If there are compelling reasons to turn off your camera, discuss them with me beforehand.

Project Management

- Projects should be aligned with organizational and team strategies and priorities.
- If there are priority conflicts, discuss them with me.
- Make a work plan and walk through it with me at the start of projects.
- Set clear timelines and manage to meet them. Tell me when you're going to miss a deadline. Don't tell me when it is due or wait for me to ask you for it. This will allow us to reallocate staff and manage stakeholder expectations if changes are required. If a timeline needs to change, bring me the implications of changing it and your recommendations for moving forward.

Decision-Making and Escalations

- You can make decisions based on your approved dollar level of $XXX. If something requires higher-level decision-making, bring me the business case for the expenditure. If applicable, include options and make a recommendation on which option you would choose.
- If a decision requires someone higher than me to approve, engage me early with an appropriate business case for the expenditure. If applicable, include options and make a recommendation on which option you would choose.
- If a stakeholder has concerns or questions, engage me as you deem appropriate. If it is something we have handled before, use your judgment. If it is a new issue or a highly visible client, come talk to me. Consider the risk involved. The higher the risk, the more I want to be involved. Keep me informed on all client concerns.

General

- Ask for help.
- Be open to new ways of doing things.
- Work in a collaborative manner with all of our stakeholders.
- Deepen and expand your network for your benefit and for your team's benefit.
- We will discuss and determine together the options of working from home or being physically present in the office. You will honor our agreement and notify me when requesting an exception.
- Be present in the office on Wednesday and Thursday of every week: If there are compelling reasons for you to not come in, discuss them with me beforehand.

After you have made your changes, I recommend that you hold on to the list for about thirty days. During that time, notice when you have been frustrated, confused, surprised, disappointed, or angry when you have interacted with a team member. Review your expectations list. Is your unmet expectation reflected on your list? If not, do you want to add it? If so, you can now credibly provide feedback to your team members regarding their failure to meet your agreed-upon or aligned expectations. (More on giving feedback later in this chapter.)

Once you feel like you have captured the essence of your expectations, share them with your team. Make sure your expectations can be captured on one page, as it is hard for people to remember more than that as they move through their daily paces. If you find that you have lots more expectations than fit on one page, I challenge you to ask yourself if you are micromanaging, exercising high-control needs, or requiring almost everything to be done your way. I know this may be a bit blunt or direct, and I think it is an important personal challenge. I can assure you with great certainty that there are many successful and productive ways of working together. I will also assure you that it is hard to be a strong team player if you are not open to accepting different ways of working together. This is at the heart of diversity and inclusion—which we discuss in chapter 12. This challenge may also take you back to chapter 1, where we talk about greater self-awareness and how you may be showing up to others.

Don't be surprised if your team members add things to your list. Be open to that. Certain expectations may be so deeply engrained that you don't even realize you have them. Recognize and communicate to your team members that this is a dynamic document and that you will periodically review it with them to remind everyone of its content. I recommend doing this once a year. You may do it as part of your annual planning or budgeting cycle, when you're setting performance objectives, or when you're kicking off a new fiscal or calendar year. It's a great reminder for consistency, reinforcement, and commitment.

I also recommend you use this expectations document as a part of your onboarding process for new employees. It helps to establish a strong foundation of working together effectively and accelerates a new employee's learning curve.

While I encourage your expectations of team members not to exceed one page, I also recognize that you may have additional expectations that are unique to a given situation. Obvious expectations could be when something is due, including milestone dates for review and deliverables. It might also include specific research or resources to be cited in your final output, or a specific person or persons you need to talk to as subject matter experts. These additional expectations require clarity and thoughtfulness on your part too. Spending a bit of extra, focused time on your part will pay great dividends as the assignment is completed.

And now, we turn the page—the expectations document page, that is. It is now your team's turn to share their expectations of you. You can help them get started by offering some things you willingly commit to do. Here is a starting example of such a list.

YOUR EXPECTATIONS OF ME

General

- Spend quality time with me at least once a year to discuss my career.

Communications

- Tell me when direction changes.

Meetings

- Allow me to lead when it's my meeting.
- Step in to add value if relevant.

Emails

- Respond within forty-eight hours unless what's expected of me requires a sooner response.
- No response means no expectation.

Direction/Instructions

- I will ask if I need more information or help–no need to check in unless I'm missing something.

continued

- Clarity of what, why, when, and how if you have specific expectations of the way something needs to be done.

Feedback

- Provide me with timely feedback—both positive and for improvement.
- If I'm missing something, tell me privately when you discover it.
- If other feedback will help my development, ask the person to share it with me, or share it if they won't.

Remember, just because a team member asks or expects you to do something, you don't have to agree to it. Make sure their expectations are within your control to meet. Saying yes to something and frequently falling short leads to mistrust and even cynicism. It also demotivates them to want to meet your expectations. In other words, it is a lose-lose proposition. Have a healthy discussion, don't be afraid to push beyond your comfort zone, and push hard to meet the expectations you have agreed to with your team and other stakeholders.

REFLECTION

- How clear are you on your expectations with your team? Your boss? Others?

- What are some first steps you want to take to—
    - Develop your expectations?
    - Communicate your expectations?
    - Align your expectations?

OBSTACLES

Obstacles. We have all faced them many times throughout our lives. From the *Oxford English Dictionary* definition, an *obstacle* is "a thing that blocks one's way or prevents or hinders progress."[3] Other words akin to *obstacle* are *roadblocks*, *challenges*, or *barriers*. Almost every major project has them, and it is the team's job to manage them, remove them, or work around them.

The following Checks and Balances tool helps you manage expectations, and it also highlights obstacles. I recommend that if you are leading a team, you start with your direct reports or team members. As a leader, it is your responsibility to see that obstacles are removed. It is not your job to remove each one yourself, though. The most effective leaders coach others on how to remove them.

TOOL: CHECKS AND BALANCES

What did I accomplish in this period?	What are my objectives for the next period?
What are my challenges/issues/obstacles?	**What are key metrics? Progress, to date?**

Obstacles can be internal or external. Internal obstacles can be lack of skills, knowledge, or experience. Another internal obstacle is negative or limiting self-talk such as, "I could never follow up with that vice president to get back to me with his response to my email, even if it means me missing my deadline" or "Who am I to speak up about this potential problem? Everyone else in this meeting is so much more experienced than I am." External obstacles that will block progress might include a lack of equipment, lack of resources (people, time, and money), antiquated policies or processes, dysfunctional relationships, and possibly even YOU. You can be the obstacle if you have not communicated and aligned expectations, removed other obstacles soon enough, been available to your team when they have questions or need clarification, or provided feedback and coaching for greater performance productivity and effectiveness.

OVERCOMING OBSTACLES

Let's imagine you are having a weekly one-on-one update meeting with one of your team members. They are giving you a status report of their project or assignment, and they have failed to deliver on a commitment. They are further explaining the obstacle they have encountered that has prevented them from making progress. Your first question is, "What have you done to overcome this obstacle?"

This is an important question from several perspectives:

- It sends the message that you expect them to manage or overcome most obstacles.
- It allows you to determine if they believe it is their responsibility to manage or overcome obstacles.
- It allows you to assess whether or not they have done everything they can to manage or overcome the obstacle.

Based on your team member's response to the previous question, you now have three options:

- **Option 1**: If you believe they have not done everything they can do, you can now coach them on how to further follow through. This helps to develop their critical thinking skills. If they say they don't know what else they could do, ask them, "If you did know, what would you do?" This may sound like a silly question, but I will tell you that in most situations, the person knows or has a good idea about what needs to happen. The reason they are not acting on it could be that they fear doing the wrong thing, they don't think they have effective skills to address managing the obstacle, or they don't have the positional power or authority to address the obstacle with the appropriate person. As the team member's leader, try to determine which of these reasons is the culprit. You can then coach the team member accordingly.

Remember, it is your job to create greater capacity in others (e.g., developing them to manage or overcome most obstacles they encounter), and it is your role to see that problems get solved or obstacles are overcome rather than being the person to actually manage or remove the obstacle yourself.

- **Option 2**: If you think your team member has done everything in their power to effectively manage or overcome the obstacle, you can ask them, "What do you need from me to manage or overcome this obstacle?" Again, you are teaching them critical thinking and problem-solving skills.
- **Option 3**: This is a hybrid of options 1 and 2. There may be things your team member needs to do, and there may be things you need to do.

LEARNING AGILITY QUESTIONS

At the end of the process for managing or overcoming obstacles, I encourage you to use these three learning agility questions:

1. What did you do? (Describe the obstacle and what you specifically did to manage or overcome the obstacle.)
2. What did you learn? (Describe the skills you developed, the courage you displayed, and perhaps even the relationships you built or strengthened.) As the team's leader, you can help your team members see what occurred as a developmental experience.
3. How will this learning help you going forward? (Look for responses such as, "I will start earlier in communicating the reason behind or the urgency of the deadline," "I will be more clear on my expectations on the front end," "I will do more research to understand better how long it takes to perform some tasks or produce some deliverables," "I will be more aware that even

though something is important or a priority for me, others have their own list of important and priority tasks.")

REFLECTION

- What obstacles exist on your team?

- What will you do with your team to identify obstacles so you can better manage or overcome those obstacles?

  Note (and this is very important) that it's easy to identify people or teams as obstacles. I have been teaching this framework for many years. Be very clear when you are identifying obstacles–focus on the obstacles you are responsible for and can control. Also remember that when you are in a room pointing fingers at everyone else, there is another room with people pointing fingers at you and your team. Finger-pointing solves nothing. Clean up your obstacles first. Also, be honest about yourself being the obstacle. What do you need to do to not be the obstacle?

- What first steps do you need to take?

FEEDBACK

Feedback is a major component of the Reina Trust Model that includes Trust of Communication®, and it is worth discussing in length. The bottom-line purpose of giving and receiving feedback is to help people learn, grow, and perform better. Always know *your* intention when giving feedback. Is it in a moment of frustration? Is it venting your own anger? Or is it because you believe your feedback can help the other person do better next time around?

Also remember to provide feedback when someone has done something really well. When that person receives your positive feedback, they are more likely to display those behaviors again in the future. I can offer a tool to support you when you give constructive feedback. I have been using this Seven-Step Feedback Model for decades—I developed it from experience and extensive reading about giving effective feedback.

SEVEN-STEP FEEDBACK MODEL

FEEDBACK FRAMEWORK

- **Step 1**–State the behavior as specifically as you can.
- **Step 2**–Describe the impact of such behavior. This could be the impact on the budget, a contract, a customer or potential customer, a relationship, or even your views on being able to trust that person.
- **Step 3**–Describe your feelings and own them. For example, "I'm disappointed," rather than "You disappointed me." We choose how to feel (and respond) no matter what the circumstances.
- **Step 4**–Ask the individual to help you understand . . . and then listen. There are always two sides to every story. You will likely learn some new information. Be careful not to let them blame someone else. Don't discuss someone else's actions or behaviors. Your conversation is about the individual's specific behaviors (see step 1).

- **Step 5**—State what your expectations are going forward. (Remember, the trust behavior of managing expectations is in the Reina Trust Model's Trust of Character® section.) If you haven't developed, shared, and aligned expectations with this person previously, now is the time. If you have communicated them previously, restate or reinforce your expectations. If there is a new or different expectation, share the expectation and get alignment around it. And always ensure that your expectation is within their control. This avoids finger-pointing.
- **Step 6**—Ensure that they understand and agree to meet your expectation. This is a "look me in the eye and give me your word" moment. This is serious. You don't want a flippant, insincere, or begrudging agreement. Let them know you will hold them accountable for meeting your expectation. Accountability is a key ingredient, and there is no accountability without consequences. These are not hollow words from you. You have to be clear about what accountability and consequences you are thinking about. The best way to ensure understanding and alignment is to walk through a real example.
- **Step 7**—Determine whether the other person needs anything from you to ensure their success in meeting your expectation. Be careful not to take on too much, inevitably letting them off the hook for achieving the desired result. If it is a more junior or less experienced person, you may want more oversight, or it may require you to do a bit more reviewing and checking. If it is a more senior or experienced person, you may want to give them more autonomy.

Now, let's walk through a conversational example so you can see how I would apply the preceding process, step-by-step. The following demonstrates for you how I would navigate a scenario in which an expectation has not been met.

- **Step 1**—You have missed your last three project deliverable deadlines. Project A was due on October 1, and you delivered it on October 5 with no communication with me that it was going to be late. Project B was due November 3, and I had to ask you about it on November 4. Project C was due December 8, and I still don't know when it will be completed.

- **Step 2**—The impact of these missed deadlines is significant. The customer is unhappy with us and is about to trigger the penalty clause in our contract for missed deadlines. These financial penalties are serious and will be reviewed by senior leaders. Your team members have had to work overtime in order to keep subsequent deadlines from also being missed. My trust, as well as the trust of your peers, has been negatively impacted, given your track record of missed deadlines.
- **Step 3**—I am frustrated and disappointed in this pattern of missing deadlines. Each time we've discussed this, you have told me it won't happen again, and then it does.
- **Step 4**—Help me understand what is going on with all these missed deadlines. (The other person gives you their side of the story. Regardless of their explanation, the following steps will still be communicated.)
- **Step 5**—What I expect from you going forward is to let me know the minute you think you might miss the deadline. Knowing ahead of time gives me more desirable and effective options. I can reallocate resources. I can remove potential or real obstacles you may be facing, and I can let the customer know what is going on so we can work things out.
- **Step 6**—Do you agree to let me know the minute you think you might miss a deadline? (Wait for their response.) You have two deadlines coming up. Is everything on track to hit those? (They might say, "No, I can't guarantee that I won't miss a deadline." Well, of course they can't, and that is not your expectation. Your expectation is that they communicate with you in a timely fashion. That is totally within their control.)
- **Step 7**—Do you need anything from me to meet my expectations? (Then you would agree to—or not agree to—what the other person is asking from you.)

When we hear the word *feedback*, we almost always assume it means negative feedback. This model can be used for positive constructive feedback as well. Cite the effective or outstanding behaviors the person displayed. Perhaps your Step 5 expectation in this scenario is to keep up the good work or even teach and mentor others.

I recommend that as you begin to use this tool, you write out your script word for word and practice in front of the mirror. You want the content, the specific words, and the tone to be effective in helping the other person improve or keep doing effective things. It is absolutely okay to bring your notes with you and to refer to them throughout the conversation. Let the other person know you have some notes and will be referring to them in order to cover everything. Knowing you have documented notes brings a seriousness to the conversation. If the feedback doesn't result in improvement, you now have documentation required for other potential performance management scenarios.

By *giving* constructive feedback, you are telling the other person, "I care about you, and you can trust me to provide feedback that will help you learn, grow, take on bigger responsibilities, and achieve career aspirations."

By *receiving* constructive feedback, you are telling the other person, "I trust and value your observations and desire to help me improve." Once you've heard the feedback, it is your choice as to what to do with it. If it is similar to feedback you've received before, you may want to refocus your efforts. If it is new feedback and seems contradictory to other feedback you've received, you may want to check it out with someone you work with frequently or someone you know has your best interest at heart. Just because you may not like the person giving you the feedback doesn't mean you should ignore it. There may be real value in what they are offering.

One last point on feedback: It is my experience that the higher you go in the organization, the less feedback you receive. It is also my anecdotal experience that women want feedback more frequently than men do; this is not good or bad, just different. Something to consider is that if you keep asking for feedback, you may be perceived as needy, insecure, or lacking confidence. Let me offer a way to get the kind of feedback you want without ever using the word *feedback*. Here is an example:

Boss, we've just completed Big Project Alpha. It was a real learning experience, and I'm proud of my team as well as my leadership. As I review this project, here is what I thought worked well [then share your bullet points]. Here is what I learned that will really help me going forward [then share your bullet points]. From your perspective, have I missed anything? You have led a lot of projects, and I would appreciate your insights [then listen].

Generally speaking, you are helping your boss to help you. It's much easier to fill in the blanks than it is to start with a blank sheet of paper. I encourage you to provide a follow-up email thanking them for their input (or stating your happiness that you hadn't missed anything) and incorporate their input if any was given. This communicates to your boss that you are a learner, confident, and self-sufficient, and gives you recognition for the good work you did. Be sincere. Be balanced. Be high level. Don't get caught in every detail or line-item task of the project. That can backfire. If your boss is smart, she'll file that email away and use it when she completes your performance review. (Remember: Results + Recognition = Influence.)

CELEBRATING SUCCESSES

Not celebrating success may be one of the biggest oversights a leader can have. We are so busy focusing on just getting everything done that we may forget to recognize and celebrate our accomplishments. Stop. Take a breath. Recognize. Celebrate. Reengage.

Here are a few tips regarding recognition and celebrations:

- Make it appropriate to the level of performance or achievements. Big results warrant big celebrations.
- Don't overlook the small, consistent, reliable contributions and contributors. Their steadiness and consistency often enable other bigger things to happen.
- "The higher the value of the recognition reward, the lower the frequency. So a simple thanks from a co-worker can happen as frequently as an employee does recognition-worthy work."[4]

When I share that last statement, many leaders comment that they fear creating a needy or entitled team, so they just forego all recognition or celebration. I call this the "I told you that I loved you when I married you. If anything changes, I'll let you know" story. Another common phrase is, "No news is good news." I offer that there are rarely situations when recognition or celebration is overdone. Your judgment has to be developed and honed on how to balance appropriate recognition and celebration versus too little or too much.

I have come to appreciate the framework from the book *The 5 Love Languages* by Gary Chapman.[5] Admittedly, this book was originally intended for couples as a way of expressing "Heartfelt Commitment to Your Mate." The popularity of the book led to a subsequent book, *The 5 Languages of Appreciation in the Workplace* by Gary Chapman and Paul White.[6] I have adapted their work and provide a description of each of the love languages and affirmations below, one for our personal lives and one for our professional lives.

THE 5 LOVE LANGUAGES

- **Words of Affirmation**–As the label for this language implies, you might prefer a verbal or written "I love you" or other compliments. Words both elate *and* hurt you. Sending a specially selected card will give you that feeling of elation. Hurtful words or insulting comments will hit you hard and are not easily forgotten or forgiven.

continued

- **Quality Time**–The basic tenet of this love language is to give another person your undivided attention. You are not on your phone or multitasking. You are listening intently with no distractions. And **remember**, don't postpone or reschedule repeatedly. Deprioritizing their **quality** time with you is hurtful to them.
- **Acts of Service**–Providing help without being asked (or nagged) reflects this love language. You are telling the other person you care about them and want to give them a hand. And if you say you are going to do something, follow through and do it. Broken promises matter to the person who values acts of service.
- **Receiving Gifts**–This love language includes giving gifts that are meaningful and thoughtful. It doesn't mean the person is materialistic. The thoughtfulness of the gift is what counts. And don't give them the gift you want, give them the gift they want (wink, wink)!
- **Physical Touch–**The person who values this love language loves to hold hands, lock arms, and feel your arm around their shoulders. It is a hug or a kiss. A reassuring and appreciative closeness.

THE 5 LANGUAGES OF APPRECIATION

- **Words of Affirmation**–Words are the essence of this language of appreciation. Verbally expressing your thanks is an example of words of affirmation. Be specific in what actions, behaviors, or results support your "thank you." Other examples include the written word–emails, cards, handwritten notes. Again, be specific. Remember, rewarded performance is repeated.
- **Quality Time**–This particular language **of appreciation** is rooted in the belief that you consider someone "worthy" of your time. When you choose to plan for and prioritize quality-time meetings, you are saying that you value the other person's time and you want your time together to focus on the other person's agenda. This is in contrast to status-update meeting time together. I always wanted to have at least two quality-time meetings with my direct reports each year to discuss their career aspirations and how I could support them in achieving those aspirations. No status updates, no task or project assignments. These meetings were only about them and their career hopes and dreams.
- **Acts of Service**–This language of appreciation includes small gestures such as helping out with a project, covering for someone so that they can attend their child's graduation or special program, helping someone with a technology challenge,

and even bringing them their favorite morning coffee. There are also large gestures such as sending food, yard service, or housekeeping services when someone is deep into a work project that requires long hours. These gestures, small and large, are valued and communicate that you care about and appreciate the other person.

- **Receiving Gifts**–Some employees value gifts as a way of showing appreciation. This could be gift cards, flowers on special occasions, or personalized gifts that show you know what they like (e.g., sporting game tickets, musical concert tickets, or camping equipment to support their family's lifestyle). Remember there are tax implications based on the commercial value of the gift. Work with your human resources department or your tax team to understand the situation. Some organizations develop reward or appreciation platforms that allow employees to earn points and redeem those points for specific gifts. People who prefer this language of appreciation often love such fulfillment programs as long as their redemption gift choices include gifts they really want.
- **Physical Touch**–When I teach about this one in my programs, the more acceptable physical touch examples in a professional work setting include handshakes, fist bumps, or a literal pat on the back for a job well done. Do be mindful not to overdo or go to an extreme on this. Too much physical touch can be just that–too much. Know and maintain your boundaries and respect the other person's boundaries when it pertains to this language of appreciation. When in doubt, err on the side of "light" physical touch.

I believe that the key to using this love and appreciation language is KYP—know your people. For instance, don't give opera tickets to someone who hates opera . . . or sports . . . or concerts . . . or amusement parks. Also, take into account whether the recognition is best delivered publicly or privately. You can have the best intentions and not get the desired outcome if you get this wrong—as in public recognition of a deeply private person.

Back in my early leadership experience, I used index cards as my reference tool for knowing my people. I noted the spouse's name, children's names, weekend activities, hobbies, outside interests, and so on. I would pick up things in our casual conversations and capture notes on my index cards. Today there are automated tools for capturing information. Use what is comfortable for you. Bottom line—KYP!

WHEN TO CELEBRATE SUCCESSES

Here are some thoughts for determining when and for what you might want to recognize or celebrate a team or a specific team member.

- When a team member or team exceeds expectations
- When they consistently meet expectations
- When they respond to feedback and coaching and are making progress toward achieving performance standards or meeting your expectations

REFLECTION

- Who deserves recognition on your team and for what reason? (Make sure you identify what they did specifically to earn such recognition.)
- What team accomplishments deserve celebration?
- What kind of recognition or celebration is appropriate?

Note

1. There may be tax implications concerning individual recognition. Do your homework.
2. Rewarded/recognized performance is motivation for continuous high levels of performance.
3. Find something to recognize or celebrate.

Applying this framework isn't about adding meetings or conversations to your already busy calendar. It's about integrating them into your existing conversations, meetings, or touchpoints. *Run the company so the best people love it.* If you're spending most of your time with team members who are not meeting your acceptable levels of performance, dare I say, you want to challenge yourself on whether that is the best use of your time. You will get a greater return on the investment of your focus and energy by making decisions that benefit your best team members. See Image 4.2.

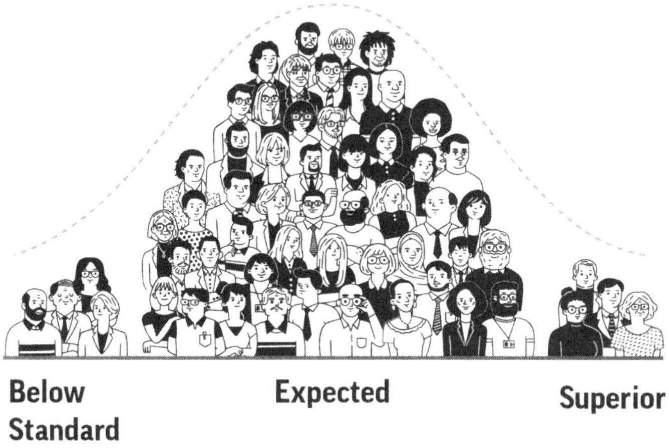

Image 4.2: Coaching High Performers

REFLECTION

- Which of these high-performing team elements do you think you do well? Describe how you implement and sustain that element.

- Which of these high-performing team elements do you want to work on? How will you go about that desired improvement?

- How will you involve your team and other stakeholder groups to ensure you have a more comprehensive view and perspective on building and sustaining your high-performing team?

CHAPTER 5

GROUP DYNAMICS

"Groups operate to their capacity because members choose to know and express themselves fully and to create a structure that elicits and uses everyone's contribution. Everyone tells the truth. Each person takes full responsibility for his or her behavior and feelings."[1]

—Will Schutz

There are many models to describe group or team dynamics. I shared the Bruce Tuckman model, developed in 1965 and updated along with Mary Ann Jensen in 1977, of forming, storming, norming, performing, and adjourning. Tuckman and Jensen said that these phases are all necessary and inevitable in order for a team to grow, face up to challenges, tackle problems, find solutions, plan work, and deliver results. This model has been very useful for describing and explaining group dynamics for more than fifty years.

Fast-forward to 2002. Patrick Lencioni wrote *The Five Dysfunctions of a Team: A Leadership Fable*.[2] Lencioni's book explores how teams fail to work cohesively together through a dynamic, five-part model of dysfunction. The five dysfunctions are 1) absence of trust, 2) fear of conflict, 3) lack of commitment, 4) avoidance of accountability, and 5) inattention to results. Through identifying these root causes of poor teamwork, teams can develop strategies for overcoming each of them.

A current search for books about team and group dynamics results in no shortage of titles ranging from psychology to sports analogies to family dynamics to emotional intelligence. I share this information to reflect the many lenses through which you can examine team dynamics. To accompany these books, there are many workshops you can attend or bring into your organization to further examine the topic.

THE HUMAN ELEMENT

The model I'm going to share with you is from Will Schutz, who served on the faculties of Harvard University, the University of California at Berkeley, and the Albert Einstein Medical School. His Fundamental Interpersonal Relations Orientation-Behavior (FIRO-B®) questionnaire is internationally recognized as one of the premier instruments in the field of human relations. After many years of practical use, Schutz created the next generation of the instrument, called Element B®, and a series of further FIRO instruments, intended specifically for development purposes. He used these as the basis of his approach, called The Human Element®. I was first introduced to Schutz's work in my master's program, and I was totally enamored by his body of work. It looks at our wants in the areas of inclusion, control, and openness from the perspective both of what we do (initiate) and what we get from others. Will's work is reflected in his model he calls The Human Element, which presents a well-tested theory and methods aimed at helping you increase your self-awareness, self-acceptance, and self-esteem and thus realize your full human potential, both individually and as a member of a group.[3]

Several fundamental principles lie behind The Human Element:

- At the heart of all human functioning is the self.
- Best solutions to organizational and leadership issues require self-awareness as an essential first step.
- Deeper self-awareness leads to self-acceptance and then self-esteem.
- As individuals gain self-awareness and self-esteem, they become more open and honest with their co-workers. They redirect the energy they now use for defensiveness, withholding, and other interpersonal struggles into productive work.[4]

• • •

Let me also offer Will's descriptions of the following from his book, *The Human Element*:[5]

- "***Self-awareness*** is the extent to which I let myself know my own experience. If I'm afraid of, ashamed of, or guilty about some things that have to do with me, I may repress or deny them. The part of my experience that I choose not to let myself know about can be called my unaware part, or my *unconscious*. When I'm aware of my experience, I can decide consciously what I want to do. When I'm not aware of my experience, it may control me in a way I do not understand."[6]
- "***Self-concept*** is my individual sense of how I experience myself, how I perceive myself."[7]
- "***Self-esteem*** is the way I feel about my self-concept. When I feel good about my self-concept, I have strong self-esteem."[8]

- "Self-concept and self-esteem are crucial to personal and professional effectiveness because if they are not fully positive, I may act in mystifying and sometimes destructive ways."[9]

Merriam-Webster.com describes *self-acceptance* as "the act or state of understanding and recognizing one's own abilities and limitations."[10] It seems to me that self-acceptance is a choice, and you make a more informed and intentional choice once you have greater self-awareness and understand your self-concept and self-esteem. Your choice is, for any given situation, you will either practice self-acceptance or will judge or criticize yourself, and that is an important choice you make every day, many times, and day after day.

Unlike some assessment instruments, such as the Myers-Briggs Type Indicator (MBTI) that describe your individual results as innate (i.e., your results rarely change no matter how many times you take the instrument), your FIRO Element B wants vary from time to time and group to group. Think about how your wants vary from your family group to various work groups to your book club and so on. In addition, your wants are different in your twenties, thirties, and forties, as well as when you are single, married, or married with children.

Working with women and looking at the research as a woman myself, I believe there are some insights that would be particularly useful on life's journey.

According to the jacket cover of Schutz's book *The Human Element: Productivity, Self-Esteem, and the Bottom Line*, "Teams perform to their potential only when members accept themselves, take responsibility for their feelings, and interact constructively with others. Only leaders who possess the self-esteem and confidence needed to speak the truth gain the loyalty of their followers. And groups make effective decisions only when they create a structure that elicits and uses everyone's contributions."[11] I couldn't agree more!

In its simplest form, there are eight principles behind The Human Element model.

1. **Truth**—Truth is the grand simplifier. Relationships—in the long run and, usually, in the short run—are greatly simplified, energized, and clarified when they exist in the atmosphere of truth.
2. **Choice**—You choose your own life—your thoughts, feelings, sensations, memories, health, everything—or you choose not to know you have a choice. (Anyone who knows me knows this is a fundamental tenet of my work and how I live my life. Each of us has been given the gift of free will to make myriad choices every day of our lives.)
3. **Simplicity**—The most profound solutions are simple. Simple is best.
4. **Limitlessness**—Human beings have no limits to their potential. Our only limits are limits of belief.
5. **Holism**—All aspects of a person (thoughts, behavior, feelings, and the body) are interrelated.
6. **Completion**—Effectiveness and joy are enhanced by the completion of unfinished experiences.
7. **Dimensions**—The basic dimensions of human functioning are inclusion, control, and openness.
8. **Self-Esteem**—All behavior derives from self-esteem.[12]

REFLECTION

How do you relate to each of these principles?

- Truth:
- Choice:
- Simplicity:
- Limitlessness:
- Holism:
- Completion:
- Dimensions:
- Self-Esteem:

FIRO ELEMENT B

Initially, Will Schutz spoke about our needs (versus our wants). Will's son Ethan writes, "We really do not know if or how much people *need* inclusion, control, and openness, so it is more helpful to assume that people *want* some amount of each of these. In Will Schutz's words, 'It is much more valuable to assume you have the capacity to change anything you do not like about your behavior, if you allow yourself to learn how.' This reorients problem solving by keeping people focused on their own role in their lives. In other words, it pushes people to take ownership of their own behaviors and choices."[13] Schutz's FIRO Element B instrument looks at our wants. *Oxford English Dictionary* defines *want* as a "desire to possess or do something." The *Merriam-Webster Dictionary* describes *want* as a "desire, wish: to feel or have the need of." And Vocabulary.com describes the concept of *want* as "In all its forms, want has to do with the lack of having and the desire to have. You can want or desire something you like, or you can be in want of something you need."[14] I don't mean to talk in circles, and I hope these definitions help you frame the subsequent content of this chapter. "Exploring wants instead of needs changes the conversation. Wants prompt exploration and inquiry."[15]

I also want to lay a bit of groundwork about the word *interpersonal* in the Fundamental Interpersonal Relations Orientation (FIRO). *Interpersonal* means any interaction, real or imagined, occurring between people. When I share this point, I often get puzzled looks, so let me explain. A *real* interaction is when the other person or people can participate in or observe the interaction. Examples are face-to-face conversations, emails, meetings, and even nonverbal body language. So, what is an *imagined* interaction? Think for a minute. Have you ever had a conversation in your head with someone else even though the other person wasn't there? Maybe it was preparing for a meeting presentation or a difficult conversation. "I will say this, and then he will likely say that." Or maybe I'm reliving an interaction that didn't go well. "I should have said . . ." or "I can't believe [the other person] blindsided me." I bet you can relate to these imaginary interactions. And on a personal front, you could swear you told someone something, and they declare you never did. (My parenthetical here is that if someone were following me around with a video recorder, I have a fifty-fifty chance that I actually did share that something with the other person.) The point here is that in our brains, the same neural pathways occur regardless of whether the interaction was real or imagined. Now, read that sentence again. Yes, it is true. So you have to be really careful that you tell yourself (your brain) what is real and what is imagined. Otherwise, you can get labeled as forgetful, delusional, or needing always to be right. When I acknowledge and understand this, it opens up a whole new world of choice and opportunity, which is at the heart of Will's and now Ethan Schutz's work.

If your physical or psychological wants are not met, it can lead to a state of discomfort or anxiety. To avoid such unpleasant outcomes, you are motivated to take action to get your wants met. Keep in mind, you can do this in a healthy and effective way by having self-awareness about your wants and being very intentional about how you can get your wants met (or not). (Note: I will use the terms *wants*, *desires*, and *wishes* interchangeably.) This is reflected by making intentional choices. You can also try to get your wants met in unhealthy ways ranging from being a needy or high-maintenance person or engaging in extreme behaviors such as addiction, alcoholism, sabotage, or other toxic psychological behaviors. I think about this as being unconscious or even blind to my wants and, therefore, making unintentional choices. This is a perfect reason why understanding these things about myself allows for better choices regarding my behavior.

Once you recognize, acknowledge, and understand your own desires, you can begin to recognize, acknowledge, and understand the desires of others and manage yourself in a more healthy, effective way.

Let me share Image 5.1 to use as a framework to understand the dimensions. These dimensions constitute the basis of the Human Element approach.

	See	Want
Do	I include people.	I want to include people.
Get	People include me.	I want people to include me.

	See	Want
Do	I control people.	I want to control people.
Get	People control me.	I want people to control me.

	See	Want
Do	I am open with people.	I want to be open with people.
Get	People are open with me.	I want people to be open with me.

These dimensions constitute the basis of the entire Human Element approach. Study them until you feel confident that you understand them well.

Image 5.1 Courtesy of Ethan Schutz

UNDERLYING FEELINGS

Also, there are underlying feelings for each of the three dimensions. These are reflected in the FIRO Element F: Feelings instrument. The underlying feeling for inclusion is *significance*. How significant do you consider me to be so you invite me to your meetings or add me to your email distribution list? And how significant do I consider you to do the same?

The underlying feeling for control is *competence*. How willing I am to allow you to take control of the meeting or conversation depends on how competent I believe you to be and vice versa.

The underlying feeling for openness is *likability*. How open can I be with you and ensure that you still like me and vice versa? This is closely tied to your willingness to take risks and be vulnerable. Let's see how all of this plays out in our day-to-day lives.

INCLUSION

In this chapter (and in my programs), I focus on principle number seven of The Human Element model: inclusion, control, and openness. Let's start with inclusion.

Inclusion, as a concept in team dynamics, refers to associations between and among people: the desire for attention, interaction, belonging, uniqueness. Being unique implies that I am interested enough in you to discover who you are. In the initial testing of a relationship, you present yourself to me so I can discover what part of you will interest me. If you aren't sure I care about what you say, you may be silent or withdrawn. Inclusion does not entail strong emotional involvement with another person. One's concern over being included is a preoccupation with prominence. Because inclusion is crucial to the process of group formation, it is usually the interpersonal dynamic in the life of a group. Your first decision is whether you want to be part of the group—whether you want to be *in* or *out*.

A general summary of inclusion—both what you do and what you get—includes:

- A behavior reflecting how much you want to be IN or OUT of the group
- How much you include others and want attention, contact, and recognition from others
- Associations between people regarding their desires to interact, to belong, and to be unique
- Determining the extent of contact and prominence a person seeks

Remember, inclusion is the **first stage** of group development. It is often reflected in the language of being in the inner circle or part of the in crowd. Now, let's break down our inclusion behavior into what you do, what you receive, and what you want.

INITIATING INCLUSION

Think about a group to which you belong. Maybe you are the positional leader of the group; maybe you are a member of the group. Got it?

ACTIVITY

As you read each of the following behavioral statements, how well do they describe you on that team? Mark an *X* on the Low-Medium-High continuum (Image 5.2) as an overall assessment of the collective behavioral statements. Please note, you could be low on some of the statements, high on others, or somewhere in between.

Behavioral Statements—Including Others

- I make an effort to include others in my activities.
- I encourage participation in activities (both for myself and others).
- I try to be with people as much as possible.
- I invite others into conversations or to social events.
- If someone appears distant, I reach out to them and invite them to join.

Where do you see yourself on this dimension?

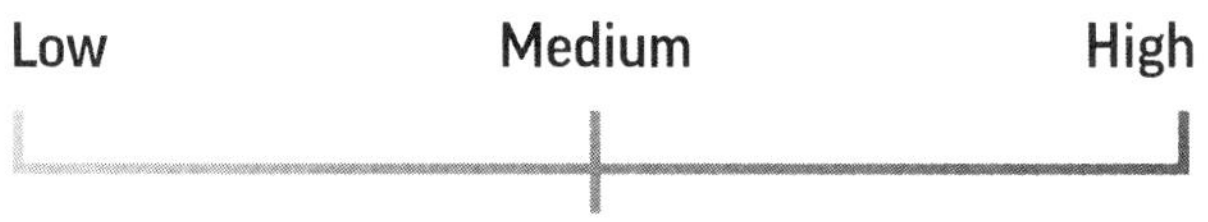

Image 5.2

Let me share an example. Imagine you are standing in the hall talking to someone, and you spy someone from your team walking by. If you have a higher desire to include people, you will likely turn to invite them into your conversation, bring them up to speed on what you were chatting about, and ask them for their thoughts or perspective. Now, let me share a few teaching points regarding this example. By inviting the person in, you are getting *your* wants met. You may or may not be getting anyone else's wants met—either the person you were originally talking to or the person you invited to join the conversation. This depends on whether or not the two other people have low, medium, or high wanted inclusion. (More on wanted inclusion later in this chapter.) This is a case of you projecting your wants onto them. In simple terms, projection is unconsciously attributing that if I have a desire for inclusion, everyone else must have a similar wish. This is a prime example of getting my wants met in a healthy, effective way . . . or not. A more effective way would be to give that teammate walking down the hall an option to join you rather than assuming they want to be included.

Next, let's look at *wanted inclusion*.

WANTED INCLUSION

Think about the same group from the previous activity.

ACTIVITY

As you read each of the following behavioral statements, how well do they describe you on that team? Mark an X on the Low-Medium-High continuum (Image 5.3) as an overall assessment of the collective behavioral statements. Please note, you could be low on some of the statements, high on others, or somewhere in between.

Behavioral Statements–Wanted Inclusion

- I want other people to include me.
- I want to be invited to belong or to events.
- I am let down if I do not get an invitation to a party or event.
- I make an effort to belong to groups and join in social activities.
- I want to be part of others' activities.
- I like working on team activities.

Where do you see yourself on this dimension?

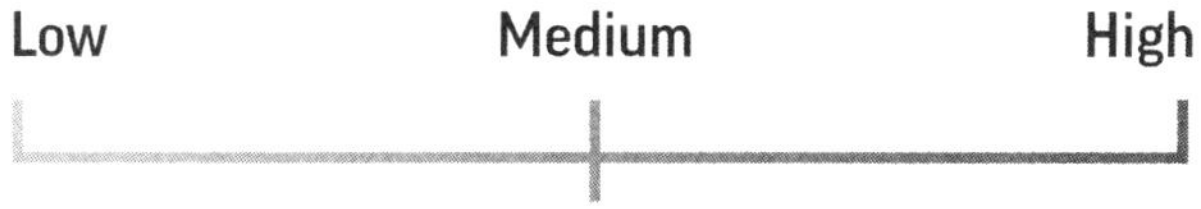

Image 5.3

An important thing to note regarding wanted inclusion is that the most important inclusion aspect is the invitation. It doesn't necessarily mean you want to go to the party, event, or social activity. Let me share an example.

Everyone at work knows that Maria hosts the best holiday party. If you get invited to her party, you are a part of the in crowd. Maria has invited you to her party for the last three years. You love that you were invited, though you have never actually attended the party. This year, Maria is reviewing her guest list. She removes your name since you have never attended. It's now about two weeks away from the time she usually has the party, and you have not received your invitation. In order to get your inclusion wants met, you might act in this way:

You to Co-Worker 1: Have you received your invitation to Maria's party?

Co-Worker 1: Yes, I did. I'm so excited.

You to Co-Worker 1: When did you get it?

Co-Worker 1: Last week sometime.

You to Co-Worker 1: Oh, okay.

This example reflects the difference between what you get and what you want to get from others in terms of inclusion. You then repeat this conversation with several other co-workers. You walk away from those conversations a bit perplexed and with a touch of devastation. You ask yourself, "What might I have said or done to Maria that caused her not to invite me?" In other words, you are having an imagined interaction with Maria. Add to this the fact that women have an overdeveloped guilt center, and now you are really concerned. You don't quite know how to act toward Maria. Should you confront her? Throw your own party and not invite her?

There is no magic answer. If Maria is a close friend, you might ask her about it. If you are self-aware about your own inclusion wants, you might recognize what is happening and come to the conclusion that Maria made a logical choice in taking you off her invite list based on you never showing up.

Here is another example. Someone comes to you and asks about the group of people who meet in the conference room next to your office. "Who are they? What are they working on? How can I be a part of that group?" Often, the person asking these questions gets labeled as nosy, annoying, or high maintenance. You may even say to yourself, this person doesn't have enough to do. In reality, they may be trying to get their high inclusion wants met. This is another example of someone lacking the self-awareness of their wants and trying ineffectively to get them met. If you are that person's leader, you might ask them what they are looking for by seeking to be included in that particular group. It could be about building a broader network, working on a high-visibility project, or FOMO (fear of missing out). You can help them find a more effective way of managing their wants for inclusion after first helping them get clearer about what their wants are. And remember, it's not your job to meet everyone else's wants.

To round out this inclusion dimension, I'll share an exercise from *The Human Element Leaders Manual* that I do in my programs that is quite an eye-opener. The exercise is called "X" Marks the Spot. The exercise instructs people to arrange themselves around the *X* based on how significant they feel as part of their cohort group (remember that feelings of significance underlie inclusion). I ask questions of various people to surface their thought process about why they chose a specific place to stand. The outcome of my questions reflects a rather wide spectrum on how individuals define significance. For example:

- "I define significance based on how much I am contributing to this learning group."
- "I define significance by how much I am getting out of this program."
- "I feel like we are all equal and that we are all significant."
- "I don't feel particularly significant. If I wasn't here, the class would still go on."

Teaching Points

There are a few teaching points here:

- Different people define significance differently. Be careful assuming everyone defines it the same way you do.

- Ask your team members or teammates what contributes to them feeling significant. This is a tip for you knowing how to inspire or recognize them.
- There is no right or wrong place to stand. The dissonance felt is when someone has high wanted inclusion and is standing in the periphery of the space. In other words, that person's wants are likely not being met in this group.
- There is also a flip side to the above bullet. Someone might find themselves standing close to or even on top of the *X* because they feel a sense of responsibility to show up in all scenarios. If the person has high inclusion wants, standing on or near the *X* works for them, but if they have lower inclusion wants, it can feel almost burdensome.
- If someone leaves or joins the group, the array might change. If the person leaving was a person feeling very significant and considered him- or herself part of the inner circle, it may leave a void to be filled, and someone may now feel more significant than they felt before that person left.

Themes

In doing this exercise for over twenty years around the world with both women only as well as co-ed groups, I have noticed some themes:

1. Men are generally not hesitant in claiming their significance in the group.
2. Significance is often related to a hierarchical structure. The person with the biggest title is often by default the most significant person in the group. This occurs most often when I am working with an intact group doing an in-house program.
3. Some organizations define significance based on seniority: The

people who have been with the organization the longest are the most significant. Other organizations define significance by level of education: Those with PhDs are more significant than those with master's degrees; people with master's degrees are more significant than people with bachelor's degrees, and so on. Still others define significance by functions. For example, in an engineering firm, the engineers are considered the most significant, and those who perform support functions are considered less significant.

4. In many women's leadership programs, there is a strong pull for everyone to feel significant. In fact, women will literally pull a woman closer to the *X* to signify more equal significance for all. That is another example of projecting our wants onto another person.
5. It's not unusual for some women to almost want to appear invisible. Women share that they prefer invisibility to the risk of being a visible target for rejection, particularly from other women.
6. I always try to notice the energy in the room while doing this exercise. There is generally a bit of nervous laughter because participants are unsure of the "right answer" in the exercise. Again, I emphasize there is no right or wrong answer. I think that's why our conversations are so rich (and, therefore, why I love this body of work).

At this point in the program, women have had two lenses through which to view their significance and inclusion wants. First, by selecting a team and assessing their behaviors with that team as low, medium, or high. And second, as a learning team and member of a cohort program. In my programs, participants also do an online assessment to give yet a third lens. Remember, our wants change from group to group and also as we move through life's phases or seasons.

REFLECTION

What stands out for you after reading this material on inclusion?

Identify various teams or groups of which you are a member—such as, a team you lead, your boss's team, your immediate family, or other groups to which you belong. How would you assess your inclusion wants in each of those groups? You might consider making a table like the following one.

Put a check mark in the column that best describes your wants.

	Low	Medium	High
My Team			
My Boss's Team			
My Immediate Family			
Other			

What new insights about others—family members, colleagues/peers, or friends—did you consider regarding their inclusion wants?

Here is a quick summary of inclusion:

- **Issue**—How much do I want to be *in* or *out*? How much prominence do I seek?
- **Underlying Feeling**—Significance
- **Interpersonal or Group Fear**—Being ignored, missing out, or being abandoned
- **Personal Fear**—Being insignificant or unimportant[16]

My wish is that everyone feels a sense of significance always. When you feel significant within yourself, you know you make a difference. Your feelings about yourself, how you feel about other people, and how you behave toward other people are all connected. Feelings of significance come, in large part, from your early years. Sometimes you get stuck, and your own self-perceptions can limit you. By being aware of and understanding your own wants, you can manage your wants. This is part of you showing up as a powerful, authentic leader—one who inspires her team to be their most powerful and authentic selves too.

CONTROL

Now, let's talk about our control wants. As inclusion is about being in or out of the group, control is about being at the *top* or *bottom* of the group. Control refers to power, influence, and authority between people. If, in an argument, you are seeking inclusion, then you want to be one of the participants in the argument. If you're seeking control, you want competence (the underlying feeling for control), and you want to be on the winning side of the argument.

UNDERLYING DOMINANCE

Let's talk about how many of us view or interpret the word *control.* It is often interpreted as a desire to be dominant. *Merriam-Webster's* dictionary defines *dominant* as "commanding, controlling, or having great influence over all others; very important, powerful or successful."[17] In my programs, I am very clear that being dominant is not the same as being dominating. *Merriam-Webster* has several definitions of *dominate,* and the one I want to offer in this context is "to occupy a more elevated or superior position; to exert the supreme determining or guiding influence on."[18] The way I see it, *dominance* is having a commanding presence and being able to influence others. *Dominating* is having an attitude or persona of being superior to another, almost in a hierarchical or one-up, one-down kind of way. For myself, I want to be dominant; I don't want to be dominating. And in the context of Schutz's work, I want to be competent. I hope this brings you some clarity. I don't want the words themselves to distract from the message.

Remember that each of the dimensions is a separate assessment or designation. In the case of control, my wish for control shows up in my desire to be in charge and direct others. Control behavior may also be manifested in your degree of resistance to someone else trying to control you. Expressions of independence or rebellion indicate resistance to someone else trying to control you. Conversely, compliance and willingness to take orders indicate an acceptance of higher wanted control.

UNDERLYING CONTROL

"Underlying control behavior is the experience that accompanies feeling or not feeling competent." According to Schutz, "Central to the dimension of control is choice, also referred to as self-determination or autonomy."[19] "No one has yet tested the limits of human capacity; however, a key factor in extending capacity is to assume that you determine your own life and are capable of making the changes you wish for yourself, as well as in your relationships or work situations. As a pragmatic statement, this gives you a way of operating that allows you to transcend self-imposed limit ations."[20]

"Once you accept that you determine your life, everything is different. You accept your power."[21] This includes the several steps required to get here: acknowledging that you have power, understanding your power, embracing your power, and expanding your power. Wow! That is amazing!

Please read this next paragraph carefully. If you are willing to take on this concept of choice and power, you have real freedom. Others don't get to define you.

You understand that such things as group pressure, manipulation, using people, brainwashing, or scapegoating will no longer be done to you. You cannot be pressured or manipulated or used unless you allow yourself to be.[22]

This choice principle reorients your search for solutions. Before, when things didn't go well, you blamed others and maybe even cursed the fate that made you a victim of the circumstances. When you assume that you choose a situation or a response to a situation, you move beyond blaming. You look for the payoff you get for contributing to the situation in which you find yourself.[23] From my own personal experience, when I find myself in an unwanted situation and I know I have contributed to it, I ask myself, "What am I getting, and what am I giving up if I continue this behavior or action?" This is how I hold myself accountable. One of my ways of describing leadership is "being accountable for the intended and unintended consequences of my choices." And I can always choose differently; it is all within my control.

CONTROL SUMMARY

Let's now lay out a general summary of control—what you do, what you receive, and what you want:

- A behavior reflecting how much you want to be TOP or BOTTOM in a group
- How much responsibility and influence you want and how much you desire to be led and influenced by others
- Relations between people regarding power, influence, and authority
- The extent of power or dominance a person seeks

Control is the **second stage** of group development. If you have seen my YouTube video about Foundational Elements,[24] I offer that "in absence of a plan, create one. In absence of a leader, be one." I think this accurately reflects this dimension of control.

INITIATING CONTROL

Think about the same group you identified in the inclusion activities.

ACTIVITY

As you read each of the following behavioral statements, how well do they describe you on that team? Mark an *X* on the Low-Medium-High continuum (Image 5.4) as an overall assessment of the collective behavioral statements. Please note, you could be low on some of the statements, high on others, or somewhere in between.

Behavioral Statements–Controlling Others

- I try to take control of situations–directly or indirectly.
- I strive to influence others in given situations.
- I enjoy directing others.
- I work hard to get my way.
- I enjoy organizing things (events, meetings, vacations, closets, etc.).
- I am comfortable taking responsibility.
- I am comfortable assuming authority.

Where do you see yourself on this dimension?

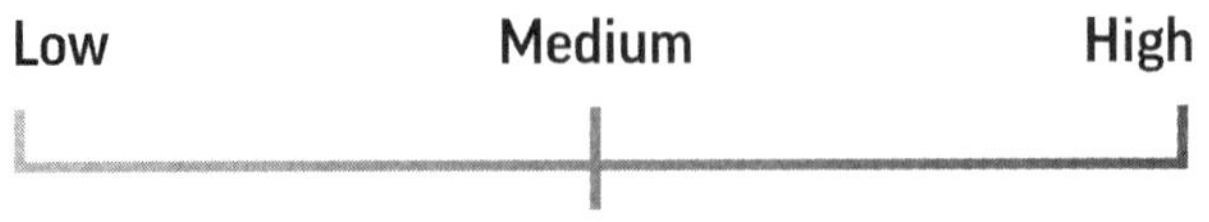

Image 5.4

If you often find yourself volunteering or being asked to lead projects or initiatives (and you always say yes), you might have higher desire for control. When I teach this content, I ask my program participants, "If you can picture your clothes closet, how many of you have grouped your dresses, dress slacks, casual slacks, jeans, long-sleeve shirts, short-sleeve shirts, and so on?" In one particular program at a technical company with a good number of engineers in the room, almost everyone raised their hands. There was one lone gentleman from marketing who laughed out loud and said, "I'm feeling good if I even hang up my clothes!" And there you have the ends of this continuum. Remember, there are no right or wrong answers!

Now, let's talk about control wants.

WANTED CONTROL

Think about the same group you identified in the previous activities.

ACTIVITY

As you read each of the following behavioral statements, how well do they describe you on that team? Mark an *X* on the Low-Medium-High continuum (Image 5.5) as an overall assessment of the collective behavioral statements. Please note, you could be low on some of the statements, high on others, or somewhere in between.

Behavioral Statements–Wanted Control

- I am most comfortable working in well-defined situations.
- I like to get clear on expectations.
- I like instructions spelled out well on activities.
- I am apt to ask permission for a task that has specific outcomes when I am not totally clear about what is desired.

continued

- I am comfortable with others taking the lead.
- I am receptive to others' influence.

Where do you see yourself on this dimension?

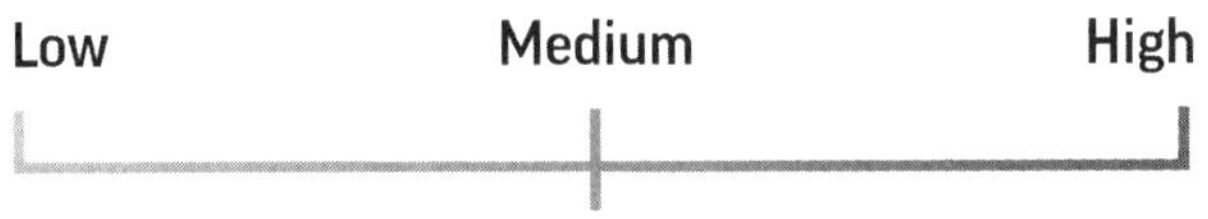

Image 5.5

If you find it hard to get started on a task or project without getting all of the instructions, requirements, expectations, and specific outcomes, you might have higher wanted control. In other words, you want someone else to provide the information and direction and command the work.

CONTROL EXERCISE

This is an opportunity for another exercise called the Dominance Line from *The Human Element Leaders Manual.* I instruct participants to line up shoulder-to-shoulder facing me and from left to right representing least to most dominant in the group. They now come face-to-face with their wanted control.

The participants are then asked to indicate if they are positioned correctly according to the instructions, as well as others being positioned correctly according to the instructions given. They are then invited to move people to the place in the line they think that person belongs. This looks at the program participants as a learning team and gives them another look at their wishes in a group—one that is different than the one they used in the continuum activities. This is a very uncomfortable assignment for almost every group. There is a higher noise level than in the inclusion exercise.

The noise level and nervous laughter are very evident. In most groups, there is moving someone up, then someone else moves, and this continues for about three to five minutes. Most often, women are moved to the more dominant end of this dominance line. There are many variations, so let's dissect this exercise and identify the teaching points.

I tell the participants that I have been intentionally serious because this is often when their control wants show up. I am trying to elicit or trigger a wanted control response.

I then tell the participants that in several situations, participants have refused to do the exercise—or as one person said, "I will not play this silly game." I ask the participants what they think about that. There are a wide range of responses, such as, "They don't want to admit to or show their high wanted control," "They don't need to demonstrate their dominance," "They don't care," or "They have no control wants."

Let me share how to interpret this refusal to participate. *Withholding or withdrawing is the ultimate form of control.* You learned it as a child when you said, "I'm taking my ball (or doll, or Legos) and going home." Let that sink in. Think about situations when you may have a disagreement or even a conflict with someone and they won't engage or respond to you. Consciously or unconsciously, this is a control move or strategy. I want to be clear: Withholding or withdrawing is a tool in your tool kit. Use it wisely, intentionally, or strategically. A word of caution—don't overuse the tool. If you are always withholding, you can appear to be a blank screen and others can make up their own story about you or the situation. Withholding can be a temporary or long-term strategic choice. If it's your temporary choice, you may be buying time to get clearer—slowing down to be intentional and strategic in your response. If it's your long-term choice, you may be moving out of a toxic situation either personally or professionally. If you are withholding because you lack the skills or courage to have a difficult conversation, seek out support or guidance from a trusted mentor, boss, or even a coach. If withholding is the ultimate form of control, insisting on the same definition is the penultimate form of control, and even more so that we agree to use *my* definition.

This exercise also has country or cultural norms. For example, in many Asian countries, program participants defer to elders or those with higher positional power to be the most dominant. In Germany, one man positioned himself as the middle of the line and was steadfast in staying there no matter how many others tried to move him toward the most dominant end of the line. His control wants were reflected in him positioning himself as "in the middle" and refusing to be moved. One of the most memorable experiences of this exercise came in India. I was working with an in-house team with multiple hierarchical levels. When we spent too much time trying to get everyone's agreement on how people should be lined up, the site manager (the most senior person in the room) stood in front of me and told the participants, "Give her your thumbs-up; this is taking too long." The participants in the dominance line grew quiet, and their eyes widened. What was going to happen? Since I had been facilitating this exercise for a while, I remembered my withholding tool. I said nothing, and after a moment of silence, the site manager returned to his position as the most dominant in the line. I was not willing to give away my power as facilitator, and I said, "That would be a great example of wanted control," and then went right on with the exercise. When I reflected on that scenario, I had several insights about different wants at different times in my life. If I had been my twenty-something self, I likely would have acquiesced and accepted his directive without protest. If I had been my forty-something self, who had just been named a corporate officer of a Fortune 50 company, I likely would have been dominating (versus dominant) and told him to get back in line and that I was facilitating the exercise. In my late fifties, I was most intent on providing a valuable learning experience. Admittedly and upon reflection, I'm embarrassed to consider my response as a forty-something, and I have to own it.

Additional Insights: Control Exercise

As we continue to debrief the exercise, there are additional insights to be discovered.

- Our control wants tend to show up most when it is time to make a decision (and note that this is when conflict often occurs). At decision-making time, if you offer up your position or point of view, you will be seen as competent by others, and thus, your contributions will be given weight and consideration. Will you be dominant enough to even offer your position or point of view to begin with? If you choose not to offer your thoughts and have a high desire for control, it is most likely that your control wants will not be met relating to the underlying feeling of competence. If you offer your thoughts, and others ignore them or diminish them, your control wants will also not be met. Now you are back to the concept of choice. Remember, others don't get to define you. You cannot be pressured or manipulated or used unless you allow yourself to be. Make a deliberate choice to hold on to or give away your power.
- Other times your control wants show up during a crisis or when there is chaos or confusion. Remember, in the absence of a plan, create one. Your control wants will drive you to handle the crisis and bring order to the chaos or confusion.
- Who would you guess does most of the moving of others in that part of the dominance line exercise? Anecdotally speaking, in approximately 80 percent of the cases, people lined up in the more dominant part of the line do the moving. Around 10

percent of the time, the moving comes from people standing in the middle of the line. In the last 10 percent of the cases, people in the least dominant part of the line do the moving. It isn't too surprising that 80 percent of the time the moving is coming from the higher dominance end of the line. The surprise often shows up when the lesser dominant part of the line does the moving. There are two plausible possibilities when this occurs. First, some people will exert or act upon their control wants only when given an invitation or given permission to do so. Second, their want for control may be higher than they realized and may be a blind spot for them. Our discussions around this often yield some greater self-awareness moments.

- You can have different control wants around the *what* versus the *how*. In my case, I have higher wanted control around how we arrive at decisions. I want to make sure everyone has an opportunity to contribute their best ideas or thinking. Whatever we come up with is fine with me. What is true for you? You likely have heard the following two phrases, and they can help you learn about someone else's wanted control. The first phrase is, "This is *what* I want; now go make it happen." The second phrase is, "Make sure you include these people before you decide what to do [the *how*]." Not to confuse you, but I want to offer that often there are two opportunities for our *how* control needs to show up. Initially, there is *how* you want to arrive at the *what*. Once you have arrived at the *what*, there is a second *how* that defines the process for achieving it.

Teaching Points: Control

Here are the teaching points around control:

- There is no right or wrong lineup as it relates to the dominance line exercise and how dominance shows up in your life.
- Control needs often appear during times of crisis, decision-making, conflict, and chaos or confusion.
- Withholding or withdrawing is the ultimate form of control and is a tool in your tool kit. Use it thoughtfully and intentionally.
- Dominance is not the same thing as dominating.
- Being in control is not the same thing as being controlling.
- Some people have a desire to control the *what* (the outcome, result, or deliverable); other people have a desire to control the *how* (the process, method, or way they go about achieving the *what*); and still others have a need to control both the *what* and the *how*.
- Control wants may vary from country to country based on the country's cultural norms.
- Lineups, such as the dominance line, are often difficult for women. This is related to our feminine tendencies for flat structures, as Dr. Patricia Heim explains in her video *The Power Dead-Even Rule.*[25] Women tend to be more comfortable with circles or random arrays versus a differentiating line.
- Some people will display wanted control behavior only when invited or given permission.

REFLECTION

What stands out for you after reading this material on control?

Identify various teams or groups of which you are a member—for instance, a team you lead, your boss's team, your immediate family, or other groups. How would you assess your wanted control in each of those groups? You might consider making a table like the following one.

Put a check mark in the column that best describes your wants.

	Low	Medium	High
My Team			
My Boss's Team			
My Immediate Family			
Other Groups			

What new insights about others—family members, colleagues/peers, or friends—did you consider regarding their wanted control?

Here is a quick summary of control:[26]

- **Issue**—How much do I want to be *top* or *bottom*?
- **Underlying Feeling**—Competence
- **Interpersonal or Group Fear**—Being humiliated, embarrassed, or vulnerable

- **Personal Fear**—Being incompetent, incapable, or phony

My wish is that we all recognize that being in control is not a bad thing and is not the same thing as being controlling. If you are in a hierarchical role that requires positional power leading teams, your team members are counting on you to be in control and provide the organization with assertiveness to represent the team effectively. For your own benefit, I hope you attain the freedom that comes from not being pressured, manipulated, or used, knowing you have choices and trusting yourself to make competent and courageous decisions.

OPENNESS

We wrap up this chapter by discussing our openness wants.

This third dimension of openness is the degree to which you are willing to be *open* or *closed* to another person. Another way to think about this is how public or private you might be. Openness varies across time, among individuals, and within relationships. In *The Human Element*, Schutz states, "Sometimes you might enjoy a relationship in which you and another person share your feelings, secrets, and innermost thoughts. You enjoy having one person—or, at most, a few people—in whom you confide."

"At other times, you avoid being open with others. You would rather keep things impersonal, and you prefer to have acquaintances rather than a few close friends. You have some desire for both open or more public relationships and more privacy. Because openness is based on building deeper ties, it's usually the last dimension or phase to emerge in the development of a human relationship or of relations within a group. Inclusion involves how much we want to encounter each other, as well as our decision to continue the relationship or not. As our relationship continues, openness has to do with the degree to which we literally or figuratively embrace each other."

"Your behavior with openness is a function of two aspects: the rational and the defensive. The rational part results from your preference for a certain amount of openness in your life. The defensive aspect results from your fear of being too open and thus vulnerable to being rejected and unloved. When you are flexible and rational, you can adapt to different situations. When you are rigid and defensive, you react the same way to all circumstances. You are some mixture of the rational and the defensive, depending on how you feel about yourself. The worse you feel, the more defensive you are."[27]

INTERPERSONAL RELATIONS

"When your interpersonal relations are *under-personal* (rigidly low in openness), you avoid revealing yourself to others. You maintain one-to-one relationships on a superficial, distant level, and you are most comfortable when other people do the same with you. You maintain emotional distance and do not become emotionally involved. You are afraid no one likes you, and you anticipate not being liked. You have great difficulty genuinely liking people, and you distrust their feelings toward you."

"When you are *over-personal* (rigidly high in openness), you tell everyone about your feelings, and you want everyone to do the same with you. Being liked is essential to you. Your direct technique is to attempt to gain approval by being extremely personal, ingratiating, intimate, and confiding. Your subtle technique is to be manipulative and possessive."

"When you are personal (appropriately open) and have successfully resolved issues of openness—most likely from childhood—your level of interaction with others varies with the individual and the circumstances. You are comfortable in a close relationship, as well as in a situation that requires distance. You feel comfortable both giving and receiving affection. You enjoy being liked, and if you are not liked, you can accept that this simply means that someone doesn't like you. You don't generalize from this one reaction and conclude that you are unlikable or unlovable."[28]

UNDERLYING OPENNESS

Underlying the behavior of openness is the feeling of being likable or unlikable, lovable or unlovable. I find you likable if I like myself in your presence, if you create an atmosphere within which I like myself. I feel you like me when you confide in me, are friendly toward me, respond warmly to my overtures, and seek my friendship.[29]

Issues of openness to yourself (that is, your self-awareness) and your openness to others are strongly intertwined. *You cannot be open to someone else in a meaningful way if you are not open to yourself.* This is another important statement. I recommend you read it again.

OPENNESS SUMMARY

A general summary of openness—both expressed and wanted includes:

- A behavior reflecting how much you want to be OPEN or CLOSED
- The degree to which you want to be open to others and how much you want others to be open to you
- Being close to others or keeping your distance—both physically and emotionally
- These factors determine the extent of closeness that a person seeks.

Openness is the **third stage** of group development. The underlying feeling for openness is likability.

BEING OPEN WITH OTHERS

Go back to the group you identified in the inclusion and control activities.

ACTIVITY

As you read each of the following behavioral statements, how well do they describe you on that team? Mark an *X* on the Low-Medium-High continuum (Image 5.6) as an overall assessment of the collective behavioral statements. Please note, you could be low on some of the statements, high on others, or somewhere in between.

Behavioral Statements–Being Open with Others

- I encourage warmth and closeness in my relationships.
- I am comfortable expressing personal feelings.
- I make an effort to get close to people.
- I am supportive of other people.
- I am willing to take risks when sharing personal details.
- I am comfortable sharing personal opinions.
- I am comfortable showing concern for others.

Where do you see yourself on this dimension?

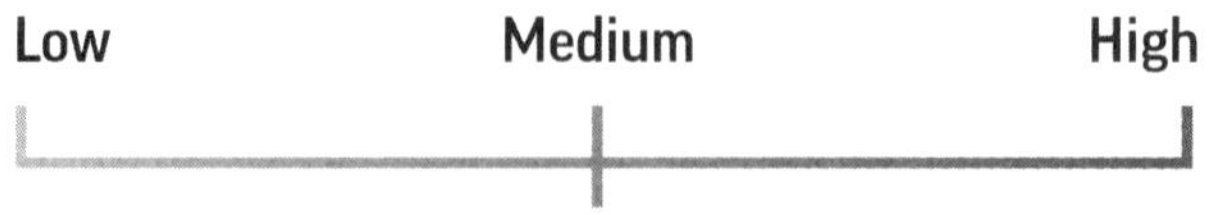

Image 5.6

When I was president of EDS's Health Care Business Unit, I was charged with a mandate to fix several things—customer relations, employee engagement, and financial performance were the highest priorities. I had a wonderful man working for me as a direct report who managed about half of the people in our business unit (about twelve hundred people). We partnered closely to get things turned around, and each afternoon at 5:00 p.m., we would meet in the hall just outside of our side-by-side offices. Admittedly, I had high desire to be open, and this dear man, twenty years my senior, did not. As we talked, I unconsciously would move toward him (physical closeness), and as I stepped forward, he would step back. At the end of our fifteen-minute touchpoint meetings, we would find ourselves at the other end of the hallway from our office doors.

And I have to tell you two other parts of this story. First, I learned that our daily meetings became an event to watch. Some of our team would come just to watch us "dance" down the hallway. And second, when this wonderful man retired, he asked me to speak at his retirement celebration. It was my honor and, of course, I told this story because it had become our thing—our bond, our connection. This man's wife spoke up after I told the story and said, "You have just described the forty years of our marriage!" As you can imagine, there was laughter all around.

Now, let's look at wanted openness.

WANTED OPENNESS

Think about the same group you identified in the previous activities.

ACTIVITY

As you read each of the following behavioral statements, how well do they describe you on that team? Mark an *X* on the Low-Medium-High continuum (Image 5.7) as an overall assessment of the collective behavioral statements. Please note, you could be low on some of the statements, high on others, or somewhere in between.

Behavioral Statements–Wanted Openness

- I want others to act warmly toward me.
- I like to have my efforts encouraged.
- I enjoy others sharing their feelings with me.
- I desire the closeness of others around me.
- I like to be trusted with secrets.
- I listen carefully to others.
- I want others to take an interest in me.
- I make myself available to others.

Where do you see yourself on this dimension?

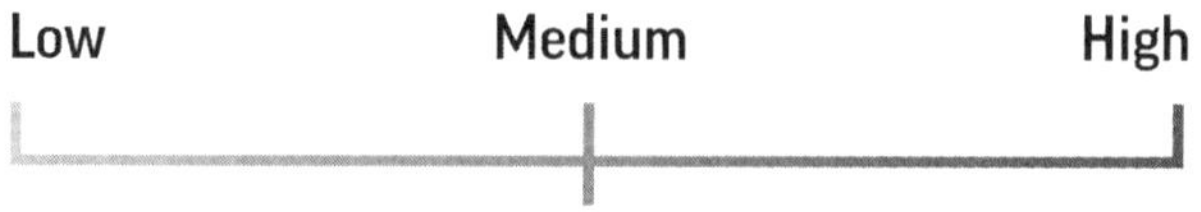

Image 5.7

Here is the way this can show up. You have just received your performance review. Your boss tells you he wants you to speak up more. Maybe you have heard this from others over the course of your career. How willing are you to share with your boss that when you have spoken up in the past, you have been criticized, ridiculed, or ignored? How vulnerable are you willing to be? What would happen if you went even deeper about your childhood experiences of being punished if you spoke up or disagreed? How much and how deep you are willing to go reflects your wanted openness.

A second example was given to me by a program participant, and it has rung true for many participants through the years. Think about different work teams you have been a part of over your professional life. Was there often someone who seemed to always know lots of things about everyone else's personal lives? They knew who got a new puppy, whose in-laws were coming in for the weekend, who was having marital issues, and on and on. Almost everyone smiles when I ask this rhetorical question, and they share that they can think of that person almost immediately. I then ask them to picture that person's workspace. I ask if they see a candy dish. Anecdotally speaking, there is a high correlation between candy dishes and the person who always seems to be in the know. It's a "take a piece of candy, tell me a story" kind of scenario. In many cases, participants laugh out loud and confess that they are the person with the candy dish.

Now, let me share the exercise we do in support of deepening our understanding of openness.

OPENNESS EXERCISE

Once again, from *The Human Element Leaders Manual*, this exercise is called the "I pretend" exercise. This activity encourages participants to share behaviors and feelings honestly and to be vulnerable in regard to perhaps previously guarded or even unknown parts of themselves. I instruct the groups to break into smaller groups of three to four people in each group. We then move through a process of sharing what we are pretending.

I always clarify what pretending means. *Oxford Languages* defines *pretending* as "speaking and acting so as to make it appear that something is the case when in fact it is not."[30] I offer some examples I have collected over the years, such as "I pretend I am going to make my budget numbers this year," "I pretend to like all the people I work with," "I pretend my child is an honor student," or "I pretend my spouse isn't an alcoholic." These are both personal and professional examples that have actually been shared over the years. Some of the examples I offer are quite personal and are intended to get participants thinking broadly and deeply. It is surprising what comes up in these small groups. They then thank each other for sharing.

Once the participants have completed the exercise, they come back to their seats and tables, and we debrief the exercise. General feedback about this sharing experience sounds like:

- "It felt cathartic, like a weight had been lifted off of me. No laughter. No judgment. No shame. Very liberating."
- "It is the first time I have ever thought about what I was pretending. Speaking the words and giving it voice was scary."
- "If I am open, I might be rejected or not liked. I always thought it was easier to pretend. Now I'm not so sure."
- "I felt really honored that people shared with me what they were pretending."
- "From a body standpoint, I was holding my breath before I actually shared what I was pretending. After I shared it, I could breathe easier."

I then ask the group how many of them heard someone else's "I pretend" and if it was something they, too, were pretending. Almost everyone raises their hand. Next I ask how much energy it takes to pretend. Almost in unison, the answer comes back, "A lot!" I then offer a new possibility: If so many of us are pretending the same or similar things, and it takes so much of our energy, what would happen if we shared our pretends, supported one another, and redirected that energy to something more productive? I can almost see the light bulbs going off.

Finally, I ask how many heard someone say what they were pretending and thought, *We all know you are pretending that.* We often trick ourselves into thinking that we have fooled everyone, that we have it all under control, when everyone else knows things may be falling short or falling apart altogether.

I've discovered some gender differences in my almost twenty-five years of doing this exercise. With women-only groups, the sharing is deeper, and there are frequently tears. With a group of all men, the sharing is often superficial, such as, "I pretend to be a scratch golfer" or "I pretend to bench-press 250 pounds." When I do this exercise in a mixed group, usually as part of an in-house program, there are typically more men than women. When I create the small groups, I try to have at least one woman in each small group. The women will help the men go a little deeper, and the men will not let the women go so deep that it gets too awkward or she feels too vulnerable.

REFLECTION

What stands out for you after reading this material on openness?

Identify various teams or groups of which you are a member–a team you lead, your boss's team, your immediate family, or other groups to which you belong. How would you assess your openness wants in each of those groups? You might consider making a table like the following one.

Put a check mark in the column that best describes your wants.

	Low	Medium	High
My Team			
My Boss's Team			
My Immediate Family			
Other Groups			

What new insights about others–family members, colleagues/peers, or friends–did you consider regarding their openness wants?

Here is a quick summary of openness:[31]

- **Issue**—Open or closed, public or private
- **Underlying Feeling**—Likability, lovability
- **Interpersonal or Group Fear**—Being rejected, disliked, despised
- **Personal Fear**—Being unlikable, unlovable

Additional Insights: Openness

"After years of tolerating distortion and secrecy in most aspects of organizational life, the public is ever more cognizant of, alert to, and intolerant of such behavior. The breakthrough possibilities and actualities are twofold. First, many old cliches turn out to be absolutely correct. The truth *does* set you free—personally, interpersonally, organizationally, and even bodily. Second, the tools and techniques—specifically feedback, imagery, and understanding of the body—are available to test the effects of self-disclosure and withholding on the body, relationships, and performance in organizations. When you are open, your body feels good. Distortion or withholding often expresses itself in your body as some form of discomfort—shortness of breath, neck pain, tightness in the stomach, sweaty palms, a dry throat, a headache—and expresses itself as well by creating distance in relationships, loss of motivation, burnout, illness, absenteeism, and declining productivity on the job. The more open you are, the healthier you are."[32]

That said, I am not suggesting that you blurt out whatever you might be thinking without clarity and intentionality. Once when I was teaching a session and asked the rhetorical question, "What do you pretend?," a woman at the front table shared, "I pretended that I enjoyed having sex with my husband last night!" Mind you, this was a co-ed group of about half men and half women. It caught me off guard and caused a great deal of laughter in the one hundred or so people in the room. The only clever thing I could think to say in that moment was, "That would be an example of high expressed openness." Gulp!

One last thought for your consideration:

- Openness leads to . . . intimacy.
- Intimacy leads to . . . trust.
- Trust leads to . . . safety.

When you share meaningfully with another person, the relationship bond between you is strengthened, leading to a more intimate connection and greater trust. (Think about how even as young girls, we loved to share our secrets.)

Trust Behaviors: Openness

I want to connect this content to information regarding building and sustaining trust. The model I share is the Reina Trust Model from the Reinas' book *Trust and Betrayal in the Workplace*. The specific trust behaviors related to this level of openness are:

- Sharing information
- Telling the truth
- Maintaining confidentiality

Last, trust leads to safety. Creating psychological safety (discussed earlier in chapter 2) is at the core of both interpersonal relationships and team effectiveness. Such safety encourages everyone to contribute their best thinking and their best work.

Teaching Points

Here are the teaching points around openness:

- It takes a great deal of energy to pretend. What if you were more open (especially since many of us are pretending the same or similar things) and redirected that energy toward more productive things?
- Often, we think our pretending is not visible to others. That is often not true.
- Each of us is some mix of the rational and the defensive. When you are flexible and rational, you can adapt to different situations. When you are rigid and defensive, you react the same way to all situations. You are some mixture of the rational and defensive depending on how you feel about yourself.
- You can't be open to someone else in a meaningful way if you are not open yourself.

SUMMARY

As I summarize this chapter, it comes down to three powerful leadership questions:

1. How can you honor your orientation to the wants of the team or group—*and* choose to feel inherently significant—just because you are in the room? (Inclusion)
2. How can you acknowledge your reactions to past life experiences and cultural conditioning around dominance and competence—*and* choose to be in control of situations where you wish to have influence and get what you want? (Control)
3. How can you create a spirit of openness with others that allows truth telling—*and* create an atmosphere where everyone, including yourself, feels likable? (Openness)

With practice and greater self-awareness, you will find you have the ability to hold both sides of the previous questions and then you can make authentic, powerful, and intentional choices. And that, dear reader, can set you free.

If you would like to learn more about the information shared in this chapter, please contact Ethan Schutz at ethan@theschutzcompany.com.

REFLECTION

- What insights about yourself did you discover about your inclusion, control, and openness wants?

- How will you notice and manage your inclusion, control, and openness wants going forward?

- How can this information help you be a better leader?

CHAPTER 6

THE MORE THINGS CHANGE, THE MORE PEOPLE STAY THE SAME

"Change has a considerable psychological impact on the human mind. To the fearful, it is threatening because it means that things may get worse. To the hopeful, it is encouraging because things may get better. To the confident, it is inspiring because the challenge exists to make things better."

—King Whitney Jr.

In addition to the quote above, reflect on the adage, "The only thing constant is change." I remember giving one of my first presentations regarding change about thirty-five years ago. Since I worked at a technology company, I found this great headline that read, "Technological change is happening faster than ever." Then I noticed the source—wait for it—the *London Times* in the early 1800s!

Yes, change is always happening—at home, at work, in our local communities, and all over the world. I have been involved in about one thousand change initiatives—as a leader of the change, as a participant working on the change, as a recipient to whom the change is happening, and as a coach and consultant supporting others through change. Over the years, I have been a student of the human factor of change. And I want to give credit to a treasured colleague, Jerry Magar, for all that he has shared with me regarding change. Much of what I am sharing with you in this chapter is based on our work together.

WHAT IS CHANGE?

In its simplest form, according to the *American Heritage Dictionary*, *change* means "to cause to be different, to alter."[1] That definition can cover a lot of ground. As I was preparing my workbook materials, I looked for a visual image of change. Look at Image 6.1. How does it represent or reflect change for you? (Notice the shades of gray.)

Image 6.1: It's a Journey

First, the title—"It's a Journey." Don't you wish you could snap your fingers and all aspects of change would be achieved? The process, the structure, the market, the technology upgrade, the training, the relationships, and on and on. Notice the winding road. It zigs and zags. Change is rarely a straight line. That winding road takes us to some dark places, and we cannot see where it ends. The tree trunks and foliage are different shades, representing lots of people and functions, all with different perspectives, experiences, and points of view. What may be less visible in this shades-of-gray image is a blue sky between the trees and in the background. That blue sky represents hope and clarity.

REFLECTION

- How is your experience with change reflected in this image?

- What was the best change initiative you have experienced? What made it the best?

- What was the worst change initiative you have experienced? What made it the worst?

- Reading the introductory quote, are you the fearful, the hopeful, or the confident?

As a leader of one team or multiple teams, it's a big responsibility to successfully lead those teams through a successful change initiative. I hope the thoughts, tips, and tools in this chapter are valuable in supporting you as a leader taking your teams through changes.

CHANGE AND TRUST

No matter how high the trust is in your organization, change will create suspicion and lower trust. Change management equals trust management. All of your strategies need to focus on building and restoring trust in the midst of change. People must trust the leader, the future destination, the process you have adopted to reach that future destination, each other, and themselves. And no matter how well planned, you are going to run into challenges you didn't anticipate. Sharing information in a timely manner and admitting mistakes will actually build trust when those unexpected challenges occur.

Here are some additional thoughts to consider and share with your team as you continue to provide context and lay the groundwork for the change initiative. And remember the Reina Trust Model from *Embracing Your Power*? One of the trust behaviors included in Trust of Character® is predictability. When I lose my ability to predict your behavior and responses, my trust goes down. When you are in a state of uncertainty or unpredictability, you may also experience a feeling of being out of control of the situation, so you may be calling on your coping mechanisms to help you regain a sense of control. You or your team members may strongly defend the more familiar way, the old way, and it can often be perceived as resistance to the change. To be clear, though, you may or may not be conscious that you are doing this.

Be on alert for noticing your reaction to the connection between trust and change. Expect these behaviors in yourself and your team members. And before we get too far along in this chapter, I want to offer that contributing to successful change is everyone's responsibility, not just the executives or leaders. Embodying that we are all in this together will contribute to everyone being more engaged, productive, and successful. We can all relate to change happening more frequently in varying degrees of complexity and scope. I want to be part of a better way, and I trust you do too.

CHANGE EXERCISE

Let me take you through an exercise I often facilitate with teams during times of change.

Facilitator: "*Find a partner about your same height and stand facing each other. Now, turn around so you are no longer facing one another.*"

- Each person then changes three things about their appearance. (Examples—taking glasses on or off, rolling up shirt sleeves, turning up a collar.)
- Each pair then turns back around, facing each other, and tries to identify what the other person has changed. Some can easily spot and describe the changes, while others may struggle. Of course, there are many variables that drive either of those outcomes.

Teaching Points

In general, here is the list of results that I refer to as teaching points. Reflect on how you might relate to each one:

- We tend to quickly revert back to the familiar. As soon as the exercise is over, almost everyone shifts back to their original appearance.
- People generally take something off—this aligns and often equates to losing something. You can be losing the familiar and predictable—a familiar process, a familiar computer screen, or a familiar timeline.
- You can sometimes make it hard for the other person to see the changes you are making. It's almost as if you are trying to slip something by the other person. It can be as subtle as

unbuttoning or buttoning a shirt or jacket or changing your belt to a different notch.

- You sometimes make change competitive rather than collaborative. If I can spot your three changes and you can only spot two of my changes, I win!

You can do a second round of this exercise while also changing partners. The results can get rather chaotic—just like many change initiatives. The overarching point is to have a fun way to learn some change principles.

PRODUCTIVITY CURVE

In my experience of leading literally hundreds of change efforts, I have learned that employee productivity can seriously decline during times of change. The distractions that underlie this loss of productivity are many. You can spend unproductive time commiserating with your colleagues, you may spend time looking for another job, or maybe you come in late more often or even miss work altogether. So, let's look more closely at Image 6.2, the Productivity Curve during times of change.

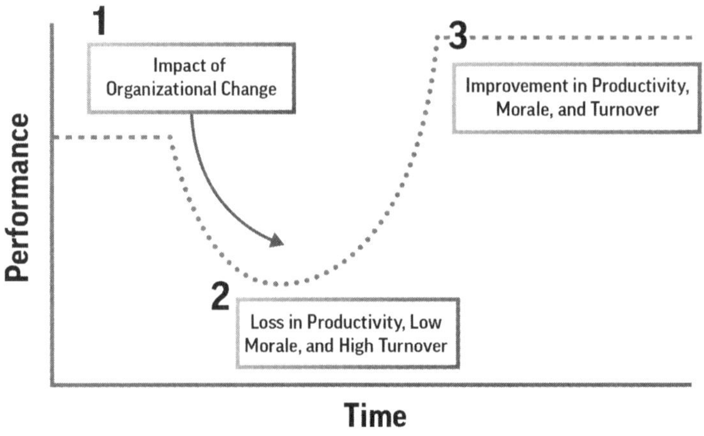

Image 6.2: Productivity Curve Chart. Courtesy of Jerry Magar

As you can see from Image 6.2, productivity or performance is moving along at a consistent level. At Step 1, you introduce the change to your team. Immediately, productivity starts to decline. Step 2 represents the reduction in productivity and employee morale along with the possible increase in unwanted resignations. Over time, you hope to lead your team through the change initiative, eventually resulting in greater productivity (one of many often-cited objectives of change initiatives).

Here is a very important message as you lead your team through change: It is your responsibility to manage both the *depth* and the *duration* of the productivity curve. In other words, how low will productivity drop, and how long will your team languish in this low-productivity place? The remainder of this chapter can help you minimize the depth and duration of diminishing productivity.

THE GRIEF CYCLE

Now, let's couple the Productivity Curve with the Grief Cycle. The first stage is one of perceived **Betrayal**. Your organization announces a change initiative, and as an employee, you feel betrayed, shocked, even angry. The organization is upsetting your familiar world. Maybe the organizational structure is changing, and you will be getting a new boss. Maybe your job is being outsourced or sent offshore, and you don't even know if you will have a job. Maybe your company is being acquired, going public, or going private, and suddenly you have new owners. The list goes on and on regarding the many kinds of changes. On a personal level, it can involve the loss of a loved one or a divorce. For many of us, we feel a sense of betrayal. The uncertainty can be overwhelming.

Then we move to the second stage, often referred to as the **Denial** stage. You may convince yourself that the change isn't really going to happen. You may even mount a business case for why the announced change is a bad idea. I've heard phrases like "This too shall pass," "If we put up enough resistance, they will change their minds," "This will never work," "This is just another 'flavor of the month.'" These statements are all related to denial and even disbelief that this is happening. And the productivity continues to decline.

Now, on to the third stage, called **Identity Crisis**. Typically, productivity has now hit the bottom of the curve. At this stage, it comes down to whether or not you believe you can do your work in the new way, with a new boss, or with new technology. Maybe the new technology system, new machinery, or new process has automated what you used to do manually. The struggle is real, and until you gain an understanding of the "new way," you will lack confidence in your ability to fulfill your role and responsibilities. And, of course, all kinds of fears follow that. This stage is all about the duration of the productivity curve. The sooner you retrain your team members, the shorter the duration of the loss of productivity will be.

I will refer you back to the RASIN responsibility material found in chapter 3. This chart can also help you during change when you find yourself in the Identity Crisis phase of change.

Once there is clarity on roles and responsibilities, you can provide training, and you and your team members can begin to regain productivity and achieve the objectives identified to justify the change in the first place. That leads us to the last stage.

The fourth stage is labeled **Renewal**. Resistance is waning. You and your team are gaining greater confidence in the new way of working. Go back and review the Productivity Curve image (Image 6.2). You will see that as productivity trends are improving, they eventually lead to even greater productivity—at least that is the goal. As a leader, be on the lookout for when you see confidence and productivity rising. Let your team know—and celebrate the progress!

PRODUCTIVITY EXERCISE

Let me offer you another exercise that relates specifically to productivity. This is a very short exercise you can do with your team to acknowledge the reality of change.

Facilitator: "*With your dominant writing hand (left or right), write your first name on a piece of paper as many times as you can in thirty seconds.*"

The facilitator starts and stops the team regarding the thirty-second time frame. Once the thirty seconds is up, the facilitator then asks the team members to count how many times they wrote their name and write down that number.

Facilitator: "*With your nondominant writing hand, write your first name on a piece of paper as many times as you can in thirty seconds.*"

Again, the facilitator starts and stops the team regarding the thirty-second time frame. And again, once the thirty seconds is complete, the facilitator asks the team members to count and document how many times they wrote their name.

Next comes the significant learning moment.

By a show of thumbs-up or thumbs-down, the facilitator asks the following questions, comparing the second time the participants wrote their name to the first time:

1. Did quantity go up or down the second time?
2. Did quality go up or down the second time?
3. Did effort go up or down the second time?

In the hundreds of times I have done this exercise, the answers have been the same 100 percent of the time. *Quantity and quality go down, and effort goes up.* This is the essence of change, and leaders need to remember this as they lead their teams through change efforts. When a leader acknowledges these results, it builds trust.

REACTION TO CHANGE

I want to offer another framework I developed many years ago amid those five-hundred-plus change initiatives in my corporate days. After observing and tracking the trends of the human readiness and reaction-to-change exercises, I saw people falling into the following categories:

- "I'm on board."
- "I'll be politically correct."
- "I have issues and questions."
- "I'm trying."
- "No way."

TOOL: CHANGE READINESS ASSESSMENT

Category	Definition	Strategy
"I'm on board."	Full speed ahead!	Reward them.
"I'll be politically correct."	I'll learn the new language. I may speak negatively about it to close confidantes but never to senior management.	Determine and communicate the consequences of their continued passive/aggressive behavior.
"I have issues."	I'll need to identify and resolve specific issues in order to support change.	Listen to their issues and resolve as many as you can.
"I'm trying."	I want to get on board, but I'm not sure what I'm supposed to do.	Determine how much time and resources you are willing to commit to get them on board.
"No way."	There is no way this will work, and I'll say so publicly and loudly.	Determine how much time you are going to give them to get on board.

Image 6.3

Let's look at each box in Image 6.3.

The first category is "*I'm on board.*" These team members (or peers, colleagues, stakeholders, etc.) are supportive of the change initiative. They see the value of the change and are ready to go. As you think about who your change agents or influencers might be, these team members will likely fit that profile. Your strategy for engaging them might be to assign them roles that give them an opportunity to highlight their support of the change. Remember, if the boss says something is good, that's one thing. If a peer or colleague also says it's good, it carries some extra weight because the peer is "one of us."

The second category is "*I'll be politically correct.*" This reflects the person who smiles and nods in the meetings when the change is being discussed. They may even learn all the new lingo or buzz words relating to the change. By all accounts, you would interpret their behavior and language as supportive of the change. And then . . . you hear about several scenarios when this person has spoken negatively about the change to others. In short, they smile to the leader's face and undermine the change behind the leader's back. Basically, they are displaying passive-aggressive behavior (the pattern of indirectly expressing negative feelings instead of openly addressing them). Your strategy for engaging this person is to let them know you see the disconnect between what they are saying to you and what they are saying to others. Be clear about how you see the impact of their behavior, and let them know that everyone is accountable for making this change successful. Remind them that there is no accountability without consequences. Probe to understand their concerns. Address their concerns and check with them periodically to help them stay on track.

The third category is "*I have issues.*" In reality—and as we reviewed in the very first image of change in this chapter—the change path is a winding one with some dark and unknown areas. At either a conscious (they are willfully resisting change) or an unconscious (they are a lower-risk person and need more certainty) level, they are resisting the change. Your strategy for engaging this person is to listen to their issues and questions. Address the issues that you can, and answer the questions if you truly have the answers. Be transparent with them that you don't have all the answers. Don't make things up to make them feel better. Let them know where you are in the process and, if possible, when you think you will have the answer. Let them know that you need them to keep moving forward to get to those answers. Check with them periodically, and keep them informed and up to date. For your own benefit, take their issues and questions seriously. They may know things you don't know and can help you avoid some of the unknowns related to the change.

The fourth category is "*I'm trying*." There are several variations on this one. Maybe this person has never been through a major change initiative and simply doesn't know what to do. Maybe they started off in a strong, supportive way, and now they're not sure of next steps. I often try to give a visual for this one. Imagine you are a team traveling from the West to the East to get to New York City. Some people are starting in Sydney, Australia, others in Honolulu, Hawaii, and others in Los Angeles, California. You can travel a lot of miles and still be a long way from New York City. The big question for you as their leader is to determine how much time, energy, and resources you are willing to commit to get them fully on board. Can you assign them a change partner? Can you meet with them more frequently? Do you need to move them to a different role? There are so many variables attached to answering this question. Are change partners available? Can you afford to spend more time with them and still fulfill your role as a change leader? Is there someone who would be more effective, and are they available? There are no magic answers. I hope these questions are valuable in helping you determine the most effective strategy for your change initiative and your "I'm trying" team member.

The last category is "*No way*." This is the person who declares loudly in a public way that this change will not work, and they are not going to support it. In some ways, this category is one of the easiest to work your way through. You know where they stand and don't have to guess. Your strategy for engaging this person is to meet with them and acknowledge their declaration of nonsupport of the change. You make sure they have all the facts and the business reason for making the change. Ask them if anything could change their mind to support the change. If there are legitimate concerns, you may want to do some homework to address them. If their concerns are more about fears or what the change means to them personally, address those as well.

If there is nothing that will get them on board, you are now at a tough crossroads as a leader. If you leave them in place and they continue to speak negatively of the change, you can set an expectation of them to stop speaking negatively. If they continue their negative talk, let them know it will be noted on their performance review (consequence). I'm going to bet that many of you reading this have experienced this "no way" person. In most cases, they go along with the change kicking and screaming. It isn't pleasant, but you eventually get through it. The goal here is to let them know that their negative comments can have a negative impact on team morale and slow the change process down, causing more anxiety for everyone. Be clear about your expectations.

If they are more extreme in their behaviors by not completing assignments or preventing others from completing their assignments, your role as a leader becomes very clear. They are insubordinate and not fulfilling their job responsibilities. Talk to them, clarify your expectations, and let them know the consequences of not completing their assignments up to and including termination. This may sound harsh, but as a leader, it is your responsibility to lead your team through this change initiative. The longer you let someone continue their "no way" behavior, the more you are contributing to the problem. Recognize that this person is no longer a good fit for where this team, department, or organization is headed. In your head (and your heart), this makes it easier to make such a hard decision. Remember, others are watching. If you do nothing, you may be sending the unintended message that everyone can be negative or adopt the "no way" approach. That can be a disaster and is certainly not leadership behavior.

Let me offer a couple of last thoughts on this Change Readiness Assessment. Your team members can fall into different categories based on the different change initiatives you are leading. One person could be "I'm on board" on change initiative ABC, but "I have issues and questions" on change initiative XYZ. As if leading change isn't hard enough, this adds yet another layer of complexity. I hope this framework helps you by giving you language to determine where each team member may be on any given change as well as strategies for engaging them more fully in the change.

TIMING MATTERS

It's my turn to ask, "Where was this when I needed it?" It was always a challenge to keep my team aligned and moving forward. The model I have included next explains it well. As human beings, we all will go through the stages of change. Some of us will go faster and others slower. If a change is first defined and known by the executive team, we will call that Month 0. The executives go through **Betrayal** at Month 0, **Denial** a few months in (as reality sets in), **Identity Crisis** at around Month 3, and **Renewal** by Months 5 or 6. Middle managers are often brought into the change initiative around Month 3 and then have their own stages to go through on the change path. And finally, employees are brought in around Month 6; they start at the Betrayal stage. Executives by then are in the Renewal stage, and middle managers are in the Identity Crisis stage. Okay, so now I understand the disconnects!

Timing Matters

Example

Stage 1	Stage 2	Stage 3	Stage 4
Betrayal	Denial	Search for solutions	Renewal
Point zero: first news about change	Months 1 and 2	Months 3 and 4	Months 5 and 6

Note: Actual times will vary from change to change, organization to organization, and person to person.

Image 6.4

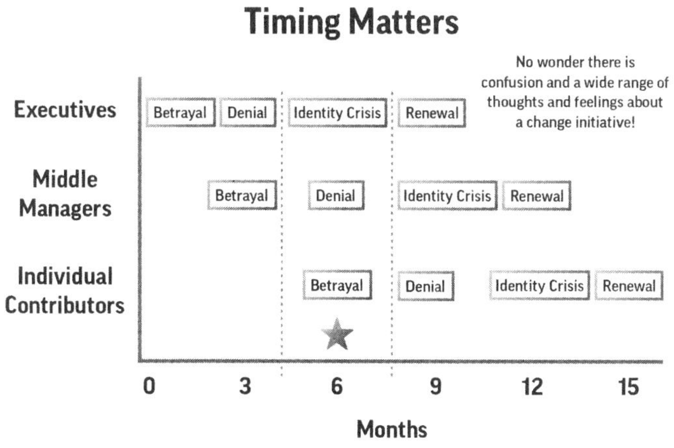

Image 6.5

After being exposed to these charts, I now use them when discussing change at all levels of the organization. I liken it to the maps at the shopping mall—the ones with the "you are here" label. In other words, the organization is not on the same page. No wonder change can be so chaotic! The executives are less likely to lose heart and start second-guessing themselves. The managers recognize they are still trying to figure things out while answering questions from the employees about what is really happening. The employees are somewhere in the "we are doing *what*?" stage. A wise colleague, Phil Novick, once shared this adage, and I have quoted him many times since: "If you're *two* steps ahead, you're a leader. If you're *ten* steps ahead, you're a target." I want to be that two-steps-ahead leader!

SUPPORTING OTHERS THROUGH THE CHANGE CYCLE

Now that you better understand some of the human dynamics of change, what are you going to do about it?

BETRAYAL

In this initial stage of change, your team feels some level of betrayal and a sense of loss. Here are some leadership tips:

- **Share as much information as possible.** Give people information on a timely basis. Be transparent. Communicate early and often.
- **Be realistic.** In times of change, people will want certainties and even guarantees. **DO NOT** make guarantees. There are too many variables to consider. New information often surfaces and has to be considered moving forward.
- **Be prepared for a reaction.** Depending on the kind of change, the magnitude of the change, how the change might affect your team, and what problem the change is trying to solve, your team may react in a variety of ways. Maybe they will be happy ("I'm on board"). Maybe they will be angry ("No way"). Be ready for them all. Listen to their concerns. Answer the questions you can, make

note of the ones you can't, and follow up with team members once you secure the answers.

- **Give yourself and others grace.** I am a strong believer that executives are *not* trying to destroy the organization. I believe that the vast majority of people are trying to do the right thing. During change, there are unknowns and, therefore, uncertainties. Have patience and give yourself and others grace as you work through the issues, challenges, and questions.
- **Know the reasons behind the change.** There is no need to apologize or defend the change initiative. At the same time, make sure you know the basis for making the change. In other words, what opportunity will this change enable (e.g., new products or services, greater quality or productivity, new markets, creating a competitive advantage, and so on)? What problem are you trying to solve (e.g., greater safety measures, quality errors, declining customer satisfaction, compliance requirements, declining revenue or profit, and so on)? Do not reply with "Because the CEO said so" when asked why you are making this change. Be informed.
- **Review work products carefully.** Remember that your team members will be distracted, and their distraction can lead to errors and lower quality, in spite of increased effort.
- **Regulate or manage your emotions.** I'm a big believer in allowing myself and letting others feel the way we feel. I don't like it when someone tries to tell me how I should or shouldn't feel, and I don't want to do that to anyone else. Listen to your team members. Let them vent. I call these BMW sessions—bitch, moan, and whine. We've all been there. It may take a few BMW sessions with a team member before they can move on. At some point, however, they need to recognize it's time to move on, and it's your job to help make that happen. My go-to language went

something like this: "It's clear that you are unhappy or upset with this change, but we *are* moving ahead with this change. You will have to decide what it's going to take for you to get on board and be part of the team making this change happen." I would acknowledge what the person may be getting or giving up as part of their choice to get on board or not. For example, they may be giving up the familiarity with the process or technology, being known as the subject matter expert, or the ease with which they fulfill their roles and responsibilities. What they may be getting is the opportunity to learn new skills, acquire new knowledge, enhance their resume, and be a role model as a change agent—all of which potentially gives them greater career opportunities. I admit this all sounds good on paper and is much harder when you are dealing with a hard-core resister. At the end of the day, it's the team member's choice. Are they happier being miserable or getting on board? And for another reminder from earlier in this chapter, it is everyone's responsibility to make the change successful.

DENIAL

In the Denial stage, team members fool themselves that the change isn't really happening. They may even convince themselves that if they complain loudly enough or try to slow things down, "they" will change their minds about this new way and go back to the old way. Here are some leadership tips:

- **Be clear and crisp when sharing information.** Depending on the magnitude and complexity of the change, it's a lot to take in. When possible, write things down for team members. Continue to refine the information as you gather feedback from those completing the new tasks or assignments and as the change progresses.

- **Ensure understanding on their part and yours too.** When things are changing—processes, technology, and organizational structure—recognize that your thinking potentially needs to change too. Ask these questions:
  - What are we trying to accomplish?
  - What is the impact of this change? Consider both the upstream and downstream in the process.
  - Who will be impacted, and have I communicated with them regarding the impact?
  - What are the next steps?
  - Also, keep in mind that everyone can check for understanding and challenge assumptions. Be careful not to automatically *assume* they are challenging your authority (or getting on your last nerve). Assume good intent. Answer or discuss patiently and thoroughly.

- **Be clear and specific when assigning tasks and roles.** As things are changing, roles and responsibilities also may change. This is where the RASIN chart framework can be introduced and implemented. Documenting the RASIN chart and providing copies to all involved is extremely helpful and can reduce confusion. Continue to review the RASIN chart, as you are sure to find more effective and efficient ways as you move through the change.
- **Establish more frequent checkpoints.** The need to check more frequently for accuracy and quality lends itself to smaller "course corrections" if you get off track. There is less rework and reinforced learning. Remember our earlier exercise where quantity and quality go down and effort goes up. Reassure your team members that you are not micromanaging but rather exercising appropriate check-and-review activities for more efficient learning and producing quality results.

IDENTITY CRISIS

In this third stage, team members are asking themselves if they can be successful learning the new way. This includes processes, technology, and people. Their doubts, concerns, and fears may resurface louder than ever. Here are some leadership tips:

- **Listen to your team's concerns.** Listen and be supportive. Your role is to listen, acknowledge their thoughts and feelings, and answer questions. Encourage your team members, assuring them that you trust their abilities and skills to grasp the new way.
- **Acknowledge success to build momentum.** Recognize and celebrate those successes. This is a form of encouraging your team members that they are indeed learning the new way, building the new relationships, and achieving the new (and hopefully better) results. This builds confidence as well as momentum toward the desired outcomes.
- **Keep your team engaged.** Your team members are closest to the work and will be gathering insights as the new way unfolds and progresses. Regular feedback sessions can be hugely helpful in identifying problems, breakdowns, and breakthroughs, as well as hearing from multiple points of view. This is a perfect place for people to be seen, heard, and valued (see chapter 2).
- **Work to retain your best.** This is more than paying retention bonuses. Let your best performers know that you appreciate them, their work, and their leadership. Be aware that if your organization's change is a very public one, your competitors as well as executive recruiters are making calls to woo your best performers away. Of course, we all need to show our appreciation year-round. At the same time, you can acknowledge to your best performers that you understand they may be getting those recruiting calls. That will build trust that you are on top of the reality of the

situation. Don't make promises you can't keep, though. If possible, assign them to influential roles that potentially help them build new skills, then reward them appropriately.

- **Identify barriers and strive to remove them.** If you have team members who are back and forth on "I'm on board" to "I have issues and questions," help them identify what it will take for them to be all in. Keep them informed as issues are addressed, challenges are overcome, and questions are answered as you eliminate or resolve their resistance checklist items.
- **Ensure adequate one-on-one time.** You will have team meetings to share information updates along with status on progress being made. In addition, you will want to spend one-on-one time with each team member. This includes your best performers to encourage their continued performance and leadership. This also includes any unhappy or concerned team members so you can address their individual issues and questions rather than bogging down team meetings. And don't forget those team members who come in every day and get the work done. They need your time and attention too.

COMMUNICATING RULES OF THUMB

Here are some general rules of thumb regarding communication. These tips apply to individual conversations, team meetings, stakeholder meetings, and town halls.

- **Know the facts and share the facts.** It's a dangerous practice to start speculating, much less making things up. Instead, describe where you are in the process and share at what point you expect to have answers. Your transparency will build trust. Having to backpedal due to your speculation or even your assumptions will likely lead to trouble and even a break in trust if it happens routinely.

- **Be transparent and be available.** The gaps in information will be filled by the grapevine or the gossip mill. Be transparent. Tell them what you do know as well as what you don't know. Managers at all levels are often in lots of meetings as major changes are happening. That reduces the amount of time you are available to be with your team. Make sure your meetings are necessary, are at the right cadence, and are run efficiently. It is the only hope you have of being able to fit in all the meetings and communication.
- **Have sincere conversations.** In other words, be real. Be authentic. It increases your credibility and helps you uncover bad news before it potentially becomes terrible news. Years ago, when I went through my company's first layoff, I was sick to my stomach for weeks. I was running a global function with responsibility for approximately twelve hundred employees around the world, and it took us about a week to complete all the one-on-one conversations. It seemed like the longest week of my life. Because this was our first ever corporate layoff, none of my direct reports had ever gone through this before. Every day at 7:00 a.m., I got all of my direct reports on a conference call. We each checked in with what we had done the day before and what we were doing that day. I also made sure to ask them how they were feeling. Men and women shared tears, stories of sleepless nights, and the numbing required to get through the day. By supporting one another, we made it through. I believe we carried out this difficult task by acknowledging how hard it was and treating one another with understanding, dignity, and respect. I later heard from many employees who were laid off that they had been treated with respect and given support. For me, that's what it means to be real. Your team members can see through the scripted messages. Bottom line, they want to know you care—no matter what the change initiative might be.

- **Continue to hone and refine your plans for achieving the change objectives.** A vision—an end state—helps people focus and keeps them from drifting. Remember that image of a winding path with a few dark areas along the way. If you have ever taken a long-distance car trip, you have likely had to take some detours along the way. Yet you always came back to the road map, still headed toward your destination.

CHANGE TIPS

I have shared a lot of information so far in this chapter, and there are a few last thoughts I would like to offer. As a leader during a change initiative, your responsibilities can be overwhelming. These last tips will hopefully help you get through with greater ease and efficiency.

BE REALISTIC WITH EXPECTATIONS AND TIMELINES

Set expectations to meet reality. You want to hope for the best, strive to avoid the worst, and plan for somewhere in between. Although I'm not a fan of the "underpromise and overdeliver" approach, realistically things likely are going to take longer. Set expectations accordingly.

RECOGNIZE AND CELEBRATE PROGRESS AND SUCCESS

Recognize inconspicuous successes. In one of our earlier exercises, you saw that effort increases even while quantity and quality decrease. In order to build some momentum and increase confidence, recognize and celebrate smaller wins more frequently than you normally might. It will encourage your team to keep trying.

COMMUNICATE EARLY AND OFTEN, AND REINFORCE THE MESSAGES

Generally speaking, we need to see something new eight times before we accept it as the new normal. Repeating accurate messages consistently helps people absorb the new way. You may think the repetitiveness will be off-putting. In fact, your team members will appreciate the reminders as the changes sink in. Use all communication avenues available to you—individual conversations, team meetings, stakeholder meetings, newsletters, emails, and announcements.

FOCUS ON WHAT YOU CAN CONTROL

Influence what you can and let the rest go. I have developed an exercise that I hope will help this tip come to fruition. I call it Operationalizing the Serenity Prayer. In case you are not familiar with the *Serenity Prayer*, here it is:

> *"God grant me the serenity*
> *to accept the things I cannot change;*
> *the courage to change the things I can;*
> *and the wisdom to know the difference."*[2]
>
> —*Reinhold Niebuhr*

EXERCISE: OPERATIONALIZING THE SERENITY PRAYER

OPERATIONALIZING THE SERENITY PRAYER

This is a tool for gaining focus during times of change.

Objectives

- To get employees focused on things over which they have control
- To encourage employees to "let go" of those things over which they have no control
- To get some shared view in a work group of the difference

Step 1–Each person writes down their issues, challenges, and/or questions–one per page (large sticky notepads work well for this exercise).

Step 2–Each person then separates their individual sheets into one of two stacks: 1) those issues over which I have control, and 2) those issues over which I have no control.

Step 3–Collect the sheets from everyone, keeping them separated by "Control Over" and "No Control Over." Post the sheets (if using sticky notepads) or lay them out by category. Notice that some people may have identified the same issue in both categories. Discuss why each person put the issue in the respective stack. Try to reach some consensus on which stack the group thinks the issue should go in.

Step 4–Ask the group to combine like issues. Don't lose sight of how many times an issue is cited; this data helps you to know where your high-leverage opportunities or greatest challenges might be.

continued

Step 5–Once you have combined groups, focus on the group with the "Control Over" category issues. Divide the group (as appropriate based on number of issues and number of individuals in the group), and ask each group to develop an action plan to address each issue. This may be a short-term or long-term assignment based on the complexity and/or urgency of the issue.

Step 6–Next, focus on the "No Control Over" issues. Determine if the group thinks they have some influence over these issues. If so, what recommendations might they have for influencing the issues? Capture that information. Generally speaking, my experience is that the leader of the group takes on the responsibility for communicating the recommendations to senior leadership. If appropriate, you may want to include members of your work group in communicating and facilitating the recommendations.

I have used this tool many times as a leader of teams involved in change initiatives. Many of my clients have also used it to help their team members focus on those things over which they have control. I hope you find it helpful too.

SUMMARY

Organizations tend to focus change efforts on the processes, the technology, or the new structure. This chapter is intended to help you manage the people side of change. As human beings, no matter what the change is, we are likely to go through the stages described in this chapter. Change is hard. Your job as a leader of a team or teams is to manage your own personal challenges and considerations as well as leading your team through their challenges and considerations. Here's to you being that confident leader who inspires her team because the opportunity exists to make things better.

REFLECTION

- What is your typical response when a new change initiative is announced?

- What new concepts did you learn about leading change initiatives?

- Are you currently in the midst of a change? Which of the tools might help you lead or positively influence the change?

    - Change Exercise–Identify Three Changes
    - Productivity Curve–Depth and Duration
    - Grief Cycle: Betrayal, Denial, Identity Crisis, Renewal
    - Productivity Exercise: Writing Your Name: Quantity, Quality, Effort
    - Change Readiness Assessment
    - Timing Matters
    - Supporting Others Through the Change Cycle
    - BMW Sessions
    - Communicating Rules of Thumb
    - Change Tips
    - Operationalizing "The Serenity Prayer"

- How might you share the information and tools with others?

CHAPTER 7

ENDING WELL AND STARTING STRONG

"Every ending is a new beginning."

–Marianne Williamson

I chose to add this chapter after the change chapter so I could share two important tools that are among the most requested and valued tools by my clients: 1) The Ending Well tool and 2) The First Sixty Days tool. These tools provide a framework when you are leaving one role and taking on a new role.

ENDING WELL

When you are about to start a new role, it's very exciting! New learning, new possibilities, new opportunities, and new career growth. As a result, most of your attention is focused on what is ahead and making a great first impression. What you may overlook is "ending well"—putting a bow on your last role and leaving a great *last* impression. The following framework is intended to help you transition with a smooth handoff to your successor. When you have completed the handoff, you can then give all of your attention to your new role by minimizing the distractions of getting calls and questions about your former role.

SAYING GOODBYE/THANK YOU

We almost always have lots of help in achieving success no matter what the role. Therefore, who do you need to thank? Different people may require different messages and different means of communicating. Make a list of everyone to whom you want to say goodbye. Indicate next to each person's name whether it is a) face-to-face, b) by telephone, c) an email, or d) a handwritten note. In some cases, it might be more than one of these interactions. Determine which people you want to remain in your network. Ensure that you have their contact information in whatever form of "address book" you are taking with you. Possibilities of messages in your goodbyes: a) thank you—be as specific as you can, b) state your intent to stay in touch, as applicable, and c) provide your contact information so they can remain in contact with you as well.

Be as specific as you can when citing the behavior, advice, coaching, mentoring, and support they've provided along the way.

TOOL: ENDING WELL

Goodbye/Thank You Spreadsheet

Name	Email	Phone Number	Physical Address	Remain in Contact?	Notes on Specifics

UPDATE AND RETENTION

Make sure you have contact information for the people you want to maintain in your network. Be sure to do this before they "wipe your laptop clean." Identify documents in your files (electronic and paper) that you want to take with you. Give yourself time to copy files if necessary and of course, honor copyright and intellectual property rights. Update your information on whatever social media sites are applicable—for instance, LinkedIn, Facebook, websites, and so on. Update your resume, bio, and curriculum vitae. If you are a member of any professional organizations, communicate your new contact information. If you have the option and there will be a public announcement—either internal or external—develop a first draft so you can have some influence on the message.

Write letters of introduction to vendor partners or key stakeholders, letting them know who their new point of contact is. You may also want to add a sentiment in your message along these lines: "I appreciate the support you've provided me in this role, and I trust that you will provide my successor that same outstanding support." This reflects true leadership wanting to support others' success as well as your own.

TOOL: ENDING WELL

Update and Retention Spreadsheet

Documents to Retain	Location of Documents	Date Secured	Notes

Social Media	Date Updated
LinkedIn	
Facebook	
Google	
Websites	
Resume	
Bio	
Curriculum Vitae	
Professional Networks & Organizations	

Key messages for public announcement:

1. ____

____

____

____

2. ____

____

____

3. ____

____

____

4. ____

____

____

THE HANDOFF

I'm going to go old-school here and share with you what I did for my successors across many years and many role changes. You can adapt this to your current technology tools as you deem appropriate. I used the tried-and-true three-ring binder with tab dividers. I would hand this binder to my successor, and we would review the material in it. This was not only valuable to my successor, but it was also valuable to me because it reduced the likelihood of someone pulling me back into my old job when I was focusing on my new job. It reduced the number of breakdowns and reinforced my reputation as a strong and competent leader. I also learned to set boundaries regarding my availability for the next thirty days following the formal handoff.

TOOL: ENDING WELL—THE HANDOFF TEMPLATE

Sample

Tab 1: Immediate

- A summary of major events, deadlines, and deliverables broken into thirty-, sixty-, and ninety-day timetables.

Tab 2: Projects

- Priorities—a list reflecting the most important projects to be completed for the year. The list may be broken into Must Do, Should Do, and Like to Do.
- Project—a brief summary of each prioritized project. This summary will include:
    - Objective(s)
    - Project owner
    - Key stakeholders
    - Project status (e.g., green, yellow, red)
    - Major deliverables and timeline
    - Any outstanding issues
    - Budget

Tab 3: People

- Organization chart of boss, peers, and direct reports with high-level roles and responsibilities
- A brief summary of each person on the organization chart—for instance, style, hot buttons, amount of interaction
- For each of your direct reports, include:
    - Name
    - Job title
    - Pay
    - Last performance rating

  - Current performance objectives/priorities
  - Career aspirations
  - Any other related, pertinent information (on medical leave, going to school at night, has special needs, has an approved second job, etc.)

Tab 4: Communication/Meetings

- A list of recurring communication:
  - Articles
  - Blogs
  - Conference calls
  - Email updates
  - Newsletters
  - Periodic reports

Note–Include frequency (for example, monthly–first Monday of the month) and points of contact who support or have responsibility for each communication delivery method

- A list of all recurring meetings:
  - Town halls
  - One-on-ones
  - Stakeholder meetings
  - Include date, time, location, phone numbers, meeting owner, meeting objective, and whether virtual and on what platform (Teams, WebEx, Zoom, etc.) or in person
  - Identify the role your successor plays in each meeting (facilitator, information provider, status update provider, etc.)

Tab 5: Resources

- A list of sources of information that may be useful:
  - People
  - Share drive

continued

- Reference materials
- Annual operating plan
- Strategic plan
- Standard operating procedures/Desktop procedures
- Road maps
- Budget

I have often heard the comment, "I wish someone had done this for me." I frequently thought that as well. Over the years, I received enormous gratification in the form of feedback from successors, former bosses, and stakeholders expressing their appreciation for such a smooth handoff. I felt good knowing I had done everything I could do to help my successor make a good first impression.

There are two additional variations in the application of this tool:

1. When I got a new boss, I shared some version of this information. It conveyed to my new boss that I was an organized and competent leader who was "on top of my role."
2. This is the kind of information you want to gather as a leader in a new role. This structure for collecting information helps to accelerate your learning, minimize breakdowns, and better ensure your success in the new role.

STARTING STRONG—THE FIRST SIXTY DAYS

Much as the Ending Well information can be used in multiple ways, so can this First Sixty Days information. First, you can use it as a framework for documenting your thoughts for that often-asked interview question, "What is your plan for your first thirty/sixty/ninety days in the role?" Many interviewees think they need to have a more specific plan. I view that as a trap—beware! Don't pretend to have all the answers when you have never had the job before. You can add your expertise and experience to this document. Recognizing that you need more information from stakeholders reflects a mature and practical leadership approach when taking on a new role. Second, you can use this framework when you have a new leader joining your team; it will help accelerate their learning curve. Third, you can use the framework to guide your first few months on the job to accelerate your learning curve and contribute to your great first impression opportunity.

Here is the overview of the First Sixty Days activities:

First Thirty Days

- Know Your Mandate
- Conduct Stakeholder Interviews
- Communicate Interview Results with Priorities
- Assess Existing Talent
- Develop a Communication Plan
- Review Your Calendar

Second Thirty Days

- Create and Execute Your Plan
    - Determine Performance Management Measures
    - Use the Checks and Balances Tool
    - Understand and Manage Your Budget

THE FIRST THIRTY DAYS

Know Your Mandate

This is critical to ensure clarity about what you are expected to accomplish in your new role or with your added responsibilities. There are several ways you can think about and talk about your mandate. One way is to think about success factors. You might ask your new boss, "What do I need to do in the first three, six, nine, or twelve months for you to consider me a successful hire or a successful performer?" Another way to ask is, "What does success look like in my new role?" A second way to think about your mandate is to fast-forward to a year from now and imagine you are receiving your performance review from your boss. Are there certain things you need to achieve or accomplish to be considered a strong performer in your new role? This could include building trusting and respectful relationships with stakeholders, delivering specific projects on time and within budget, growing revenue by a certain percentage, improving employee productivity by a certain percentage, increasing market share by a certain percentage, strengthening your team's performance by adding certain skills or expertise, or standing up a whole new team to deliver new products or services. The possibilities are endless.

And let's be fully realistic: Some bosses won't be prepared to answer this question crisply and succinctly, if at all. That doesn't lessen the importance of knowing your mandate. If your boss is vague or can't really answer your question, I recommend you conduct a variety of interviews with various stakeholders. Once you have completed the interviews and analyzed the input, *you* develop your mandate and share it with your boss. After sharing your thoughts, ask your boss if you have missed anything. It's much like soliciting feedback. Sometimes it's easier to fill in the blanks or add to a response or recommendation than to start with a blank sheet of paper. It also lets your boss know that you are confident in setting the agenda for your first year in your new role.

Conduct Stakeholder Interviews

Once you know your mandate, you are ready to start gathering additional information. Listed below are your key stakeholder groups: direct reports, customers, peers, and vendors/suppliers. Based on your specific situation, you may have additional stakeholder groups to interview. I have suggested some possible questions. Feel free to modify them to better support your specific situation. The overarching objective in conducting these interviews is to gather a considerable amount of information quickly in order to accelerate your learning curve. You want to ask the same questions of multiple stakeholder groups to determine if something is an isolated problem with one stakeholder group or a pervasive problem across multiple stakeholder groups.

TOOL: THE FIRST SIXTY DAYS

Meetings (One-on-One)

Direct Reports

What do you want to know about me (in this new role)? Share your leadership style.

Ask them:

- What does this team do well?
- Where does this team fall short?
- What are this team's top three priorities?
- What are the biggest challenges in achieving these priorities?
- If you had my job, what are the first three to five things you would do?
- What do you want me to know about you?
- What are your expectations of me?

continued

- What, if anything, do you need from me right now?
- Is there anything else we should talk about?

Tips for Meetings with Direct Reports

- I recommend not sending the questions ahead of time. My experience is that "top of mind" responses are more relevant. Always leave the door open to receive additional or subsequent thoughts.
- "What" and "how" questions are powerful and will yield more useful information than "why" questions, which often put people on the defensive.
- Listen for clarity around people, process, financial, operational, and customer considerations.
- Take notes in every meeting. Look for themes, patterns, disconnects, contradictions, and alignment/lack of alignment from person to person. For example . . .
    - Is there agreement/alignment on the top three priorities?
    - Do people see the strengths and challenges of the organization in a similar way?
- Once you've met with each of your direct reports, consolidate the information you've gathered and share it with the team in a collective session. Get their feedback on whether or not you've captured the information accurately. My experience is that it's insightful and useful to share the information with the team.

Customers

- What do you want to know about me (in this new role)?
- On a scale of one to ten, how would you rate the quality of our service to you?
    - What do we do well?
    - What do we need to work on?
    - Are there things you want to ensure that we keep doing? If so, what are they?
- What are the key things I should be focused on in these first thirty days to ensure that we serve your needs? If you had my job, what are the first three to five things you would do?

- What are your ongoing expectations of me? My expectations of you are . . .
- Is there anything else we should talk about?

Peers

- Is there anything you want to know about me (in this new role)?
- How do our teams interact—regarding workflow, meetings, shared projects?
- Are there any "thorny" issues or contentious relationships that exist between your team and my team? Has anything been done to address these issues? If so, what, and with what result?
- What are your expectations of me? My expectations of you are . . .
- What is your perspective on how to best relate to the boss or other key stakeholders?
- Is there anything you need from me right now?
- Is there anything else we should talk about?

Vendors and Suppliers/Other Stakeholders

- Understand your relationships and contracts.
- Understand the rules of engagement.
- Understand who is on point for the relationship—on their side and yours.
- Understand the escalation procedures—people and process.
- Understand payment structures.
- Understand if there are any thorny issues—such as project status, timelines, next steps, your role (if applicable).

Tips for Meeting with Customers, Peers, and Other Key Stakeholders

- Depending on the time frame for collecting this information, share as much as possible with your direct reports. Help them see the big picture.
- Depending on the situation, solicit their help in aligning priorities, addressing thorny issues, developing solutions for immediate problems, and strengthening relationships in this time of change.

continued

- Map the political landscape. Identify a) decision-makers, b) allies, c) adversaries, d) influencers, and e) gatekeepers (those people who enable or disable access to people, meetings, information, etc.).

Summary

- Consolidate your findings, and identify themes and patterns within and across stakeholder groups.
- Prioritize action items based on these themes by asking, "Where is my greatest leverage or greatest return on investment of my time and focus?"
- Share your summary findings and priorities with all stakeholder groups.

Communicate Interview Results with Priorities

Once you have conducted all the interviews, consolidate your findings and identify themes and patterns within and across stakeholder groups. You will then use this information first to identify your Year One Mandate, if not already known, and second to prioritize action items based on these themes. You are striving to determine your greatest leverage and the greatest return on your investment of time, energy, and focus, as well as allocation of resources (people and dollars). You also will want to share your collective findings about themes and priorities with each stakeholder you interviewed. This is an important step—be careful not to skip it. By sharing this information, you accomplish several things:

- You let stakeholders know you listened well and heard their feedback—the good things as well as their concerns.
- You let them know how their feedback aligns with (or not) the larger stakeholder group's feedback. Were they an outlier, or were they part of the consistently themed feedback?

- You let them know where their concerns fit in with your priorities. If they were an outlier, their concerns may be lower on your list of priorities as you address concerns that will benefit the masses. Ensure the outliers that you are not ignoring or dismissing their concerns and then make sure you come back to them as you complete the higher priorities.

I also recommend meeting with your various stakeholder groups periodically to share the progress you are making on your priority line items. This builds trust and credibility that you do what you say you are going to do. It also offers you an opportunity to hear updates from them on how things are going.

Assess Existing Talent

Based on your mandate, your stakeholder interview results, and your initial strategy or plan, you have to determine if you have the right people on your team of direct reports. In determining this, remember: A Players choose A Players . . . B Players choose C Players. You may be required to make some hard decisions, such as removing people who are good people and have been effective performers in the past but don't fit the current role profile that you need. Leadership courage is required. Treat them with dignity, respect, and humanity. Focus on the situation being one of a "bad fit" rather than that of a "bad person"; if they have a track record of good performance, focus on "good fit." Place them elsewhere in the organization if possible.

Be thoughtful in your assessment. Define your threshold (for keeping/letting go) before you do the actual assessments. For example, an 80 percent match to the profile description is required for keeping the person on the team. You may need to adjust your threshold as you review your people. Try to balance your head and heart feelings and decisions.

Ensure that those who remain in the organization receive a reassuring message. Generally, this occurs through providing individual feedback. Language is important. Preparation is important. For example, "In looking at the future of this organization and what we need to accomplish, you currently have the skills and capabilities we need. I'm counting on you to provide critical and courageous leadership and be a positive influencer as we move ahead."

TOOL: ASSESSING EXISTING TALENT FRAMEWORK

Identify profiles that reflect a framework of knowledge, skills, and competencies. For example:

Profile	Employee A	Employee B	Etc.
Strategic Thinker			
Strong Decision-Maker			
Customer Focus			
Drive for Results			
Organizational/ Political Savvy			
Interpersonal Skills			
Coaching/Developing Others			

You can use a numeric rating (e.g., 1–5, with 1 = Low, 5 = High) or a Low, Medium, High rating. Different roles will most likely have different profiles.

Develop a Communication Plan

Communication is probably the biggest problem identified, no matter what is happening. This is a broad category that covers a wide range of breakdowns, misunderstandings, and basic lack of information. What I want to offer in the context of this chapter is a structured approach to creating and implementing a deliberate plan that provides timely and appropriate information to your stakeholder groups. It also challenges you to delete meetings that are no longer needed or don't require your attendance.

TOOL: COMMUNICATION PLANNING FRAMEWORK

- Identify what communication framework is in place: Who receives what information when and through what media?
- Overcommunicate in the first thirty days. Be visible–in person and in writing.
- Taking into account what you've learned in your various one-on-one meetings, develop a communication plan. A simple template might look something like the following:

Who	What	When	How
Examples: My Leadership Team My Entire Team My Boss My Internal Customers My External Customers Suppliers/Vendors Others	Examples: General Enterprise Info Strategic Plans Operational Plans Status Updates Performance Feedback Reorganizations Industry News	Examples: Daily Weekly Monthly Quarterly Annually Ad Hoc Deliverable-Driven Milestone-Driven	Examples: Conference Calls Group Meetings One-on-One Meetings Email Town Halls Portals Share Drives Retreats Newsletters Blogs Podcasts

In general, you want to overcommunicate in the first thirty days. There is a lot of uncertainty and, therefore, anxiety. Remember what I wrote about in chapter 6 on change. In absence of a story, people often make one up, and they are usually not flattering to you. Be visible—both in person as well as using written communication to keep everyone informed. And don't think you have to do everything yourself. If corporate or business unit communication specialists or resources are available, be sure to take advantage of what they have to offer. Use their expertise.

Here is a more tactical set of steps to help you build your plan:

Step 1—Identify what communication framework is currently in place. Identify who receives what information when and through what media.

Step 2—Taking into account what you learned during your stakeholder interviews, begin to build your template for a communication plan.

Another way to organize this communication plan is the following:

MEETINGS

Who	What	When	How
Direct Reports	Status updates using the Checks and Balances tool	Weekly	Face-to-Face One-on-One

You will need to determine the best day of the week, the month, or the year to do this. For example, Friday may be a good day for your direct reports. They can share what they have completed that week and prepare for next week's work as well. (Note—the Checks and Balances tool discussed in chapter 4 is an excellent tool for conducting these meetings with direct reports as well as your meetings with your boss.) Be aware of business cycles. For example, month-end and quarter-end can be extra busy. Schedule meetings accordingly. There is typically an annual cycle for developing strategic and operational plans as well as budgets. Know those cycles and give yourself plenty of time to do your research and planning effectively.

As a final thought, review your plan periodically to make sure it is working effectively for you and your stakeholder groups. I recommend twice a year. Of course, this is dependent on the amount and kinds of activity going on in your organization, in the market, and in the world. Communicate your plan to your stakeholder groups in order to set and maintain expectations. Three of the behaviors for building trust are managing expectations, keeping agreements, and being consistent. How you communicate and execute your communication plan can help you build those trusting relationships with your stakeholders.

Review Your Calendar

I don't know about you, but my calendar guides my days year after year after year. If it's on my calendar, it's much more likely to get done. A long time ago, someone told me, "If you want to know what is important to someone, look at their calendar and their checkbook. How someone spends their time and money tells you everything you need to know." I have found that to be pretty true. So, if your calendar guides your activities and also reflects what you value, let's give your calendar the attention it deserves.

In your new role, here are some important thoughts for you to consider as you plan your time accordingly:

TOOL: CALENDAR CHECKLIST

- Review your calendar and determine what meetings you need to continue attending and which ones you need to have someone else attend.
- Delegation is the key–you can't keep doing your old job while assuming the responsibilities of a new role.
- Recognize that it is very tempting to hang on to familiar tasks, responsibilities, and projects. Identify appropriate oversight and metrics for those responsibilities after delegating them to the appropriate person on your staff.
- Determine what new meetings you are expected to attend–choose wisely.
- Make time to execute against your communication plan activities.

Reviewing your calendar is a classic case of slowing down to speed up. When you are transitioning to a new role, time is at a premium. Take the time on the front end to be intentional about how you spend your time. You can set an example for your team as well. It will save you hours as you settle into your new role, and you will feel confident you are spending your time on things that will help you achieve your mandate and contribute real value to your organization.

THE SECOND THIRTY DAYS

Whew! Are you a bit tired after that whirlwind of activity in the first thirty days? That said, I also want to be realistic. It may take more than thirty days to get all of this done. Remember, the answer to every leadership question is, "It depends." In this case, it depends on the scope and complexity of your new role. It depends on what is going on within your organization, the marketplace, and the world. It also depends on the availability of your stakeholders and their willingness to meet with you. You have to take into account their mandates, performance goals, and staff leadership responsibilities. Bottom line—gather as much information as you can, develop your plans, and be prepared to flex and adjust as new information surfaces.

The activities in this next thirty-day period include the following:

- Activate and implement as many action plans as possible—priorities, talent assessment actions, communication delivery, and spending your time wisely.

Be sure to have the following things in place before you activate and implement:

- Determine how you will hold people accountable for performing well and delivering desired results. Remember, there is no accountability without consequence.
- Identify quantitative metrics as appropriate to measure performance and progress.
- Use the Checks and Balances tool to help stakeholders stay focused, ensure desired results, and efficiently make course corrections as needed.
- Understand the budget you have and the financial implications of your decisions and plans.
- Setting and maintaining boundaries is another important aspect. As you are wrapping up one role and moving to your new role, let your successor in your old role know that you will be available to them for the next thirty, forty-five, or sixty days. Given that you have provided comprehensive information and reviewed it with them, it is now their opportunity to lead your former team and function. If, for example, your successor calls you on the thirty-first day and asks you questions about something, you remind them where they can find that information in the transition document or advise them it is now their decision or their discretion on how to handle whatever it is they are asking about. Setting

> your boundary determines and communicates how many days you will make yourself available. Maintaining your boundary is holding true to those stated days of your availability. Of course, there may be exceptions. Just remember not to get sucked back into your previous role. That helps your successor be more successful and allows you to focus on your new role.

Continue to be visible and communicate often. Be both inspirational and aspirational in your words and actions. Don't forget to celebrate successes to keep others (and yourself) motivated, feeling appreciated, and inspired to keep doing great things. Provide thoughtful, constructive feedback (both positive and negative—remember the Seven-Step Feedback tool in chapter 4), and ask for feedback as well. Don't forget the Rules of Eight identified in chapter 6: People generally need to see something eight times before they believe it's real—the new normal. Initially, trust may decline since those around you could previously predict your behaviors as well as the behaviors of your predecessor. When they can no longer predict with great certainty how you will behave, make decisions, solve problems, and so on, trust can decline. Don't lose heart. You will have to rebuild trust based on your new behaviors. I offer to you my goal around this predictability—that they can predict with great probability that I will be thoughtful and intentional in how I lead, make decisions, and so on. Choose the best you, stick with it, and solicit feedback.

I hope this chapter is useful for you as you find yourself changing roles and taking on greater responsibilities. Wrapping up and transitioning from your previous role well will then allow you to focus on starting well and making that great first impression in your new role. Structure, plan, follow through, and execute. You will be fabulous!

PART 2

DISCUSSION QUESTIONS

Some of you will be reading this book on your own. Others may be reading and reviewing the book as a book club or a women's group. At the end of each section, I've included some reflection questions that focus on what you've learned from the section and how you plan to apply it in your life.

If you are reading the book as a group, I encourage you to answer the questions individually before discussing them as a group. You want to do your own personal work. Once you hear others' responses, you can add, change, or even delete items in your own responses. Remember, women learn through stories. Share yours freely and deeply, and listen as others do the same.

PART 2 REFLECTION QUESTIONS

- What did you learn about yourself while reading this section?

- What stands out for you about building, developing, and inspiring teams?

- What are three things you'll do differently going forward based on what you've learned?

PART 3

INFLUENCING ORGANIZATIONS

CHAPTER 8

ORGANIZATIONAL SYSTEMS

"Spatial blindness is about seeing
the part without the whole.
Temporal blindness is about seeing
the present without the past."

—Barry Oshry

In 1999, I attended a learning event called the Power Lab at the suggestion of one of my master's program classmates (thank you, Phil Novick). So many new insights, thoughts, and activities were spawned from my week at the Craigville Retreat Center in Massachusetts. I experienced and saw an organizational system I had never experienced or seen before. In fact, it was a major contributing factor in framing how I could better engage and support women. Thank you, Barry and Karen Oshry! I would be remiss if I didn't give Barry Oshry full credit and praise for the words, graphics, and concepts included in this chapter as well as in chapter 9, "In the Middle." Barry has spent his adult life studying and writing about organizational systems. I only wish I had been introduced to Barry's work earlier in my career. I had done lots, and I mean *lots*, of training programs. I can truly say none of them had the deep and meaningful impact on me that the Power Lab had. I went back to staff future Power Labs as an anthropologist and coach. I went even further and became a member of the board for the Power + Systems organization. I'm excited to share with you my Power Lab experience and the many lessons the Lab provided me as well as the corporate spin-off simulation called the Organization Workshop. The wisdom and insights that I share here are attributed to Barry Oshry.

As I cite these two experiences, I define what each one represents.

Program Name	Purpose	Duration	Roles
Power Lab	Societal Simulation	8 days (24 x 7 experience)	Elites Managers Immigrants
Organization Workshop	Workplace Simulation	4-6 hours	Tops Middles Bottoms Customers

POWER LAB

When Barry and Karen Oshry set out to create a learning environment (circa 1970), they wanted to deepen their understanding of power and powerlessness in social systems. The result was the Power + Systems Laboratory. The basic idea was to create a societal setting in which people could *experience* issues of power and powerlessness directly and dramatically, so they created a "world" with clear-cut differences in power and resource control and access. This learning environment was somewhat ironically called the Community of New Hope.

NEW HOPE

There are three social classes in New Hope. The first is the Elite (or Tops), who control the society's wealth and institutions. The second class is the Managers (or Middles), who manage the society's institutions for the Elite. The third class is the Immigrants (or Bottoms), who enter the society with no funds, few resources, and no control over the society's institutions. This Community of New Hope is compelling in that it encompasses all aspects of participants' lives—the quality of their housing, the quality and volume of their meals, the job opportunities available to them, the amount of employment opportunities available to them, the amount of New Hope money they have (the only viable currency in New Hope), their access to resources, and more.

A good play needs an appropriate theater, and the Oshrys were fortunate early on to discover the Craigville Retreat Center on Cape Cod. Craigville offered an isolated setting with a variety of housing possibilities for the three social classes as well as a huge tabernacle that could house the society's institutions—its court, newspaper, company store, employment center, pub, and theater. And importantly, over the years the Craigville staff have functioned as patient, understanding, cooperative, sometimes bemused partners in this learning venture.

The Oshrys created and honed the process to create the world into which participants are "born" as either Elites, Managers, or Immigrants. They then step back and allow the community to unfold. There are no scenarios to follow, no scripts or further instructions from the staff. What becomes of the society depends on whatever the collection of players makes of it.

When I attended the Lab in 1999, I elected to participate as an Immigrant. I wanted to explore my personal power. I had been a corporate officer of a Fortune 50 company where I had positional power (as a Top) and generally enjoyed the control and access to resources as an Elite. I was starting my own entrepreneurial business; therefore, I would have to rely more on my personal power to develop relationships, sell my services, and achieve results.

COACHING THE COMMUNITY AND OBSERVING THE LAB

I mentioned earlier that I had come back to the Lab as both a coach and an anthropologist. These are important learning partners for all participants. Each participant is assigned a coach and has access to any of the coaches who are staffing the Lab; typically, there are four coaches available for each Lab. The coaches spend five to fifteen minutes in individual coaching sessions. They use a different approach to coaching in the context of organizational systems. When I was a participant, they asked me questions I had never been asked before:

- "Where is your power in this situation?"
- "How might you be giving away your power?"
- "How could you hold on to your power in service to the Community?"

As you probably recognize by now, these are questions and concepts that are foundational to my work in supporting women.

The role of the anthropologist is to observe, take copious notes (as verbatim as possible), and never speak or interact with participants other than to observe them and take notes on what they see and hear. At the end of the weeklong learning experience, the anthropologists (referred to as Anthros) combine their notes and observations to create the "Anthro Story." Because Anthros are assigned certain roles and locations, great attention is given to covering all parts of the system to the best of the five Anthros' abilities in order to develop a comprehensive system story. There are always multiple storylines. The Anthros meet throughout the Lab (after all the participants have been "put to bed") to share information as well as to discover and discuss emerging themes and stories. The hours are long, and sleep is scarce. And I loved every minute of it!

Again, on a personal note, as a coach, I learned what systemic questions to ask, and to see things as I had never seen them. I've asked myself these questions many, many times—as an entrepreneur and as a coach to my own clients. Going all the way back to chapter 1 in my first book, *Embracing Your Power*, I discuss three different kinds of power and power sources. I first considered all of these concepts and content as a participant in the Power Lab in 1999. As an Anthro, I began to see so clearly how words and actions created ripple effects throughout the system—cause-and-effect connections. It also deepened my understanding of the power of words, the stories we make up, and the actions we subsequently take. It's the Ladder of Inference discussed in chapter 5 of *Embracing Your Power* in live action.

TIME OUT OF TIME

One other important facet of the Lab is the daily Time Out of Time (TOOT). This is when the activities of the Lab are paused. Everyone—Elites, Managers, and Immigrants—comes together. System frameworks are presented and discussed. These TOOTs last about an hour. Each participant takes the new or enhanced system sight back into their participation in the Lab.

SEEING SYSTEMS

To quote Barry from his book *Seeing Systems*—

> Generally, if we are paying attention, we know what life is like for us in our part of the system. Other parts of the system, for the most part, [are] invisible to us. We do not know what others are experiencing, what their worlds are like, what issues they are dealing with,

> what dilemmas they are facing, what stresses they are undergoing. And what makes matters worse, sometimes we think we do know when, in fact, we do not. We have our beliefs, myths, and prejudices, which we accept as the truth, and which become the bases of our actions. This blindness to other parts of the system—which we call spatial blindness—is a source of considerable misunderstanding and conflict.
>
> Temporal blindness refers to the fact that all current events in system life have a history; there is a coherent tale that has led to this particular point in time. Generally, that history is invisible to us. We experience the present but are blind to the complex set of events that have brought us to the present. And again, it is the blindness to the history of the moment that is a source of considerable misunderstanding and conflict.[1]

Considering that you live in myriad systems—family, work, community, friendships, nation, communities of faith, teams (sports and organizational), and even book clubs or bowling leagues—it will serve you well to learn more about how these systems work. No matter which system you consider, there are Tops (Elites), Middles (Managers), Bottoms (Immigrants), and Customers (internal and external). In your everyday organizational life, you can play any of these roles. If you are meeting with your direct reports, you are a Top. If you are meeting with your boss and your direct reports, you are a Middle. If you are meeting with your boss, you are a Bottom. If another department or team provides you with services or deliverables of some sort, you are a Customer. Think about your meetings this week. Make a note for each meeting, describing whether you are a Top, Middle, Bottom, or Customer. It is important to be clear about this because different system dynamics are going on for each of these roles. (Note—I use the following terms interchangeably: *role*, *world*, *space*.)

Image 8.1 is a diagram to help you visualize:

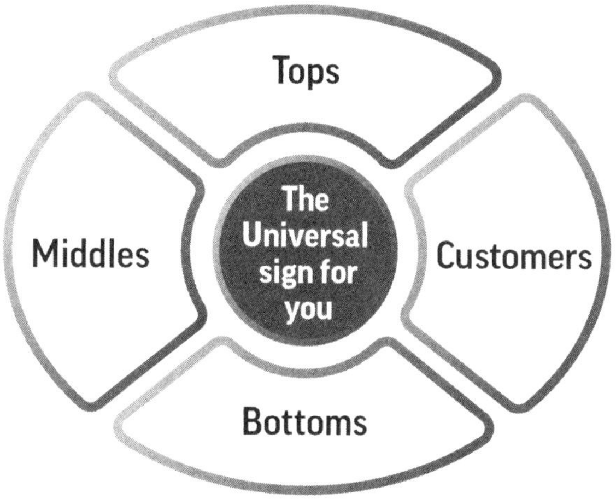

Image 8.1 Model Courtesy of Barry Oshry

This is your system, and you can play any one of those four roles. When you are in your role, you know what is going on only in your world. It's as if there are brick walls in front of all those other worlds, and you can't see what is going on behind that brick wall.

THE "STUFF"

Periodically, several kinds of "stuff" come floating into the system:

- **Good Stuff**—Your project is approved. You won the deal. You are getting a raise or promotion.
- **Noxious Stuff**—Your organization is struggling financially, and layoffs are coming. You have been working from home, and your organization announces that you have to come into the office,

adding cost and hours to complete your commute. Your company is being acquired, and you fear your job will be eliminated. Your organization is implementing new technology, and you are not sure you can learn the new technology.

- **Mysterious Stuff**—Your company announces a reorganization, and you don't know why they think that is necessary. You receive an email that says a longtime leader is leaving the organization to "spend more time with their family," and you wonder what the real story is. (By the way, I'm waiting for the organizational announcement that someone is joining the organization so they can "spend *less* time with their family.")
- **Silent Stuff**—You send an email expecting a response, and that response never comes. You have been waiting for a decision that keeps getting pushed out with no communication or explanation.

REFLECTION

Looking at your calendar for the next thirty days, focus on your meetings. Identify and note in which meetings you are a:

- **Top** with overall responsibility for the meeting
- **Middle** existing between the Tops and Bottoms, playing interpreter, reporter, and director of assignments
- **Bottom** with responsibility for rendering services or producing the deliverables of the organization
- **Customer** receiving those products and services from another part of the organization
- Where do you spend the majority of your time–Top, Middle, Bottom, or Customer?

- What stuff has recently been floating around in your organization (e.g., a change in direction, an acquisition or merger, outsourcing, hiring freezes, budget cuts, etc.)?

- How would you categorize such stuff—good, noxious, mysterious, or silent?

PARTNERSHIP APPROACH

One of my favorite principles in this work is about being in partnership—no matter what role you might be playing or what kind of "stuff" is floating into the system. I love the definition of how we want to work together in partnership: **being mutually committed to whatever process we're in . . . and to each other**. I want that! We might be in a strategic planning process, a project planning process, a contracting process, a decision-making process, a budgeting process, and on and on. Whatever process we are in, we want each other to contribute and deliver results that are good for the larger organization, or customer, or family, or community. In other words, you are not pushing your agenda to the exclusion of others, and neither is the other person for personal gain. You are working to help the other person be successful, and they are working to help you do the same.

In addition to the strategy of being and working in partnership, let's also do a deeper dive into the worlds of Tops, Middles, Bottoms, and Customers.

TOPS

Tops are trying to survive in a world of complexity and have a strong sense of being responsible for the entire system. There are lots of things bombarding Tops on a daily basis. Tops worry about making the numbers, selling new business, meeting regulatory requirements, engaging and supporting employees in bcing productive, keeping clients happy, watching the competition, ensuring that they know what is going on in the marketplace, and so on.

Image 8.2 is a simple visual of the world of a Top:

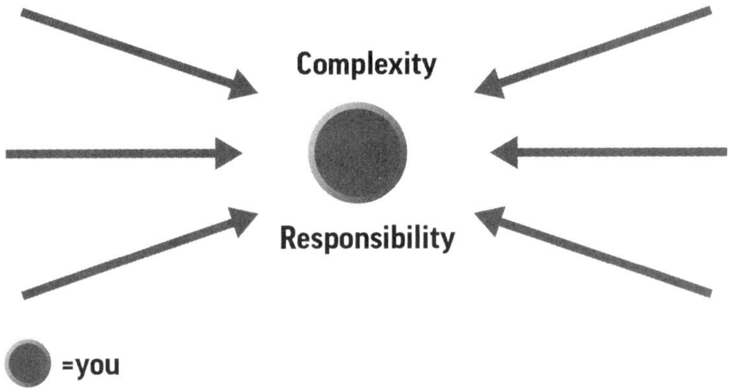

Image 8.2: Model Courtesy of Barry Oshry

BOTTOMS

What about the Bottoms? Many Bottoms are trying to survive in a vulnerable world waiting for the higher-ups (Tops and Middles) to provide direction, allocate and review work, make decisions, develop them, give feedback, and keep them informed on a wide variety of things. It's a world where noxious, mysterious, and silent stuff is ever present.

Image 8.3 is a simple visual of the Bottoms' world:

Image 8.3: Courtesy of Barry Oshry

MIDDLES

Middles feel like they are getting pulled in a million directions. The Tops want updates and results. The Bottoms are asking a million questions. Peers (other Middles) have expectations, and Customers want status updates, a good deal, and results. I see the Middle world as the master repository of information from the most sources. They are the linchpin of many organizations. I'm betting that many of you reading this find yourself living in this Middle world for a large percentage of your workday.

Image 8.4 is a simple visual of the Middles' world:

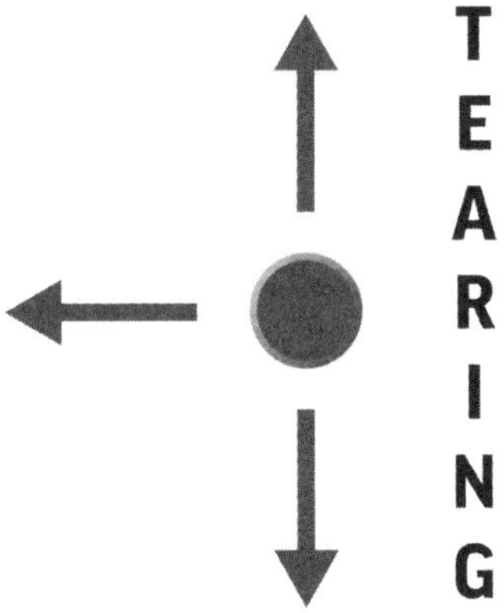

Image 8.4. Model Courtesy of Barry Oshry

CUSTOMERS

Last, though certainly not least, what about the Customers? Customers often experience a world of promises made and promises broken, excuses, delays, and disappointments. A customer can quickly feel neglected and have a sense of being dismissed.

Image 8.5 is a simple visual of the Customers' world:

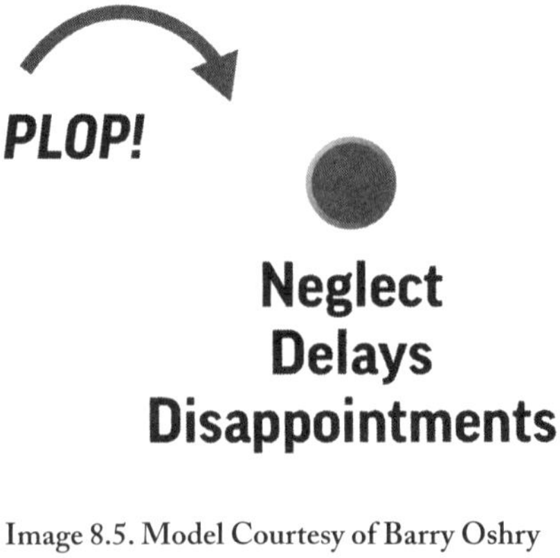

Image 8.5. Model Courtesy of Barry Oshry

THE SIDE SHOW AND CENTER RING

With all the stuff swirling about, how do you typically react? Does this sound familiar?

- **We make up a story about it.** "Those people have no idea how hard we are working! We can't keep up with the workload now. They have no idea what is really going on."
- **We evaluate others.** "They don't care how hard we have to work. They are stupid, incompetent, out-of-touch leaders."
- **We take it personally.** "I have given a lot of years and made a lot of contributions in my time here. They just see me as a number on a spreadsheet."
- **We react.** "I am mad. I'll show them. I'm doing as little as possible."
- **We lose focus.** It's no longer about making contributions or doing our best work. We are distracted with complaining conversations, high anxiety moments, and wondering if we should be looking for another job.
- **We fall out of partnership.** It's no longer about being mutually committed to whatever process we are in, much less to each other.

How long do you think it might take you to go from making up a story, evaluating others, taking it personally, reacting, losing focus, and falling out of partnership? Most likely in less time than it took you to read this paragraph. It happens quickly and almost by default. We are humans, and our brains operate this way. It's how we make sense of the world. But it doesn't serve us well.

SIDE SHOW

Our choice is not whether we will go to the Side Show. Our choice is whether or not we will stay there.

SIDE SHOW

We make up a story.
We evaluate others.
We take it personally.
We react.
We lose focus.
We fall out of partnership.

Let's ask ourselves why it is so easy to go to the Side Show. There are several explanations. The most obvious one for me is that it's easy, and I don't have any accountability. There are a lot of people in the Side Show with lots of finger-pointing, and there's plenty of blame to go around to everyone but me. What role do you usually reserve for yourself in your story?

- You are the victim, and they have done you wrong.
- You are the self-righteous one that told them it would never work; they should have listened to you.
- You are the hero or heroine riding in to save the day.

The last question to ask yourself is, "What do I have to give up to move out of and beyond the Side Show?" You have to give up your lack of accountability and blaming others. You may have to give up a bit of arrogance and ego pretending that you have all the answers. Why do you want to move beyond the Side Show? Because nothing ever gets done and things don't get better when everyone is in the Side Show. Following are a few reflection questions.

REFLECTION

- Based on the stuff you identified in the previous reflection, have you been or are you now operating from the Side Show?
- What do you need to do to move on from the Side Show?
- Who can help you?
- Who can you help?

And where will you move as you leave the Side Show? The Center Ring.

THE CENTER RING

The Center Ring choice is a more productive mindset. It requires you to acknowledge and understand that the stuff and all the challenges are coming from a world of Tops, Middles, Bottoms, and Customers rather than from a specific individual.

Remember:

- You have to diagnose the problem correctly in order to fix the problem effectively.

- You know it's a systemic or organizational problem when it exists throughout the organization. It becomes further evident of a systemic problem when you change out the person and the problem still exists.

If you are operating from the Center Ring, your thinking reflects these strategies (see Image 8.6):

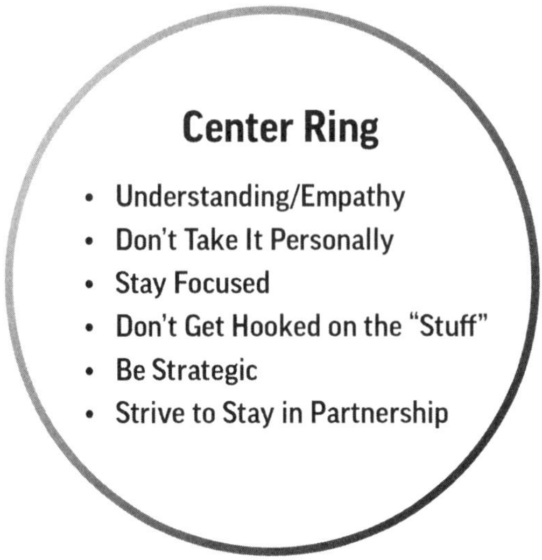
Center Ring
• Understanding/Empathy
• Don't Take It Personally
• Stay Focused
• Don't Get Hooked on the "Stuff"
• Be Strategic
• Strive to Stay in Partnership

Image 8.6

- **Understanding/Empathy**—Now that you are aware of the conditions of each world, put yourself in the shoes of a Top, Middle, Bottom, or Customer. Think about times when you have lived in that world. Acknowledge to the other person(s) that you understand, appreciate, and respect their reality in their respective world.
- **Don't Take It Personally**—Remind yourself that whatever stuff is happening, it is coming from a world. It is not about you—and

I know it's hard to see, much less admit, that it isn't about you personally. When you are in the stuff, you are often deeply in it, and it's hard to pull yourself out of it.

- **Stay Focused**—What is your desired outcome? Your work is not to get distracted and to continuously hang out in the Side Show. A phrase that reflects this Center Ring principle that you may have heard before is "Keep your eye on the ball." The ball (or desired outcome) may bounce several times and in several directions. It requires you to stay open and be flexible so that you can readily pivot when the situation requires it in order to achieve your outcome.
- **Don't Get Hooked on the Stuff**—When I find myself getting hooked or triggered, I often say to myself, "Isn't that fascinating!" Then I ask myself, "What else could be true?" This allows me to refocus and stay engaged *and* stay away from criticism, judgment, and blame. I remind myself that I made up a story—likely one that is narrow—when I have considered only my view of my world. This is in contrast to me calling on my systems sight or systems thinking.
- **Be Strategic**—Strategic thinking requires us to be big-picture, long-term thinkers. The big picture is synonymous with systems sight and systems thinking. You understand the desired outcome, and you know that working effectively with another person(s) requires you to engage in a big-picture, strategic kind of way. It's akin to when you step back, take a breath, consider everyone's points of view, and then reengage. You must get beyond seeing it from only your point of view.
- **Strive to Stay in Partnership**—Remember that if you are truly striving to operate and engage as a partner, you are committed to achieving a desired outcome so that the other person feels seen, heard, and valued.

REFLECTION

- How might you use Center Ring thinking to work through some of your current stuff?

- How can you assess, consider, and check out what is going on in the worlds of others to better understand their stuff? The situation? The person?

- What are you going to do differently as a result of your new lens (the Center Ring) through which to see and manage the stuff?

Many company cultures and even leadership development programs and books have an underlying implication that if you are a good hero or heroine and try really hard to lead well, everything is doable, so just do it. What I have described to you so far is a better, more effective leadership approach, one that provides a systemic framework to influence your thinking. If you stop and think about your own experience, you will remember that, in some cases, no matter how hard you try to lead and no matter how you will yourself to get things done, the dynamics of systemic forces are in motion. Unless you take those system dynamics into account, it's as though you are fighting Goliath while you are wearing a blindfold. You will continue to take hits and won't even be sure where those hits are coming from.

It's important to recognize that there are both individual leadership capabilities *and* systemic forces at play. To leave out either of these forces is to invite the experience of personal failure and being overwhelmed. Forgetting either element does little to rectify organizational dilemmas or answer individual anxieties.

Generally speaking, to diagnose the problem, the challenge, the issue, or the opportunity, you ask yourself the following questions:

- Is it an **individual** problem? Have you had similar problems in the past? Is it a skill issue? Are you open or resistant to new thoughts, new ways of doing things?
- Is it an **interpersonal** problem? Maybe you get along with almost everyone but struggle with one particular person.
- Is it a **team** problem? Is the team fulfilling its commitments? Are the team members difficult to work with? Do others see the team as competent? Trustworthy?
- Is it an **organizational** problem? Do your policies and procedures cause problems? If so, what changes need to be considered? How does your culture reward mediocre or even poor performance? Is your organization and even your leadership team spending more time in the Side Show or the Center Ring?

HOW COME IT GOES THE WAY IT USUALLY GOES?

Image 8.7 shows how the conditions of each world feed into themselves to further perpetuate the problems of an organization.

Predictable Conditions	Predictable Responses	Familiar Disempowering Scenarios
↑ Top Overload ⟷	"Suck it up" ⟷	Burdened
↑ Bottom Disregard ⟷	Hold "them" responsible ⟷	Oppressed
↑ Middle Crunch ⟷	Slide into the middle ⟷	Torn
↑ Customer Neglect ⟷	Hold "it" responsible ⟷	Righteously screwed

Image 8.7

You can see how crazy-making this becomes! The **Tops** take on (suck up) all the responsibility and end up feeling burdened and even more responsible, and it all adds up to overload. Notice that the horizontal arrows between each column reflect a two-way relationship. In other words, the predictable conditions of each respective world feed on themselves. The disregard for **Bottoms** prompts the **Bottoms** to hold "them" responsible and brings on a feeling of oppression, and the **Tops** also hold "them" responsible for their state of oppression, which is further evidence of their disregard of Bottoms. **Middles** feel torn and pulled apart from almost everyone, and the crunch of the Middle world holds fast. **Customer** neglect leads to **Customers** holding the system responsible and having a sense of being righteously screwed. "The system doesn't listen to me!" "They are moving so slow!" "They never stop asking questions!" Can you relate to these predictable conditions, responses, and disempowering scenarios? Can you see yourself in the chart when you are operating from the Top, Middle, Bottom, or Customer worlds?

Your predictable reflex responses are often invisible to you—you don't see your part in it. See Image 8.8 for a simple visual to understand this:

Image 8.8

Only when you understand your role in the system—through your predictable reflex response—can you choose differently.

PRINCIPLES AND STRATEGIES

So, we have now described the system and the many facets to consider as we live in the various systems of our lives. You are not destined to stay in these systems and be miserable. You have choices. The following are some specific empowerment strategies for when you are a Top, Middle, Bottom, or a Customer. Keep in mind, this is just the beginning of the list. When you are committed to living and working in partnership, much of your life is about discovering and learning new ways to make it happen.

PRINCIPLES

Here are some principles that drive the empowerment strategies:

- Be a **Top** who creates responsibility throughout the system.
- Be a **Middle** who stays out of the middle and maintains your independence of thoughts and actions aligned with your systems' strategies.
- Be a **Bottom** who is responsible for your condition *in* the system *and* the condition *of* the system.
- Be a **Customer** who gets in the middle of delivery processes and helps them work for you.

I would describe the above bullets as both a mindset as well as *what* you want to happen. The following empowerment strategies are more about the *how* and add to your leadership mindset tool kit.

TOP EMPOWERMENT STRATEGIES

When you are living in the Top world and want to create responsibility throughout the system, here are some specific things you can do:

- **Share high-quality information.** This is information that reflects big-picture and longer-term visions, which are often known only by the Tops. It also helps to share the why, what, when, and who. Teams and organizations perform better, are more engaged, and are more productive when they have high-quality information. One of my favorite leadership principles is "When we know better, we do better."
- **Provide feedback.** Review chapter 4 for a tool on giving feedback. Remember, providing feedback is about helping someone acquire new skills, gain new knowledge, deepen their understanding, and develop broader and deeper perspectives.
- **Involve others in big issues.** Invite others to provide their points of view; this is especially important when you need their psychological buy-in and need them to make it work.
- **Ask for help.** Simply stated, you don't have to do it all. It's a sign of leadership maturity to know when to ask for help.
- **Make another Top—be a coach.** I look at this strategy as delegating both responsibility *and* authority with appropriate checks and balances.
- **Invest in relationships.** Relationships matter. Bad relationships make things harder. Good relationships make things easier.
- **Invest in training and development.** Help people grow so they can help the organization grow. This can be self-study (webinars, books, TED Talks), in-person training (internal and external providers), in-place developmental assignments (special projects and assignments that build skills and provide exposure), and full job change rotations.
- **Create enrolling visions.** In chapter 11, I write about influencing others. One of the influencing strategies I share is captivating. It reflects painting a picture or telling a story that captures your

heart and mind. As a result, you definitely want to be a part of that vision.

- **Create and use teams.** This is another version of "don't think you have to do it all yourself." Allow teams to define the outcomes, design the framework or project plan, and develop the products or services. In a family, it's letting kids plan the family vacation within a certain budget.
- **Reduce differences between Tops and Bottoms.** These differences can come in several varieties—compensation, decision-making, influence, information sharing, problem-solving, customer relations, and so on. Be thoughtful and intentional. Make choices over a period of time as the Bottoms are given the invitation, permission, and encouragement to fully engage and gain broader and deeper experiences.
- **Support Middle integration.** Middle integration gets its own chapter in this book—see chapter 9.

REFLECTION

- Which of these strategies appeal to you?

- Which of these strategies do you need to deploy more often? Even right now?

MIDDLE EMPOWERMENT STRATEGIES

When you are living in the Middle world and want to avoid Middle tearing, be a Middle who stays out of the middle and maintains your independence of thoughts and actions aligned with the system's strategies.

- **Be a Top when you can.** One foundational element of all my work is "In absence of a plan, create one. In absence of a leader, be one." Step up, not in an autocratic or arrogant way but rather in a serving way to support the greater good and achieve the bigger outcomes.
- **Be a Bottom when needed.** There are times when the Bottoms need a helping hand. This requires your thoughtfulness and intentionality. Sometimes we do Bottom work because it is familiar and comfortable. Sometimes we do it because we don't know what to do as a Middle or even a Top. Sometimes we don't want to inconvenience anyone else. And sometimes we think we can do it better than everyone else. These are all danger zones. Be really clear on why you choose to provide your helping hands to a Bottom group, and make sure you stay focused on your Middle role.
- **Be a coach.** Share your expertise and guide your team(s) to achieve desired outcomes. One of my EDS colleagues shared a story that is relevant here. He was talking about the difference between being a coach and a manager in the context of coaching his son's Little League baseball team. At practice, the coaches were hitting ground balls to the infield players—ten ground balls each. A manager then assessed each player's performance—"You caught three, two went to your left, one went to your right, and four went through your legs." On the other hand, a coach, well, coaches. They teach the player to bend her knees, keep her glove on the ground, be ready to shift left or right, and keep her eye on the ball. Both are important. Start with coaching. That will yield greater capacity and improved performance.

- **Be a facilitator.** A facilitator is "a person or thing that makes an action or process easy or easier."[2] Look for ways to simplify tasks or processes. Provide information and clarify expectations.
- **Integrate with your peers.** There are multiple considerations with this strategy. First, keep Tops informed. You don't want to be blindsided with information that you expect to come from your direct report. Second, hold each other accountable. This requires an up-front conversation about how you want to work together (see chapter 9). Third, rotate leadership. This enables everyone to experience a leadership role while building empathy and understanding and also building skills and experience. And fourth, work the tough issues. The Middle world is the repository for a wealth of information—use it. Develop new ideas, make recommendations, and propose solutions. This Middle peer group can be a powerhouse.

REFLECTION

- Which of these strategies appeal to you?

- Which of these strategies do you need to deploy more often? Even right now?

BOTTOM EMPOWERMENT STRATEGIES

When you find yourself living in the Bottom world, be a Bottom who is responsible for your condition *and* the condition of the system.

- **Shift from victim to co-creator.** Move out of the Side Show and into the Center Ring.
- **Shift from complaint to potential projects.** One of my most effective career-advancing strategies was taking things off my boss's to-do list rather than putting things on my boss's to-do list. I always tried to have an idea or a recommendation whenever I had a complaint or saw an opportunity for improvement. It doesn't take very much skill or capability to identify problems. People who complain are everywhere. People who bring solutions are valuable. And people who implement those solutions are priceless.
- **Ask yourself what part you play in perpetuating this problem condition.** Holding up that mirror takes courage. Maybe you're staying too long in the Side Show. Maybe you aren't speaking up to identify problems and potential solutions. Maybe you're waiting for someone else to fix it or to ask for your help. Once you identify your role in the problem condition, make a plan and be a leader.
- **Ask yourself how you can become central in making this problem go away.** This is a more complicated strategy than it initially appears. In becoming central to making the problem go away, you are likely "signing up" for more work. Big problems require time, attention, and focus. Most of my clients are already working double time to get everything done. You have to be thoughtful and intentional when stepping into this strategy. Determine if spending some up-front time to solve this problem will save you time in the long run. When I have competing priorities, I always ask myself, "What will matter most a year from now?" Depending on the answer, I prioritize accordingly.

REFLECTION

- Which of these strategies appeal to you?

- Which of these strategies do you need to deploy more often? Even right now?

CUSTOMER EMPOWERMENT STRATEGIES

When living in the Customer world, be a Customer who gets in the middle of delivery processes and helps them work for you.

- **Find out how the system works.** There are always protocols for engaging with another organizational system. This is often referred to as chain of command. I recommend that you get very clear about how you make requests, how status updates will happen (format, frequency, participants), how problems will be resolved, how changes will be received and executed, and how decisions and approvals will be made. These protocols might also be referred to as group norms or operating principles. Take the time up front to get clarity and alignment with all parties.
- **Have clear expectations, demands, and standards.** If you are in the Customer role and are not clear, it will be a long and arduous situation. If there are some things you are very clear about, share them. If there are unknowns, identify them and collaborate on how answers will be developed and how that will be

communicated. If there are areas where your provider has discretion, share those along with any parameters or boundaries (budget, timelines, priorities) to be taken into consideration.

- **Get into the process early as a partner, not late as a judge.** Of all the strategies I have shared here, this one is my favorite. If we slow down a bit to get clear on how the system works, set clear expectations, demands, and standards, and respect the agreed-upon protocols, partnership is a much more effective and likely outcome. I practice this strategy in all the worlds of Tops, Middles, Bottoms, and Customers.
- **Stay close to the producer.** Once the protocols have been agreed upon, stay as close as reasonably possible to the Bottom doing the work. This reduces the chances of miscommunication or disappointing outcomes. Include Tops and Middles as needed, and rely on the Bottom to keep his Middles and Tops informed. If you have problems that can't be resolved by your Bottom provider, you can always invite the Middle or Top into the process.

REFLECTION

- Which of these strategies appeal to you?

- Which of these strategies do you need to deploy more often? Even right now?

Remember, this is a starting point. Add to this list as you deepen your understanding of these four worlds. Periodically reflect on your effectiveness in each of these worlds by asking yourself the learning agility questions:

- What did I do?
- What did I learn?
- How will that help me going forward?

Without taking the time for these learning agility questions, you run the chance of missing out on important leadership development and may even be destined to repeat less effective decision-making and results.

I round out this strategy section by offering more wisdom from Barry and Karen Oshry.

> "Be a person who sees others–who gets who others are and what is important to them, who gets behind them and helps move them ahead in their worlds . . .
> AND
> Be a person who puts your projects out to others–who lets others know who you are and what is important to you, who allows others to get behind you and move ahead in your world."[3]

BACK TO THE POWER LAB

Now, to come full circle, let me share a few lessons learned from my Power Lab experience back in 1999.

In my New Hope societal Immigrant world experience, I was the equivalent of an organizational system Bottom. I had access to few resources, and, in some cases, that included my own personal resources.

Shortly before I attended the Lab, my husband had to have unexpected surgery, and I almost didn't go to the Lab at all. He had regained his self-sufficiency and insisted I go. I reluctantly went and promised, as I always did when out of town, to call him every night. Keep in mind that this was before cell phones. Much to my surprise, Immigrants did not have access to phones. During our orientation, we could make a phone call to inform our loved ones that our phone calls were limited to emergency situations. Once again, I almost checked out to go home. In all my twenty-seven years of work and travel, I had always called home each day. Once again, my husband assured me he would be fine. Okay, let the learning begin.

In my Lab, there were seventeen people: four Elites (Tops), one of whom was female; four Managers (Middles), one of whom was female; and nine Immigrants (Bottoms), five of whom were female.

From the very beginning, the men began telling the women what to do. We were a strong group of seven women (one Elite, one Manager, five Immigrants), and we were not having it. In addition, the societal systems were strong at work regarding our housing and sleeping quarters, our food, and our basic rights. Here's the good part: For the first time in my life, women from all levels came together and developed strategies to improve our conditions in the system. By Day Two, I was operating as a Manager. (I must also admit, I never got the title, money, or access to resources that a Manager had in New Hope. I took it all on with no reward. See chapter 10, "Ask for What You Want." That was my personal learning experience and a familiar story.)

Our female Elite was the judge in our judicial system, and we were able to bring lawsuits protecting our rights according to the "laws" of New Hope. It was a grueling week with lots of drama and intense learning. At the end of the week, the story the Anthro Team crafted for us was entitled, "I Am Woman, Hear Me Roar." That may sound familiar as a Helen Reddy song from 1971 and part of the feminist movement of the time. The bottom-line learning was that *when the women from all parts of the system worked together, making strategic decisions and supporting one another, they changed the system*! Breathe that in. Read it again. They—we—changed the system. At age forty-seven and after thirty years of work experience and growing up in the midst of the feminist movement, I had never experienced this.

This resulted in some fundamental principles of my work:

- Define your own definition of success.
- Never let anyone else define you.
- Be authentic.
- Here's to women supporting women.

These principles still guide my work today.

Being fully transparent, the women in the Lab never got together and defined changing the system as our desired outcome. We wanted basic rights and fairness. We wanted our needs to matter. We wanted to tell our story and have our voices heard. We wanted a say in decisions that had a major impact on our quality of life. We had a bigger purpose. It took the Anthro story to help us see the system in bigger ways—and help define, design, and develop a better system for all the citizens of the community of New Hope.

If I sound passionate about these desires, it's because I am. Many things have changed in my seventy-two years—some things for the better and some for the worse. In my humble opinion, women around the world deserve the same human rights that the women of the fall 1999 Power Lab were fighting for. My learnings there gave me clarity and focus, an appetite for learning more, and a framework to focus my work to do my part. By better understanding how systems work, you have knowledge, tools, and a blueprint for doing your part too. Don't ignore or avoid organizational and societal systems thinking as you travel your life's journey.

REFLECTION

- What stands out for you when you read this chapter?

- In what role or world (Tops, Middles, Bottoms, and Customers) do you operate most frequently?

- What strategies can you deploy to be more effective in that role?

- How has your system sight changed?

CHAPTER 9

IN THE MIDDLE

"Middles tend to be a perpetual motion. They carry in their heads a seemingly endless list of items to be accomplished."

—Barry Oshry

This chapter is a deeper dive into the role of the Middle discussed in the previous chapter. Once again, this chapter is based on the brilliant work of Barry Oshry. The majority of the material in this chapter is adapted from Barry's work.[1] I am learning more and more year after year regarding the Middle space or condition. The power of this Middle condition is seemingly untapped. The possibilities, therefore, are great. I hope the material in this chapter opens up new possibilities for you when operating in this Middle space.

Middleness is not a position; it is a *condition*. It's a condition all of us experience at various times and in varying degrees, in whatever position we are in. Middleness is the condition in which you exist between two or more individuals or groups; these groups have differing priorities, goals, needs, and wants; and each of them exerts pressure on you to function on its behalf. You can be a Middle vertically, sitting between Tops and Bottoms. You can also be a Middle horizontally, sitting between peers or other departments.

Middleness is a potentially disempowering condition. It tends to weaken *individuals* in the Middle—confusing them, muddling their strategies, and sapping their energies. It tends to weaken *groups* in the Middle—alienating members from one another and diminishing their capacity to function as an integrated and effective unit. However, there is another possibility. Middleness is also a potentially empowering system condition. It offers individuals and groups unique opportunities for sensitive and effective influence over the course of system life. Which way it goes for you when you are in the Middleness condition—toward powerlessness or powerfulness—depends on your ability to understand and manage the unique dynamics of that condition.

OBSERVATIONS OF THE MIDDLE CONDITION

As you think about when you are experiencing the Middle condition, I invite you to ponder these observations.

Middles tend to be involved in a hectic work pace. Middles generally work long and hard throughout the duration of organizational system experiences. You are continually on the go, doing your management work, meeting with Tops and with Bottoms, delivering messages, structuring and restructuring the work, mediating, negotiating, and so forth. In contrast to the relatively stationary existence of Tops and Bottoms, Middles tend to be in perpetual motion. You carry in your head a seemingly endless list of items to be accomplished: quick management meetings with Tops, setting up work for Bottoms, back to Tops on some other matter, an errand to run, paperwork to be cleaned up, a piece of business to be transacted on the run between one meeting and another, and on and on it goes.

The Middle experience tends to be an ego-deflating one. As hard as Middles work, they generally receive very little positive support, reinforcement, or gratitude from either Tops or Bottoms. As a Middle, you tend to feel you are not measuring up to the standards both Tops and Bottoms hold for you. Words that Tops and Bottoms have used to describe these standards include *confused*, *uncertain*, *wishy-washy*, *unable or unwilling to take a stand*, *powerless*, *weak*. On the other hand, Middles are also described as hardworking, well meaning, and trying to please. According to Tops and Bottoms, the problems with Middles lie less with their intentions and effort than with their competence.

The Middle experience tends to be a confusing one. Middles tend not to have clear and firm positions on issues. As a Middle, your thinking is often muddled. You listen to Tops, and their position makes sense to you; you listen to Bottoms, and their position also makes sense. In the Middle, you find yourself confused and ambivalent on a variety of issues, unable to make up your mind, continually flip-flopping between contradictory positions, or, in attempting to be responsive to both Tops and Bottoms, assuming compromise positions that satisfy neither the Tops nor the Bottoms.

Middles tend to believe that the significant action in the system lies with the Tops and Bottoms and not with themselves. Middles have described themselves as "telephone wires" connecting the Tops and Bottoms, as "invisible people" through whom the feelings and actions of Tops and Bottoms flow. Despite these feelings of insignificance, Middles generally feel a heavy responsibility for keeping the system together, for making it work, and for preventing Tops and Bottoms from destroying one another in the system.

Middles tend to feel isolated and lonely. Middles are accepted by neither Tops nor Bottoms, and their own groups tend to be fractionated. Middle group members tend to be unsupportive of one another, and there is often a great deal of interpersonal tension and competition among them.

Middles tend not to take independent action. Tops are more likely to develop game plans and strategies and to initiate actions based on those plans and strategies. Bottoms execute those plans. Middles, by contrast, tend to be more reactive, acting in support of or against the plans of others or reconciling the conflicting game plans of Tops and Bottoms. As a Middle, you rarely develop a Middle perspective of your own, one which is independent of the perspectives of the Tops and the Bottoms.

Middles tend to personalize their experiences, attributing whatever difficulties they are having to their own personal failings in skill, character, experience, or intelligence. Better people, you believe, would be less confused, less ambivalent, and less wishy-washy. Better people would be able to handle their situation more competently, more powerfully.

REFLECTION

- Look at your calendar for the last thirty days. What percentage of your time was spent in the Middle space? Think of it as a condition where your boss (a Top) has given you an assignment or asked a question. As a Middle, you engage the Bottoms on your team to fulfill the assignment, conduct the research, develop the options, build the deck, and so on.

- How clear were you on what to do or how to complete the assignment?

- Were there mixed messages? Unclear requirements? Were your Bottoms asking questions or requesting resources to complete the work?

- Were there times when you felt isolated or alone? Describe the scenario. What role did you hold for yourself as you considered the situation?

- How did you respond?

Sound familiar? Read on.

DISINTEGRATION OF THE MIDDLES

Contact with many parts of the system, which is inherent to the Middle position and is the power source in that position, is also a major contributing factor to the personal disintegration of the Middles. There are other contributing factors:

Pressures from Tops and Bottoms—The more disintegrated you are and the more confused, uncertain, and weak you feel and are seen to be, the more likely Tops and Bottoms are to increase the pressure on you to bring you into line. As this pressure from Tops and/or Bottoms is increased, the more confused, uncertain, and weak you become. It is paradoxical that those Tops and Bottoms who want to gain the support of Middles are more likely to succeed by *decreasing* rather than increasing the pressure on them, by acknowledging the special tensions of their positions, and by supporting them.

The hectic work pace—Integration is more likely to develop when you are able to step back from the system periodically, remove yourself from the ongoing pressures, rest, and take a detached look at yourself, others, and the system as a whole. Getting out of the workflow from time to time is one element in this. Having a space of your own to retreat to and conduct business is another. But the more you allow yourself to be carried along in the frantic flow of activities, being ever responsive to others, putting out fires, bearing messages, cleaning up paperwork, and so forth, the less opportunity there is for you to develop your own independent perspective on the system and develop your own independent action strategies. As a Middle, you need to do the work of the system, and in order to prevent personal disintegration, you also need to pay special attention to your personal boundaries, control your own involvement in the flow of work, periodically shut off your responsiveness to others, attend more often to yourself, and develop and protect your own personal space.

Absence of support group—Middleness is a potentially disintegrating condition for groups as well as individuals. When the dynamics of Middleness go unrecognized and unmanaged, Middle group members tend to drift apart; they become increasingly independent of one another, more isolated from one another, more interpersonally distant from one another, more competitive, less interested in one another's work, less collaborative, and less personally supportive. A common business phrase used to describe this disintegration is "operating in silos." Each Middle's vertical functional team operates independently. It's this lack of peer group support that contributes to the personal disintegration of Middles. Given the diffusing dynamics of Middleness, Middles need to work harder than Tops and Bottoms to develop an effective support system. Minimally, a strong Middle team provides each Middle with emotional support in trying situations. Beyond that, it provides a setting for sharing and sorting through information about the system, stepping back from the ongoing work and using this data to gain a larger perspective on system processes and issues, and developing coherent Middle strategies.

Definition of the Middle role—The Middle role is often defined by Middles as well as Tops and Bottoms as one in which Middles are *expected* to be responsive to others. The role is positioned such that you are supposed to be emissaries *of* others, extensions *of* others, negotiators *for* others, and buffers *for* others. Such role definitions encourage Middles to see situations more from the perspective of others and less from their own perspective. Such definitions encourage Middles to act in the interests of specific others rather than the interests of the system as a whole. Middles need to recognize that Middleness is more than a "telephone wire" between Tops and Bottoms; it is its own legitimate position within the system, and there is a legitimate perspective that goes with Middleness that is different than the perspectives of Tops and Bottoms. There is a legitimacy to independent actions in the Middle, actions that may not be perceived by either Tops or Bottoms as particularly responsive but which, in fact, do serve the best interests of the system.

These are some of the factors that contribute to the personal disintegration of Middles:

- The many and varied contacts Middles have throughout the system, each of which generates its own pattern of thoughts, feelings, and action possibilities for Middles, and many of which are in conflict with one another
- The tendency of Tops and Bottoms to respond to Middle difficulties by increasing the pressure on Middles
- The hectic work pace that, when unmanaged, makes it difficult for Middles to step back and gain some perspective on themselves and the system
- The absence of a Middle support group that itself tends to disintegrate under the pressure of the Middle condition
- The tendency to define Middle positions as responsive and reactive rather than independent and proactive

Disintegration is a painful condition. Chronic disintegration experiences threaten your emotional and physical well-being. The personal dramas of organizational Middles can be examined from the perspective of the choices you make as to how to cope with the existence or possibility of disintegration.

REFLECTION

- When you find yourself in the Middle condition and are feeling pulled in a lot of directions, do you find yourself aligning with the Tops or aligning with the Bottoms?

(In my twenty-plus years as a leader in the corporate world and my twenty-five years of experience supporting women, I have found two things that are at play with many women—including myself. In an effort to please others or "get a good grade," I found myself trying to please my boss or my Top. It was a strong "good girl" pull. Women often feel more comfortable in a flat structure where we are all in this together. As a result, I would roll up my sleeves and go to work with my Bottom team, even to the detriment of my Middle responsibilities. I embodied the "I wouldn't ask my team to do anything I wouldn't do," and as a result, I didn't leave myself the capacity to do the work that was mine to do. On top of that, I felt guilty and worked even longer hours to get it all done, once again working to please my boss [my Top], be a good leader and team player to my team [my Bottoms], losing my Middle self in the process. [Remember the familiar disempowering scenarios discussed in chapter 8? I know I'm not the only woman to experience this.])

- What is your story or your example of this likely familiar situation?

- Do you see patterns that lead to your tendency to align with the Top(s)? The Bottoms?

- How has the pressure to do more and more shown up for you?

- How has that worked for you?

- How has that worked against you?

- How would you describe your performance as a Middle during these scenarios?

REACTIONS TO DISINTEGRATION

In this section, we explore some characteristic reactions to the existence or threat of personal disintegration in the Middle.

Burning Out: Staying Stuck in the Middle—Some Middles remain stuck in the Middle. As this kind of Middle, you continue to function as extensions of both Tops and Bottoms. You try to be responsive to both, be fair to both, and function as buffers for both. You work very hard, you remain confused and uncertain about a variety of issues, and you continue to carry the burden of keeping the system together. You go on being seen by others in the system as hardworking, well intentioned, but not particularly effective. You continue to work under these conditions until you are no longer able to function to either your own or others' standards. You burn out. You break down physically or emotionally. You are transferred or fired, or you quit the system. Burnout occurs when you are unable to resolve your disintegrated condition. In your role as a hardworking, fair, and responsive extension of and buffer for both Tops and Bottoms, you maintain or worsen this disintegrated condition until you break down. The great tragedy of burnout is that it is often experienced by the Middle and others as a personal failure. And the treatments, if offered, are personally oriented. All of these treatments, however beneficial, reinforce your greatest fears: that the problem lies somehow in you, that if you took better care of yourself, burnout would not occur. Burnout may, in fact, be related to personal weakness (e.g., insufficient skills, lack of knowledge or inexperience), but it is not only that. It is also a systemic condition, a set of interpersonal phenomena that are the consequences of unrecognized and unmanaged Middleness, and whatever personal weakness may exist—physical or emotional—tends to be exacerbated by those dynamics. Systemic weakness tends to multiply personal weakness. The solution to burnout, along with taking better care of yourself, involves understanding and managing the dynamics of Middleness.

Sliding Up and Sliding Down—Some Middles resolve the disintegration of Middleness by getting out of the Middle. Rather than being extensions of *both* Tops and Bottoms and rather than being *equally* responsive to both, you align yourself with one or the other. The choice to align yourself upward or downward may be made quickly and clearly at the outset of the relationship, or there may be a subtle and gradual drift over time in one direction or the other. In either case, the dilemma of disintegration is at least partially resolved. Such Middles are no longer in the Middle. You have redefined your role. You now see yourself as an extension of either Tops or Bottoms but not both. There is, under these conditions, less confusion and less uncertainty, less wishy-washiness of behavior, fewer doubts about yourself. The organizational lines are more clearly drawn. By sliding up or down, you are now clear about your position. Others know where you stand, but as we shall see, you do so at the sacrifice of Middle power. At best you now enjoy the power potential of Tops or Bottoms, but the unique power of Middleness is lost to you.

Bureaucrats: Nonresponsiveness—Some Middles resolve their dilemmas of disintegration by becoming nonresponsive to *both* Tops and Bottoms. In this case, you see yourself neither as an extension of nor in the service of either. In fact, your tendency is to define both Tops and Bottoms as antagonists to be resisted rather than supported. Your tendency is to withhold rather than to provide service. You offer little on your own. You are resistant to requests from others. You create buffers around yourself to discourage intrusions from Tops and Bottoms. You generate complex procedures and evaluation mechanisms—all of which discourage approaches from Tops and Bottoms and all of which make access to Middle resources complex, painful, and costly. This mesh of bureaucratic barriers, procedures, and complexities does enable you to avoid the dilemmas of disintegration; the problems of doubt, confusion, and uncertainty are minimized. As a Middle, you are clear about where you stand and what you do and do not do. You have your own space, and others come to you when they must. As such a Middle, you have fewer doubts about your own competencies. If there are problems in the system, you are more likely to see the fault as lying with Tops and Bottoms, with their unreasonable requests and demands, with their inability or unwillingness to cope with and manage sensible bureaucratic procedures. This nonresponsiveness to both Tops and Bottoms resolves the dilemmas of disintegration for the Middles. It does create a type of power base for Middles who control resources others need access to as well as the means of access. And this pattern of nonresponsiveness does deny to such Middles the unique power that comes from the Middle perspective.

REFLECTION

- When was the last time you experienced burnout?

- After reading this chapter thus far, how might your burnout have been connected to you being in the Middle space?

- When was the last time you found yourself caught up in or even creating bureaucracy or potential bureaucracy?

- How do you relate to bureaucracy as a coping mechanism for this condition of Middleness?

POWER IN THE MIDDLE

The power of Middleness comes from the diffusion characteristic of the Middle space, the fact that you are out there in the system, have contact with Tops and Bottoms and others in the system, and have the opportunity to see and interact with and understand the various subworlds existing within the larger world of the system as a whole. In some sense, the greater the diffusion of the position, the greater its potential for power. If you are able to stay in the Middle, to diffuse without disintegrating, you are in a position to respond sensitively to system issues because of the amount and nature of information available to you about pieces of the system and the system as a whole. You are in a position to be proactive as well as responsive, to influence Tops and Bottoms, and to influence the way Tops and Bottoms interact with one another. Read this paragraph again. In this Middle space, you are a rich repository possessing valuable information from all across the system!

The challenge for you as a Middle is to be *responsive to* Tops and Bottoms yet *independent of* them, to understand the perspectives of Tops and Bottoms while at the same time clarifying and acting on your own Middle perspective. That is, you are able to diffuse the system while at the same time remaining an independent and integrated entity within the system. Responsiveness is a central feature of your Middle position. It's often what Middles are hired to do. Yet, from a *system power perspective*, responsiveness is a means, not an end. It's a process that provides Middles with the information on which an independent Middle perspective can be developed and independent Middle action can be formulated; independence is key to Middle power. *By developing an independent position for yourself, you are able to diffuse without disintegrating, and you are able to stay in the Middle and use the special opportunities of that position.*

MIDDLES AS SYSTEM INTEGRATORS

The first part of this chapter describes the challenges of the Middle space. I was exhausted writing about it, and I bet you felt your own anxiety rising as you read and thought about your own experiences. Now, I want to explore the possibilities for Middles and the potential for exerting system power. Middles have two functions in the system. One is a local function, the other systemic.

Middles as Servicers/Managers. The local function of Middles is to service or manage specific system units. This function can be performed *individually*.

Middles as System Integrators. The systemic function of Middles is to integrate the system (or subsystem). This function can be performed only *collectively*. System integration is an appropriate function for a Middle. You are in the best position to do it. It empowers you to function as a System Integrator, and you are disempowered when you don't. In order to integrate the system, Middles must integrate themselves.

THE INTEGRATING GROUP

The integrating group is a collection of peers within a system. When this group performs its integrating function, the Middle group meets and works without the boss. The boss and others may be invited to participate from time to time when their resources are required by the group. Middle group meetings are separate from staff meetings with the boss; they have a different function and are likely to have different dynamics. Meetings with the boss may heighten issues of competitiveness among Middles, dynamics that may be present but less obtrusive when Middles meet alone. Meetings with the boss also tend to suppress problems Middles are experiencing, and they tend to promote dependence rather than independence among Middles—the boss tells you what to do, and you submit, resist, or rebel—or you bring problems to the boss, and they care for them or not. The exclusion of the boss is not an antiauthoritarian act; it is a structural arrangement promoting the independence and empowerment of the Middles. It makes it possible for Middles to function as system integrators.

THE PROCESS OF INTEGRATING THE SYSTEM

DIFFUSING OUTWARD AND INTEGRATING WITH ONE ANOTHER

Middles integrate the system (or subsystem) by moving back and forth between diffusing out to the system parts they individually service or manage and coming back to integrate with one another.

When Middles are in a *diffusing phase*:

- Each Middle functions independently of one another.
- Each Middle services or manages the specific system parts for which they are responsible.
- Each Middle attempts to influence these parts.
- Each Middle collects information about those parts. (What do the parts need? What difficulties are people experiencing? What are their attitudes? What events of significance have occurred? What problem is each Middle experiencing in servicing or managing?)

As a Middle, when you are diffusing, you have two functions: *influencing* the parts you are servicing and managing, and *data gathering* regarding the life of these parts. (Note that when Middles are diffusing, they generally have contacts with a variety of system parts—subordinates, clients, other Middles, and Tops—so opportunities for influence and data gathering extend to all of these.)

When Middles are in an *integrating phase*:

- They meet with one another. They exclude all others, including bosses (although the bosses may be included from time to time as resources for whatever the group is doing).

- They share and make use of the intelligence individual members have gathered while diffusing throughout the system. The potential intelligence pool for a Middle group is considerable. Collectively, Middles often have access to more system-wide information than any other system parts with whom they have contact, including Tops; however, this potential is realized only if Middles share the information with one another.
- Middles can choose to integrate at a number of levels ranging from light involvement with one another to heavy commitment to one another. The choice of level of integration has implications for the system power of the Middle group and for the personal power and individual freedom of its members.
- Generally, the higher the level of integration, the greater the potential for individual and system power (although Middle groups might simply jump to organize themselves as a power bloc and focus on improving their own condition within the system without concern for the consequences their demands have for system survival and growth).
- It is also true that as Middles move toward high levels of integration, members may feel more constraints on their individual freedom. As the group develops an agreed-upon mission, diagnoses of system-wide issues, and strategies for change, members might rightfully expect support and consistency from one another.
- Diffusing and integrating activities strengthen one another. The more effectively Middle group members integrate with one another—sharing and assimilating information—the more strengthened each individual Middle is in carrying out their servicing and managing functions. Middles feel more informed, have a better sense of the connections among system parts, feel more secure having a solid database for their decisions and

actions, and feel more in harmony with other Middles. The more skilled Middles become at gathering intelligence from the field, the richer the contributions they are able to make to the group's integrating activities.

LEVELS OF INTEGRATION

As with many things, there are degrees to which you can choose to integrate. These are described in the following tool.

TOOL: LEVELS OF INTEGRATION

LEVEL 0: No Integration

Middles may choose to function as individual operators and not to integrate with one another at all. The personal and system power of such Middles are low, and individual freedom is high in that each Middle is free to act as he or she chooses with no input or constraint from other Middles.

LEVEL 1: Information Sharing

Middles do nothing more than share information. Each simply puts into the common pool the intelligence gathered from his or her contacts with the system. No analysis is done, no decisions are reached, and each Middle is free to use that intelligence as he or she chooses.

LEVEL 2: Assimilating Information

Using the pooled intelligence as a basis for system diagnosis (What trends do we see? What system-wide problems are developing?), Middle commitment to one another is still minimal. They jointly work on system diagnosis, but no consensual decisions are made, and each Middle is free to use these diagnoses as he or she chooses.

continued

LEVEL 3: Mutual Consultation

Middles use one another as resources to consult on problems individual Middles are facing in their servicing or managing functions.

LEVEL 4: Joint Planning and Strategizing

Middles identify problems that cut across all Middles' areas of responsibilities and develop agreement among Middles as to how these will be handled. Middles agree to support one another and follow through on their commitments.

LEVEL 5: Power Bloc

Middles organize themselves as a power bloc within the system, identifying common grievances, needs, and conditions they want changed. They develop bargaining positions and pursue tactics aimed at bringing about the desired conditions.

When Middles function as system integrators, moving back and forth between diffusing out to the system and coming back to integrate with one another, they are able to function as a significant entity within the system. Even functioning at the lower levels of integration—sharing and assimilating information—can have major impacts on the system and on individual Middles.

There are certainly benefits for the organizational system itself. Consider these as a starting point:

- There is greater consistency throughout the system.
- Various subsystems are coordinated with one another.
- Tops, Bottoms, and other Middles have the information, materials, and direction they need to do their work more effectively and efficiently.

- Subsystems are better able to adjust performance to the needs of the system as a whole.
- The system as a whole is better able to cope and prospect in its environment.

In addition, there are benefits for those experiencing this Middle condition, including:

- Middles feel coordinated and in sync with one another.
- Middles feel supported by one another.
- Middles feel that the Middle group is a significant entity within the system, with a unique mission to perform and the capacity to carry out that mission. They experience group identity and pride.
- Each Middle feels more secure and effective in carrying out their individual servicing or managing functions. They feel smarter and more knowledgeable about the system.
- Middles feel independent and capable of making their own judgments about what the system needs.
- Middles feel powerful and able to make things happen in the system.

WHY MIDDLES DON'T INTEGRATE

If Middle integration is so valuable, why haven't Middles embraced it?

Here are some possibilities:

- **Job Definition.** Middles are hired, evaluated, and rewarded as individual contributors. Their jobs have been defined as servicers and managers of their system units, not as system integrators.

- **Do Tops Want Integrated Middles?** Many Tops require an extensive reeducation program before they will allow and encourage Middle group integration. Tops need to recognize the potential value to the system of having strong and independent Middle groups that function as system integrators. Even if Tops recognize the value to the system of Middle integration, they might not support something that has the potential for creating new power blocs within the system. Concerns for control might supersede concerns for coping and prospecting. Finally, the empowerment of another group also raises concerns regarding one's own power or powerlessness. It is, for example, the empowerment of Bottoms that menaces powerless Middles. Would not the empowerment of Middles also menace powerless Tops?
- **Do Middles Want Integrated Middle Groups?** Many don't. Of all system groups, Middles are the least oriented toward integration with one another. Middles appear to choose isolation over integration. Middle group members tend to have little interest in or zest for mutual collaboration. Relationships among Middle group members tend to be marked by interpersonal tension and competition. Middle group members tend to have little interest in forming a closer and stronger group. They doubt the possibility of forming such a group and question the potential payoff a group would have for themselves or the system.

We need to understand these dynamics. Why are Middles the most formidable barriers to their own integration? To answer this question, we need to step back once again and look at Middle dynamics and the Middle experience within the context of the larger system.

WHY TOPS, BOTTOMS, AND MIDDLES DON'T USE THEIR POWER

In general, the power of a system is measured by its capacity to cope and prospect in its environment. Each layer of the system has its unique leverage over vital system processes that can enhance the capacity of the system to cope and prospect. **Tops** have the greatest leverage over system form. They can shape the system so it is better able to cope and prospect. **Bottoms** have the greatest leverage over production processes. They can influence the process of work in ways that enhance the system's capacity to cope and prospect. **Middles** have the greatest leverage over system integration. They can influence system parts so these parts are in sync with and enhance one another, and they can adjust one another's performance to the coping and prospecting needs of the whole.

Each layer of the system, then, has its own *unique potential* for system power. Tops as Shapers, Bottoms as Producers, and Middles as Integrators. Each layer of the system also has its *unique dilemmas*, and if you are unable to successfully resolve these dilemmas, then little of your consciousness and actions are addressed to their system power potential. The unique dilemma for Tops is *complexity*; for Bottoms, it's *vulnerability*; and for Middles, it's *diffusion* (without integration). Tops who fail to master complexity do not shape systems effectively. Bottoms who do not resolve their vulnerability in the system fail to produce effectively. Middles who do not master diffusion do not integrate the system effectively. Let's discuss these further.

TOPS

Tops exist in an environment that is more *complicated* than that for either Bottoms or Middles. The inputs Tops must deal with tend to be more difficult—what isn't resolved elsewhere in the system often rises to the Tops—more varied, more changing, and more unpredictable. When Tops don't manage complications well, their energy is stuck on the complications—on not being overwhelmed, keeping up, staying afloat, or fighting fires. And there is little opportunity or inclination to step back from the system, comprehend its current structure, examine the environment and how it is changing, and address themselves to the processes of shaping the system so it's better able to cope and prospect in that environment. When the day-to-day energy of Tops is spent in fighting losing battles with complications, Tops do not function as system shapers, and, what may be more significant, they do not even *see* themselves as system shapers. System shaping is not part of their consciousness—that's not what they do, and that's not even a possibility for them.

BOTTOMS

Bottoms exist in an environment that is more *threatening* than that for either Tops or Middles. Bottoms tend to be more individually vulnerable than others in the system. Generally, they are on the receiving end of decisions affecting their lives. They often perform under the poorest working conditions. They receive the lowest pay and benefits. They also are the most expendable system members, the first to go in hard times. When Bottoms fail to satisfactorily resolve their vulnerability in the system, their energies are stuck on self-protection and security. They can become docile before authority, submissive, trusting that "goodness" will bring its own rewards. Or they may become protective, hard-lining, resistant, doing all they can to keep the Tops from influencing them. What often happens is that Bottoms fight with one another over whether to be trusting and submissive or protective and resistant. When Bottoms do not resolve the dilemma of vulnerability, neither their actions nor consciousness are inclined to producing in the sense we have defined it—actively influencing work processes in ways that enhance the system's capacity to cope and prospect. Not only do Bottoms fail to produce in this sense, but the concept of themselves as producers does not exist.

MIDDLES

Middles exist in an environment that is more *diffusing* than that for either Tops or Bottoms. Middles tend to be pulled away from one another and toward others in the system that they service or manage. Middles are pulled toward spending their time in other people's territories, not in any common Middle territory. Middles are pulled toward investing their energies in other people's agendas, not in any common Middle agenda. Middles are pulled toward servicing and managing others, not toward giving to and drawing from one another. In short, there are powerful system forces pulling Middles apart, isolating them from one another. *When Middles are unable to manage their diffusion, they are controlled by it.* When Middles are overwhelmed by diffusion, when they allow themselves to be isolated within the system, they do not function as system integrators, nor does it enter their consciousness that this is a possibility for them. When Middles are unable to manage their dilemma of diffusion, they see themselves not as integrators but as individual managers and servicers, and they view their collection of peers not as a vital system network required for the integration of the system or subsystems but as a collection of individuals each pursuing his or her own path.

EMPOWERING MIDDLES

How can Middles overcome these strong system forces? Here are some ideas and tangible actions that can help.

CONSCIOUSNESS RAISING

The first step as a Middle is to ask yourself if you want to integrate. The best prediction is you won't want to do it. You won't see it as possible. You won't be attracted to the idea of working more closely together. You won't see it as appropriate for your position to "organize." You won't see its relevance or potential for yourself or the system. We know that these feelings are *consequences* of the disintegrated state of Middles, but to the Middles, these feelings are reality—the way things are and the way they can be. Before you want to integrate, you must first understand how your current systemic condition shapes your consciousness. When the light first dawns for Middles, when you see it is a systemic condition, when you see that someone understands their condition, the first reaction you have is one of great relief. ("It's not just me!") The first phase is significant but not sufficient. As a Middle, when you come to understand the systemic nature of your condition, you may simply use that understanding as an excuse for your weaknesses. Middles need to be confronted with this important point: *If the problem is systemic, so is the solution.* Read that again. What I have seen again and again is that an organization can replace a person in that Middle space, yet the same problems continue to exist. That's a clear sign it's a systemic problem rather than an individual problem. By diagnosing the problem accurately—as a system problem—we can apply a systemic solution. As a Middle, are you willing to take responsibility for improving your own conditions? With that question, the work begins.

CHOOSING AMONG LEVELS OF INTEGRATION

As you begin to integrate, you need to make decisions regarding the level of integration at which you will function. Concerns about individual freedom versus group control are usually central to this point. Middles are accustomed to operating as loners. It's a source of weakness in the position, but it also has its benefits. Middles feel free to handle their position as they choose. Some Middles have strong negative feelings toward collective action. I generally recommend that Middles start at the lowest level of integration—information sharing—and simply meet periodically to pool the information each has gleaned from their contacts with the system, with no commitment to common action.

With LEVEL 1 Integration, all Middles are free to use this information as they choose. LEVEL 1 Integration is by itself a powerful move. Middles feel strengthened, more informed. Their day-to-day business is embedded in a larger systems context, and they are still free to act however they choose. As Middles begin to reap the benefits of LEVEL 1 Integration, they may choose to move up the integration ladder. Middles may initially be concerned with coercion by a Middle group and loss of individual freedom. Integrating initially at LEVELS 1 and 2 (Information Sharing and Assimilation) will likely minimize these concerns. But there is another issue. The emphasis on maintaining one's individuality and concerns for themselves becoming too closely enmeshed in the working of any group may themselves be symptoms of the disintegrated condition of Middles. To some extent, the issue of individuality versus solidarity is a political one, and where each Middle comes out on that issue is influenced by where they stand in the system. As a Middle moving up the scale of Integration, you may find that your freedom as well as your personal power is enhanced—that you are not only strengthened by your group membership but liberated by it and you won't feel as alone or isolated.

CONSCIOUSNESS RAISING FOR TOPS

The empowerment of Middles can proceed with or without legitimization by Tops. On one hand, Tops can recognize the value to the system of integrated Middle groups and legitimize the functioning of Middles as both servicers/managers and system integrators. Or, in the absence of such legitimization and support, Middles might simply choose to integrate themselves and deal with the resistance they will generate among Tops. The former would be a smoother path; the latter would be rockier, and it is possible that in the end, it might cement closer relations among the Middles.

STILL CIRCLING

This investigation of Middleness is not complete. It's as if we now stand before two doors when there was only one before. There is a beat-up, broken-down old door marked "Personal." Someone keeps painting it in gaudy colors, but all the coats of paint can't hide the reality of its overuse and shabbiness. Then, there is a new, barely touched door marked "Systemic." Each door takes us to a very different set of experiences about ourselves and others, and each offers a very different set of possibilities for action, change, and system contribution. We can continue to pass through the Personal door, or we can venture through the Systemic one.

You may feel that we have made great strides in unraveling the puzzle of Middleness. I think we have just opened the door and are now cautiously peeking down the hall. When we really understand that this is all systemic, when we really appreciate how much we are at the mercy of systemic forces, when we really envision the possibilities that stem from mastering the Middle space, then the fun will begin.

REFLECTION

- Where do you think you have an opportunity to explore Middle Integration?

- What are some first steps you would need to take to positively influence Middle Integration?

- What level of integration do you think would be most beneficial for you and your organization and why?

- What are potential benefits of Middle Integration–to the organization system? To the individuals experiencing the Middle condition?

- What are you committed to do to utilize Middle Integration to influence your organization?

CHAPTER 10

ASK FOR WHAT YOU WANT

"The breeze at dawn has secrets to tell you.
Don't go back to sleep.
You must ask for what you really want."

–Rumi

Teaching this content has been eye-opening. It explains so many personal experiences and is helpful research in my coaching. How many times have I heard (and said), "I could never ask for that." Well, this chapter is about quieting that inner voice. We must have clarity about what we really want. We must build the skills and have the language to ask for what we really want. We have to muster the courage to have the conversation. Before you read the remainder of this chapter, know that many of the women who swore they couldn't do something or wouldn't get what they asked for, did what they thought they couldn't and did get what they wanted. I offer this important information so that as you read this chapter, it's with a can-do spirit.

Much of the information I share is from the research of Linda Babcock, the director of the PhD Program at Carnegie Mellon University. While there, a delegation of women graduate students came to her office. The women said that many of the male graduate students were teaching classes of their own, while most of the female graduate students were assigned to work as teaching assistants to regular faculty. In other words, the male graduate students had the better jobs. Linda agreed that this didn't seem fair, so she contacted the associate dean who handled such assignments and shared what the female graduate students told her. The answer the associate dean gave her was, "More men ask. The women just don't ask."[1] This is where it begins.

MEN ASK

Men ask for things they want and initiate negotiations two to three times more often than women.[2] Men also are more likely to mention more ambiguous situations as opportunities for negotiating—situations that may or may not be construed as negotiating opportunities by women. The first experience that came to my mind when I read this research was when I was working at EDS. At the time, I worked primarily with men. One day we were sitting in a room together and having some lighthearted conversation. The men in the room began to talk about who got the best price on their dress code–required wingtip shoes. I pretty much ignored the conversation, viewing it as another silly competition among "the boys." Then I heard one man say, "Well, I just went to the department store and told the salesperson I was willing to pay this much for the shoes, and he sold them to me for that price."

That got my attention, so I asked him, "So, there was a price tag on the shoebox and you offered a lesser price, and you got that lower price?"

I asked my question with a rather incredulous tone, feeling sure I had misunderstood his story.

He answered without hesitation, "Of course." I was stunned. It would never have occurred to me to even consider that the sticker price on an item in a department store was negotiable. I then berated myself for not knowing this possibility and began to mentally calculate how much money I could have saved (or how many more shoes I could have purchased!).

I had to put this to the test. I see myself as a buyer rather than a shopper. I generally know what I want, find a place that has it, and go buy it. I also do my shoe shopping once a year and generally buy several pairs of shoes at a time. (This was before online shopping was available.) So, I went to this same department store, put three boxes of shoes on the table, and declared that I would buy all three for a certain price.

Without a blink, the salesperson said okay and rang them up. I could hardly believe it, and I learned several valuable lessons over time. First, ask—it's that simple: Ask. Second, male clerks are more likely to say yes (or give you a coupon discount you didn't even know existed). Third, timing matters. When it's time to take inventory or supplies are high and demand is low, you have more leverage.

When I share this story in my programs or with coaching clients, two things happen. You can see the wheels turning as they plan their next shopping trip, and inevitably, someone comes back to our next session and tells about a positive experience of asking *and* getting it—whatever it might be.

ASKING PROPENSITY

This leads to teaching point number one: **asking propensity**. The biggest difference in achieving maximum results is choosing to ask—or initiating negotiations—for things we may never have considered before. The simple difference in this asking propensity of men and women will inevitably lead to men having more opportunities and accumulating more resources. I also want to add—from a place of when we know better, we do better—that we have unknowingly colluded in our own marginalization by not asking in the first place. Now, don't get me wrong—there are many forces at play that contribute to women's marginalization. Many of those are outside of our control. This particular choice of asking is totally within our control, however.

The more information we have about why we may not ask or choose to negotiate, the more we can raise our awareness and understanding so we can manage this skill effectively—with new clarity, tools, language, and courage.

Women are more comfortable negotiating with their children or on behalf of others. You may remember your mother saying, "Eat your vegetables and you can have dessert," or "Clean up your room and you can go play," or "Make good grades and you can get that [fill in the blank]." That is negotiation. In the case of negotiating on behalf of others, we can ask something for our loved ones, friends, team members, and our companies much easier than we can ask on behalf of ourselves. You might fight to get one of your team members a salary increase but never ask for one yourself. One Harvard Law School article, "Negotiating on Behalf of Others; Are Women Better Agents," stated that this could be because "women felt more freedom to negotiate assertively, with less fear of being judged unfeminine, when advocating for another person."[3]

Now that I have shared that depressing news about men asking for what they want considerably more than women, let me now share some updated good news. One of the predominant newer studies, "Now Women Do Ask: A Call to Update Beliefs about the Gender Pay Gap," comes from researchers Laura Kray, Jessica Kennedy, and Margaret Lee, which was published in the *Academy of Management Discoveries* in August of 2024. Their research was based on a series of surveys and a review of the historical data around gender pay inequities and potential reasons for those gaps. They explored many of the underlying causes that have been cited over the years—systemic causes, social conditioning, and the belief that women simply weren't asking. These beliefs were grounded in the idea that women were deficient in negotiation skills and were unwilling to lean in and stand up for themselves. They discovered in their research that women were, in fact, negotiating even more often than men for higher starting salaries or for raises.

The authors of the study acknowledge a combination of factors that may have played into this shift—the first being the awareness and challenges raised by Babcock and Laschever. The study's assertion is that it is possible that popular messages across the last two decades encouraging women to be more assertive have contributed to a closing, or possibly even a reversal, of historical gender gaps in negotiating propensity.

They also point out that the nature of their study, which was focused on MBA graduates, may have contributed to the shift in women asking more often than men. They acknowledge that their findings diverge from patterns identified in other studies, such as those conducted in 2017 and 2018 by LeanIn.org and McKinsey. Those studies reflected "no gender difference in negotiation propensity, and more research is necessary to understand why, moderation by race/ethnicity and sexual orientation, they did not appear to account for cultural variation in negotiation propensity in their global sample. It could be that women and men are more identical when they have more advanced education, identical degrees, or are further along in their careers, and reside in the same cultural context."[4]

Now all of this certainly sounds like progress. I will add that another factor having potential impact is the implementation of the Paycheck Fairness Act of 2022, which bans companies from requiring a candidate to share their previous salary history. The Act declares that "to combat unequal treatment, the legislation prohibits employers from asking for salary histories. The salary history ban legislation generates a structural change to limit perpetuation of women's unequal compensation. Given that women have been disadvantaged in receiving equal pay in the past (and still in the present), the purpose of a salary history ban is to eliminate the possibility of inequality carrying over into new salary negotiations. Whatever men and women were earning previously, a salary history ban aims to give everyone a fair wage offer upon receipt of a new job offer. Research has found that a salary history ban improves outcomes for women (as well as minorities)."[5]

As time has passed from when I first wrote this chapter, and now that we are ready to go to print, I am including the current status of this proposed legislation. The Paycheck Fairness Act remains a piece of legislation that has passed in the U.S. House of Representatives but has not yet been passed into law. If so inclined, let your Congressional representatives know how you would like them to push this legislation to enactment.

One last finding that I thought was especially intriguing in the research of Kray, Kennedy, and Lee was the link between the *belief* that the gender pay gap is due to women's lower asking propensity and a reluctance to then support systemic changes like the Paycheck Fairness Act. They found that "holding the belief that women are relatively low in the propensity to negotiate may be useful in rationalizing the status quo."[6]

One last thing I want to emphasize on this topic of asking propensity is that women have historically been highly effective in asking on behalf of others and advocating and negotiating fiercely for causes and changes they believe in. So keep in mind it is vital that we all work at updating our beliefs about gender differences in asking propensity (and so many other gender areas). Incorporating this information into research, studies, textbooks, curriculum, books, talks, podcasts, and so on can help update these beliefs and contribute to more fair and equitable compensation and career opportunities.

THE LIKABILITY FACTOR

This leads us to teaching point number two: **the likability factor**. Now, before you get upset or flustered on this point, let me assure you, I don't like it either. What I believe, though, is that by knowing it, I can make choices accordingly to get what I want or need. I offer it with that sentiment.

For women who want to influence others, being likeable is critically important. In reality, a woman's influence is increased the more she is liked. I can't help but think back to the many times well-intended men told me it was more important to be respected than to be liked. It turns out that this isn't exactly true for a woman. The research further tells us that both men and women need to be assertive and able to present strong arguments, defend our interests and positions, and communicate confidence in our points of view. But here comes the tricky part: Research further reveals that assertive women are less well liked than those who are not assertive.[7] This is a classic example of a man and a woman who can do identical or almost identical things, yet are received and interpreted differently. It speaks to stereotypes of what is feminine (or not).

Research also tells us that whether or not they are liked does not affect men's ability to influence others, and there is no connection between assertiveness and likability for men. Men are equally well liked whether they are assertive or passive. Now that we have heard the hard truth revealed by research, what do we do?

There is a way of asking and getting that works for women. Pairing assertive and communal behaviors can allow women to become more successful and, in fact, the combination of these behaviors can be a real source of power.[8]

ASSERTIVE BEHAVIORS

What are assertive behaviors? These behaviors require you to come armed with ideas, facts, and information. Assertive behaviors also require you to display resolve. You can't back down. Think of it as a form of resiliency. You won't take no for an answer; you regroup, do further research to support your position, and try again. You may even choose to escalate the conversation to the next-level decision-maker if you feel strongly about your position.

COMMUNAL BEHAVIORS

And . . . you display communal behaviors. This includes smiling and being friendly, exhibiting nonthreatening social behaviors, and being nonconfrontational. In short, when you smile, your brain releases tiny molecules called neuropeptides that help fight off stress. Then other neurotransmitters such as dopamine, serotonin, and endorphins come into play. The endorphins act as a mild pain reliever, whereas the serotonin is an antidepressant. Anna B. Orlowska and colleagues, as well as others, state that there are three primary types of smiles:[9]

- **Reward smile**—conveys approval, happiness, contentment, and other positive feelings
- **Affiliation smile**—communicates positive intention, trustworthiness, belongingness, compassion, and social connection
- **Dominance smile**—intended to convey contempt, disgust, or superiority

Such smiles have been shown to increase cortisol (stress hormone) levels in people to whom they are directed.[10] I think the Affiliation smile is the one most indicative of communal behavior. Who knew that a smile could be so powerful! Consider it a tool in your tool kit.

What exactly is nonthreatening behavior? A Better Way describes it as "talking and acting so that [another person] feels safe and comfortable doing and saying things."[11] Review chapter 2, as it relates to creating psychological safety. It boils down to displaying good leadership behaviors.

The last item describing communal behaviors is avoiding being confrontational. According to *Oxford Languages*, *nonconfrontational* is defined as "tending to deal with situations calmly and diplomatically; not aggressive or hostile."[12] I want to expand on the word *aggressive*. Generally speaking, being aggressive is pushing your agenda to the exclusion of others, often for personal gain or benefit. Being assertive is standing up for what you believe in, often for the benefit of the greater good, with or without a motivation for personal gain or benefit. In my own experience, this is where the "meeting before the meeting" comes in handy. You can be more assertive in a one-on-one meeting than you can in a group meeting. Strongly pushing back in a more public group meeting can be seen as emasculating and even insubordinate in some organizations and countries' cultures. You have more leverage one-on-one.

Here's the bottom line: Do your homework, and have the facts and data to support your position. Keep standing even if you get pushback. Be professional and respectful. Always lead with what is best for the greater good (e.g., the client, the organization, the team), and every now and then, smile. I know this sounds almost silly, but I have seen it work again and again. While I wish all of this wasn't necessary, my experience confirms that if we want to influence outcomes or get what we want, using communal behaviors can help us achieve our desired results.

SELF-SCHEMA

Teaching point number three is our **self-schema**. According to the American Psychological Association, the definition for *self-schema* is "a cognitive framework comprising organized information and beliefs about the self that guides a person's perception of the world, influencing what information draws the individual's attention as well as how that information is evaluated and retained."[13] Men and women see themselves differently. Think about looking at yourself in the mirror. Rather than seeing your external physical features, a self-schema mirror would be more of an interior portrait. You would see how you experience your own personality and how you believe others see you. Our self-schema provides a filter through which we process information, understand events, and organize our memories. Have you ever been at some family gathering when one of your siblings tells a story from when you were kids? As you listen to their story, you're saying to yourself, "That is not how I remember it!" That's your self-schema at work. You processed the experience your sibling is describing differently. Therefore, your understanding or interpretation of the events are different, and furthermore, you organize the memories differently. What may have been a happy event for your sibling may have been a dreadful event for you. This is an important teaching point because our self-schema is a primary motivator of our behavior.

Let's take a deep breath and do some reflecting.

REFLECTION

- How would you describe your awareness and understanding of asking for what you want for others? For yourself?

- When was the last time you asked for something for yourself? Think about how you prepared for it. Was it a big deal? Did you get what you were asking for? How did you feel about it?

- On a scale of one to five (one = low and five = high), where would you rate your **asking propensity**? How has that worked for you? How has that worked against you?

- Describe a time when you consciously or unconsciously used likability to achieve a desired outcome. What would you tell someone you were mentoring about the **likability factor**?

- Can you think of a time when your **self-schema** led you to a different behavior, conclusion, or action—personally or professionally? How did that impact the outcome?

CHILDHOOD SOCIALIZATION

We now come to the role that **childhood socialization** plays, and this is teaching point number four. I want to provide some contrasts between boys and girls gleaned from bell-shaped-curve research; remember that there will always be exceptions and outliers. When I first read the research, I found myself identifying with the boys' socialization. I grew up with two older brothers, and, of course, that impacted me (and my self-schema portrait of myself).

THE ROLE OF A BOY'S CHILDHOOD SOCIALIZATION

Boys tend to play in larger groups, and their play is rougher. This can be physical sports like soccer and football as well as electronic games that include more physical violence. Boys learn to issue more direct orders to one another than girls do. The key word here is *direct.* Girls tend to use more indirect forms of communication. When girls and women use more direct forms of communication, they are often called "B words": *bossy*, *bully*, and *bitchy*. Boys' play involves more competition, conflict, and struggle for dominance.[14]

Men and boys can create a competition for almost any situation. Remember my story early in this chapter about who paid the least amount for their wingtip shoes? Another example happened just recently at my eight-year-old grandson's baseball game. After his game, we went to dinner and talked about the game. My dear, sweet grandson took pride in being one of the tallest and fastest boys on his team. There were comments like, "Yeah, but I'm faster than him." It was almost like a game within the game. There are many examples in our workplaces too. Who has the biggest title, the biggest budget, biggest staff—it all relates to scorekeeping and winning or losing.

I want to emphasize that I'm not saying this is good or bad; it's just prevalent enough to be reflected in the bell-shaped-curve research. As a result, a boy's agenda is one of self-assertion. He wants to win and get what he wants. The last thing boys tend to do is implement agreed-upon rules when there is a dispute.[15] The first things that come to mind are the slow-motion replay cameras used in sports. In American football, we have to watch the replay from several different camera angles to determine if a player's knee was down or the ball broke the plane for the score. Again, it's all about keeping score and winning and losing.

What boys learn from this childhood socialization is that they can be aggressive in their interactions without hurting one another or damaging their relationships. Boys also learn that competition is fun. Boys learn that asserting themselves can be a successful strategy to achieve their goals.[16] The childhood lessons we learn on the playground are the same rules we bring to the office, or the plant, or the classroom, or the hospital, or the congressional floor. We have all seen it many times.

THE ROLE OF A GIRL'S CHILDHOOD SOCIALIZATION

So, how does this compare or contrast to a girl's childhood socialization? Girls tend to play in smaller groups and form closer relationships with one or two girls. As an aside, I'm pretty sure it was little girls who came up with BFF—best friends forever. For girls, the most important goals involve increasing intimacy and preserving connection.[17] Think about creating intimacy. Girls tend to engage in activities in which everyone is equal and there are no winners and losers. There is no scorekeeping when girls are playing dolls, school, or house. Girls are also likely to take turns to maintain equality. Girls also learn that if a dispute occurs, it's better to end the game in order to protect the relationships among the players. Often, when girls are having a playdate and a conflict occurs, the host mother may send the girl home, which reinforces preserving the socialization connection. This contrasts with the way mothers may just tell the boys to "settle down in there." Two very different responses—almost always at an unconscious level.

Girls learn from this socialization to make polite suggestions with a preference to get agreement. I distinctly remember my mother telling me on several occasions, "Just go along to get along." My mother's intentions were the best; she truly believed what she was telling me. When I think about it now, her advice protects the status quo and can quiet a woman's voice. Girls learn a strong preference for cooperation and avoiding conflict. Finally, girls learn that avoiding conflict can be a successful strategy for achieving their important goal of maintaining close relationships.[18]

As I wrote that last statement, I was screaming, "Noooo!" I disagree vehemently with the thought that we can't have a conflict and also maintain our relationship. I wrote an entire chapter called "Managing Conflict and Enriching Relationships" in my first book. The quote I offered as the introduction to that chapter is a favorite one on this topic: "One can be of a different opinion and still be my friend" (Margaret Cavendish). I believe that a lot of the girl drama (and adult woman drama) could be eliminated or significantly reduced if we learned how to have hard conversations. We could speak our views, and our relationships wouldn't suffer as a result. I have always thought that if a relationship is so fragile that we can't disagree, it must not have been a very strong relationship to begin with.

These childhood socialization lessons run deep, have been around a long time, and are learned early.

REFLECTION

- How do you relate to the lessons learned from **childhood socialization**?

- How might these lessons show up in your adult life?

- How do these lessons work for you? Against you?

- What do you notice in your organizational life that reflects these childhood socialization lessons? How are you thinking about them after learning where some of those lessons were learned?

ACCUMULATION OF DISADVANTAGE

We are now coming to a big finish on the impact of not asking for what we want and need. Teaching point number five is called the **accumulation of disadvantage**. Hmm, what does that mean? In lay terms, it's when an initial inequity is so small that no one will likely even notice it, but over time it accumulates to a great disparity.

Here is a summary of accumulation of disadvantage. A young man and woman are graduating with similar grades, majors, and extracurricular activities. In other words, they have similar capabilities to bring to their first professional job. They go to the same company whose standard starting salary is $35,000 per year. On average, men negotiate a 4.3 percent increase to receive a starting salary of $36,505 per year. In contrast, women negotiate a 2.7 percent increase to receive a starting salary of $35,945 per year. The difference between $36,505 and $35,945 is $560 per year. Having managed compensation for several years, I can tell you this difference would have gotten no one's attention. And this is where *accumulation* comes into play. If you extrapolate those negotiated percentages over the years until these graduates are now sixty-five years old, the differences are exponentially greater. His salary is now $213,941 and hers is $110,052, resulting in a difference of $103,889. The man is making almost double what she is making![19]

It doesn't end there, either. If your bonus is determined as a percentage of your salary, then your bonus also will be less. In America, your Social Security contributions can also be different, resulting in a different level and quality of retirement. The same can be said of 401(K) contributions. Are you getting angry yet? It's no wonder that the gender pay gap still exists. In 2022, the Pew Research Center's analysis reflected women earning an average of 82 percent of what men earned. The results are even more dismal when you compare earnings for women of color.[20] As I said before, we—each of us—can do better! Here are some thoughts to consider.

CONSIDERATIONS FOR ASKING

These ideas apply primarily to compensation. There are also some tips when asking for bigger job titles or when asked to take on bigger responsibilities. Think broadly as you read through the following information.

- **Rule #1**—Always know your market value. Sometimes it's easier to compare what you are earning to one of your peers or colleagues. It's much more compelling to know your market value. It sends a strong message that you are informed and clear in knowing your real value, and it can leave your employer feeling vulnerable knowing they can lose you. The following language is important and useful when asked about compensation expectations:

  "*I know that the market value for this job is between $125,000 and $175,000 per year* [or whatever it actually is]. *Based on my track record of outstanding performance and my years of experience, I would expect to be paid at the high end of the range* [or wherever your experience might be reflected]."

It doesn't matter what you are making today. If you already know you are underpaid, you don't want to perpetuate that foolishness! Another helpful phrase is, "*Here is what I would need in order to say yes.*" You can then speak about compensation, bonus percentage, title, work from home, or any other items you want. And please, please, please remember that you lose all negotiating power after you say yes to the job.

Executive recruiters have shared with me what I call the executive version of the accumulation of disadvantage. An organization is looking to fill an executive role. They review the resumes. Basically, the man's and the woman's resumes are quite similar with a few exceptions. He has a higher hierarchical title, and he makes more money than she does. We also know it is often a man making the hiring or promoting decision. If he sees a higher title and compensation, he will likely see that man as the better candidate and offer the opportunity to him. Dang, there it is again!

Keep this in mind when you are asked to move into an acting role filling in until the next person is hired or when you are asked to take on more responsibility. Remember, you need to know your market value. Don't automatically say yes without thinking through what you want. It isn't all about making everyone else's life easier or being a good team player. It's being appropriately valued for your contributions. Beware of being put into a role with an acting title that will be evaluated in three to six months and then your boss will determine if you get the title and pay to go with it. Listen to all those alarms going off!

Men get promoted on potential, and women get promoted on proven performance.[21] This is a perfect place to use the "Here's what I need to say yes" strategy. If you are offered more responsibility or asked to broaden your scope of responsibility, your first response should be something like, "Tell me about the role." Listen and ask questions for clarity. Then say, "Let me think about it, and I will get back to you tomorrow [or whenever reasonable, but not too long]." Do your homework. Know what you want and need to be successful. Your list might include some of these items:

- To take on significantly more responsibility, you may want to ask to backfill your former role so you are not doing two jobs.
- You might ask for reprioritization on certain tasks or assignments, taking into account staffing and your learning curve.
- In the case of an "acting" role, you might ask for the title and compensation *now* and then, in six months if you are not performing well, they can make a different choice. This is a high-stakes strategy. First, you have to believe in yourself and your capabilities, and second, you have to speak it with confidence.

I have heard so many stories and seen so many examples of women taking on additional roles and responsibilities with no recognition through title and no remuneration through compensation. When that six-month time frame comes around, nothing happens. More often than not, nothing was put in writing, or in other cases, the boss that promised a six-month review has moved to a new role or has left the organization altogether. In other words, you are out of luck. To add a bit more misery to the story, now you are doing the bigger role with no bigger title and likely lesser compensation than your predecessor.

One more tip—if you are told they don't have a budget, in short, don't believe them. If they had to go out into the marketplace to hire someone, they would pay market rates and, in many cases, also pay an executive recruiter a fee to find them viable candidates. I suggest that you call their bluff. The last bit of coaching I offer is to know your organization's cycle for making compensation decisions. You want to manage your compensation all year round. It starts with setting performance objectives, reviewing your results with your boss throughout the year, and letting your boss know what you are expecting in the way of a performance rating and commensurate compensation. Once the names and percentages have been sent to payroll for processing, it's much harder to get changed.

INFLUENCE

One of my foundational elements woven throughout my work is Results + Recognition = Influence. The vast majority of women I work with achieve outstanding results. Their recognition for those results often falls woefully short. Therefore, influence is less. It's simple math. The teaching point around this foundational element is that when you are silent about your results or deflect the praise given to you regarding your results, you are diminishing your role in achieving those results and even taking yourself out of the story regarding the results. **When you take**

yourself out of the story, you are giving everyone else permission to do the same. Let that sink in. We have to stand up for ourselves and for one another. When you are hiring a new person, hire them at market value. It is almost impossible or takes forever to overcome a below-market starting salary.

LEADERS

If you are the leader of a team and one of your team members comes to talk to you about compensation, there is another difference between men and women to be aware of. If a man comes to you and tells you he has an offer from an outside organization, he sees this as the beginning of negotiations. If a woman comes and tells you she has an outside offer, it is likely that she is ready to leave. It's rarely a negotiating ploy. Male bosses often misread or are unaware of this difference. Women bosses can often misread this as well. Be a leader in the know and don't always wait for your team members to come and ask you about compensation. It is incumbent upon you to know the market value of the roles that report to you. If available, work with your human resources department to keep you current. I also recommend that everyone maintains a relationship with a professional recruiter. When market values are in flux or are very volatile, often these recruiters know the market best.

TOOL: PREPARATION WORKSHEET

1. What is something that you want or need? What is your ask?

2. To whom do you need to talk in order to ask for what you want?

3. Are there gender considerations (e.g., assertive plus communal behaviors, disclaimers, hedging language)?

4. What are your plans to ensure that you are being politically savvy? (For instance, know who the decision-makers are, who your allies and adversaries might be, and who can provide you the needed information to support your position.)

5. What meetings before the meeting do you need to have?

6. How much risk are you willing to take?

7. What facts, data, or information do you need to bring or present?

8. Do you have a walk-away position? (Generally speaking, this means that based on what you are hearing, you are no longer interested in pursuing your ask. This can happen for a variety of reasons, including the other person is not willing to give you what you are asking for or you have found a better deal elsewhere.)

9. Who can support you in this situation?

10. What else do you need to be successful?

SUMMARY

In summary, here are some things to remember regarding asking for what you want or need:

Women

- Typically set less aggressive goals than men
- Make more modest offers
- Concede more rapidly
- Feel unsure about what they deserve
- Worry that asking for too much will threaten a relationship
- Tend to be less optimistic regarding outcomes
- Lack confidence in their negotiating ability

All that said, I offer at the end of every bullet "until now." You now know better, so you can do better. If you are unsure, ask for help. Plan, develop your supporting facts, write it down, practice saying it out loud, and even role-play the conversation. Once again, you've got this!

CHAPTER 11

THE ART OF INFLUENCING

"Never underestimate the power of dreams
and the influence of the human spirit.
We are all the same in this notion:
the potential for greatness lives within us."

—Wilma Rudolph

You may notice that the subtitle of this book references influencing organizations, so it seems only right that I dedicate a chapter to the topic of influencing. The framework I am sharing is a compilation from several models, concepts, and research. I have adapted this material based on my own experience as a businesswoman, corporate executive, and coach, and consultant to many senior executives and client organizations. Let's first start with a definition. The *Cambridge Dictionary* defines *influence* as "to affect or change how someone or something develops, behaves, or thinks."[1]

INFLUENCING FRAMEWORK

My framework has three main components: advocacy, inquiry, and integration. Each component plays a specific role in the process of influencing.

ADVOCACY

The purpose of advocacy is to get your point of view out on the table. You want to make clear your position on whatever outcome you are trying to influence. The first step in advocacy is *framing* your position. Framing includes the assumptions you have made, the research you have done, the facts you have gathered, and any other contextual information pertinent to the second step, which is *asserting* your position. Your position might be an idea, a proposal or recommendation, or even a final decision.

In most situations, I recommend you speak first if possible. By putting your position on the table first, you build trust and display confidence. You are clear on your position, though not rigid. That's why it's important to frame your position. If someone changes your assumptions or brings additional research or facts to the table, you then want to take that into your own thinking and come up with what your potential new position might be. Influencing others doesn't mean that you are not able to be influenced. Remember, you are after the best outcomes, not competing to win.

INQUIRY

The purpose of inquiry is to get the other person's point of view out on the table. Keep in mind that a number of people's points of view might be contributing to an outcome. Others might represent different organizational functions, geographies, or stakeholder groups. Be very clear on whether you are trying to influence one person or several (and therefore the organization). When I talk about strategies later in this chapter, you may use different strategies or tools with different people even when you are trying to get everyone to see your point of view or position.

After the other person(s) have framed and asserted their positions, you then want to *probe and clarify*. This means asking questions to ensure understanding and not to attack or poke holes in their positions. Clarifying questions tend to start with *what* or *how*. Following is a list of typical questions to help you in the language of probing and clarifying.[2]

TOOL: PROBING AND CLARIFYING QUESTIONS

- How will this help us accomplish our goal/objective?
- What did you learn after doing your research?
- What other options did you consider?
- What challenges do you anticipate if we choose this option (or follow your recommended path)?
- What additional information or resources would make your proposal even more effective?

continued

- How do you think our employees/customers/vendors/partners/stakeholders might respond to this?

- What is important to you about this approach?

- What outcome are you seeking, or what problem are you trying to solve with this idea/strategy/approach/recommendation?

- What could go wrong, and how could you mitigate that risk?

- What could go right, and how do we increase that probability?

- What are the risks of waiting or doing nothing?

- What is the next best alternative?

- Is this consistent with our strategy/vision/mission? Our values and principles?

- What decisions do we need to make today?

____

____

- How can I be helpful as we make this decision?

____

____

Obviously, you don't ask every one of these questions in every situation. They are merely thought-starters to get greater clarity and understanding. Let me also add this quote from the same *Power Questions* book: "I can always tell how experienced and insightful a [person] is by the quality of their questions and how intently they listen. That's how simple it is."[3] Of course, it's simple to state this quote and much harder to develop and ask high-quality, relevant questions. You may also notice that these questions are not designed to contrast the other person's position and yours. That happens in the integration component of the framework.

The second part of inquiry is *paraphrasing*. This does not mean repeating exactly or almost exactly what the person said. That is parroting, not paraphrasing. Use your own words to recap what the other person asserted. I strongly suggest that you walk through a relevant example; this helps to make the assertion more real. It may create more questions, and that's okay. Remember, you are trying to get the best outcome for the organization.

Keep in mind that there are three levels of listening. The first level is listening with your ears, which means you can repeat back to someone what they said. The second level is listening with your head. Here you think about what the other person is saying as it relates to what you have experienced or what your research yielded. You process the information and then analyze it as useful, relevant, timely, credible, and so on. The third level of listening is with your heart. You listen for the passion and the energy of the person as they present their position. I often remind my clients that feelings are data too. This is an important consideration for those who pride themselves in being data-driven decision-makers.

Finally, I encourage you to use the probing and clarifying questions to get even clearer on your own position.

INTEGRATION

The purpose of the integration component is to potentially blend the views of all or many or to abandon your own position in support of another's position. This component invites you to challenge your thinking first before challenging the other person's thinking. Are your assumptions accurate and timely? Have you corroborated your research and facts? Have you considered all of the stakeholders that will be impacted by your position? And a very personal question for you: Are you holding tightly to your position for ego reasons or for the best possible outcome?

The next—and last—step is to *bridge*. You are building a bridge between others' positions and your own. This almost always results in a negotiated or collaborated approach or strategy.

I often think of the continuum represented in Image 11.1:

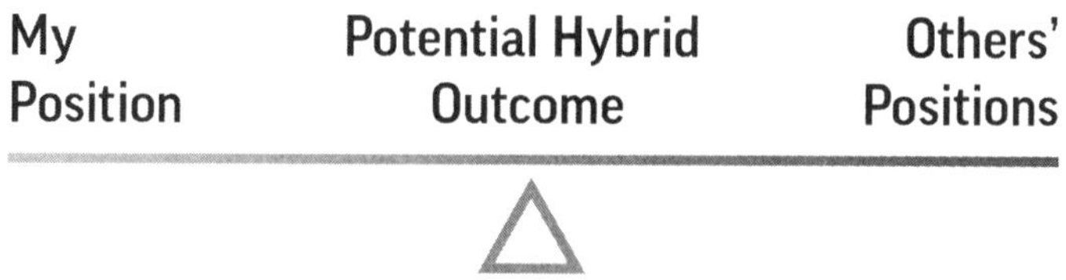

Image 11.1

I have included Image 11.2 to help you visualize the full framework:

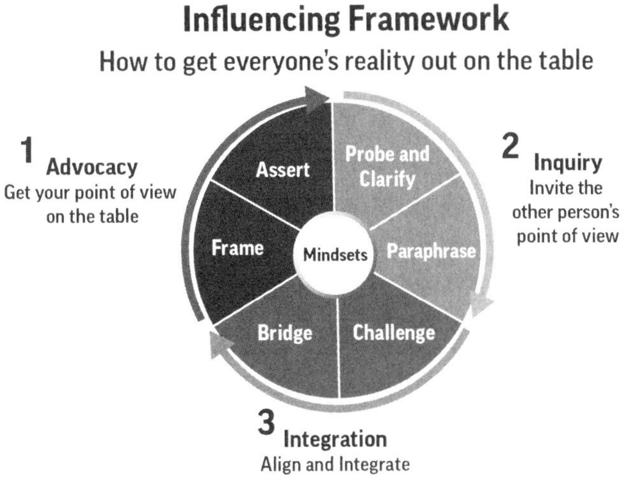

Image 11.2

Here is another important question for you: Do you spend more time in the advocacy, inquiry, or integration components of the framework? The balance of advocacy and inquiry is very useful in influencing. "Advocacy with inquiry is a powerful technique that promotes discussion and helps identify the underlying drivers of thought or behavior."[4] The two components come together to get all the information out on the table so you can integrate more effectively. Coming as no surprise, we tend to advocate more than inquire or integrate. Getting super conscious about this will help you engage more effectively and thus be a greater influencer.

The next big thing to remember to be an effective influencer is to take a mindful (versus reflex) approach. You may have heard that when you're angry, you should count to ten before you respond. In my younger years, this made no sense to me. *What good would that do?* I wondered. I've since learned that waiting even just ten seconds can help us take a breath and get clearer and, therefore, be more intentional when we respond. Taking a deep breath (or even a few deep breaths) helps to spread the flow of blood throughout your body, and it's your bloodstream that carries oxygen. Getting oxygen to your brain helps you think more clearly.

When it's your turn to listen to another person, know that most of us speak about 125 to 150 words per minute. On average, we can listen and comprehend up to six hundred words per minute. Our brains deal with the excess capacity by 1) making up stories and 2) letting that "little voice" in our heads speak to us. In the first case, you often make up stories about the other person or what is happening. Examples might be, "They have no idea what they are talking about" or "This is not going well—they just looked at me in a funny way." In the second case, that "little voice" is often your inner critic. Examples might be, "I shouldn't have said that" or "You are not performing at your best today." When you recognize the stories and acknowledge your inner critic, you can manage your response and overall engagement even more effectively.

INFLUENCING APPROACHES

There are six different influencing strategies I want to share with you: partnering, coaching, negotiating, captivating, selling, and directing. Think of these strategies as six new tools in your tool kit. The strategy you choose requires you to consider several variables, such as the strength (or not) of your relationship with the other person; your hierarchical role compared to the other person; your desired outcomes; and your strengths, skills, and experience. You can even use different strategies with different people in order to influence everyone to get to a desired outcome.

PARTNERING

My favorite definition of partnership is adapted from Barry Oshry's work: "Being mutually committed to whatever process we're in . . . and to each other."[5] This is a more collaborative approach in which you are as committed to the other person's success as you are your own. This strategy lends itself to deliberately building the relationship with the other person or persons. You ensure joint problem-solving and decision-making. You also declare your intentions up front—a commitment to work together to jointly set goals and establish processes to address issues. Bottom line, you want to show that you have the other person's interest in mind as well as your own.

COACHING

You might think that coaching would be useful only with your direct reports or peers. I can assure you that I also have used the coaching approach with bosses, executives, prospects, and clients. This approach helps the other person get clearer regarding their thinking on challenges, complex problems, ambiguous situations, and decision-making. Helping the person to achieve greater clarity is the goal. In reality, you are coaching the process to influence greater clarity rather than influencing a specific outcome. Coaching often includes asking thought-provoking questions, such as helping others face a challenging situation or owning their role and responsibilities. Other questions might challenge them to see other options, points of view, perspectives, or possibilities. Your questions can also help guide their thinking around obstacles, roadblocks, and challenges so they can be better prepared for questions or pushback. You can also help them get clear on the underlying reasons their desired outcome is so important to them, as well as important to the organization, various stakeholder groups, the marketplace, or the world in general. Finally, your questions can stimulate the other person to identify actions they can take to achieve their desired outcome. If it's a large, complex, highly visible, or high-stakes situation, helping them get clear on next steps can be immensely helpful to get them unstuck or out of the fog.

NEGOTIATING

As the name implies, the negotiating strategy engages the other person in a process of give-and-take that focuses on both parties providing and receiving a fair exchange. You want to ensure that your exchange results in mutual value. Feeling like you have given up more than you have gotten can lead to frustration or even ill feelings. You may be frustrated with yourself or the other person.

Make sure you prepare effectively. This includes being clear about what you want and what you are willing to exchange to get it. I recommend you make two lists. The first list includes what you want with an estimated value attached to each line item. The second list includes what you are willing to give up with the estimated value attached to those line items. Prioritize your two lists. What do you want the most? What are the first things you are willing to exchange?

There are various approaches you can take at this point. One approach is to work down your list from highest to lowest priority. Another approach is to handle the lower, more easily negotiated priorities before engaging in higher priority exchanges. This demonstrates goodwill and may be more effective with someone you don't know as well and with whom you have yet to build a mutually trusting relationship. To use the negotiating strategy effectively, you want to focus on *mutual* exchange. What you give up needs to be considered valuable to the other person and vice versa. Negotiating requires compromise. It is not a "winner takes all" mentality.

Another recommendation is that you are also very clear about what is *not* negotiable. I literally draw a line on a piece of paper. What is negotiable is above the line in priority order with respective estimated value. My nonnegotiables are listed below the line.

My last recommendation is that you make sure you know what authority you have as it relates to what you are giving up in the exchange. Related to this, if applicable, is to know the regulations, the legal requirements, and the terms and conditions of any particular contract.

CAPTIVATING

I must admit, I am most drawn to this strategy, though it is one that is rarely considered or used. This strategy is about telling a story or painting a picture that energizes and inspires others to action. You gain others' buy-in with a powerful vision or a common cause. This strategy appeals to shared goals, mission, and values. It creates enthusiasm and uses inspiration to spur action.

My two favorite examples, admittedly, are dated. The first one is a President John F. Kennedy quote:

> We choose to go to the moon in this decade and do the other things, not because they are easy, but because they are hard, because that goal will serve to organize and measure the best of our energies and skills, because that challenge is one that we are willing to accept, one we are unwilling to postpone, and one which we intend to win.[6]

We had no idea how we were going to make this happen when President Kennedy said this in 1962. In his speech, Kennedy characterized space as a new frontier, invoking the pioneer spirit that dominated America's history. He infused the speech with a sense of urgency and destiny and emphasized the freedom enjoyed by Americans to choose their destiny rather than have it chosen for them. The speech resonated widely and is still remembered. Kennedy's goal was realized posthumously in July 1969 with the success of the Apollo 11 mission.

My second favorite example is Martin Luther King Jr.'s "I Have a Dream" speech that he delivered on August 28, 1963. I was eleven years old and was inspired even at my young age. King delivered his speech on the steps of the Lincoln Memorial, which added to the inspiration—of the speech, of the moment in history. Though there are many moving parts of his speech, the one that stands out for me is, "I have a dream that my four children will one day live in a nation where they will not be judged by the color of their skin but by the content of their character."[7] I want that for every child, and I am still inspired by those words today!

SELLING

This strategy is the one I see often used in organizations. I often refer to it as options-based selling. It is focused on presenting facts, data, evidence, and objective criteria in order to persuade others to accept recommendations or ideas. The following is the template I use for this.

TOOL: OPTIONS TEMPLATE

	Option 1	Option 2	Option 3
Pros			
Cons			
Upside Opportunity			
Downside Risk			
Benefits			
Estimated Costs			

You would complete this template for as many options that you deem are viable. You would not only present these options—you would also make a recommendation on which option you think is the best option based on specific criteria. I would also add that it's not unusual for a group to arrive at a hybrid option through discussion and based on the input of multiple stakeholders. In my mind, this enhances your influence. You arrive at a decision based on you presenting options, and you garner the buy-in of your audience by encouraging and considering their input.

This selling or option-based influencing strategy is also very helpful when you are guiding your team in the transition from "order taker" to "owner" of the direction of their respective functions. Even at more senior levels, cultures may have evolved into directive-based leadership styles, resulting in leaders becoming order takers rather than accountable, strategic thinkers. A common phrase reflecting this kind of culture is, "Just tell me what you want, and I will make it happen." When shifting to the owner-based leadership style, you communicate your expectations that your functional leaders (at all levels) will bring you recommendations that are fact-based, well researched, and provide the greatest benefits to the organization and the clients served.

Generally speaking, since different kinds of organizations have different stakeholders as well as different nomenclature, you'll want to consider key elements in the context of your recommendations. Following is a starting list of key questions that could be a useful checklist.

TOOL: SELLING-STRATEGY-INFLUENCING STYLE CHECKLIST

- Does it increase revenue/donor contributions? If so, how much?
- How does it improve profits or margins?
- How does it improve productivity (e.g., people, process, or technology)?
- How does it improve quality?
- How does it align with our Mission? Vision? Strategy?
- How does it improve customer/stakeholder satisfaction?
- How does it improve time to market for our products and services?
- How does it create or enhance competitive advantage?
- How does it increase market share?
- Are there any legal, regulatory, compliance, contract, or audit requirements to consider?
- How does it take into account the impact on other parts of the organization?

I encourage you to set an expectation with your team that this checklist will be used for all major decisions, projects, initiatives, proposals, or recommendations. It will begin to change the way people think and bring their ideas forward. It also enables you to hold them accountable for true leadership of their respective functions or areas of responsibility. In the words of Steve Jobs, "It doesn't make sense to hire [or promote] smart people and tell them what to do. We hire smart people so they can tell us what to do."[8]

DIRECTING

Sometimes we don't consider directing or telling others what to do as influencing. When you consider the definition offered at the beginning of this chapter, telling others what you want and even how to do it has an "effect on their behavior." Though I don't recommend this strategy in all situations, it is appropriate and useful when there is a specific outcome required. This is typically the case when you are tasked with legal, regulatory, compliance, contractual, or audit requirements. You are clear on *what* needs to be done; you may have some flexibility on *how* it needs to be done. This is also a strategy that may be reliant on your positional or hierarchical power. Don't be apologetic if something is required. Explain directly what you want or need. State your expectations clearly. And, because there are nonnegotiable requirements, you may need to work with your team members, peers, or stakeholders to shift priorities.

BEING POLITICALLY SAVVY

No matter which influencing style you choose, I encourage you to be politically savvy. First, let me contrast being *political* and being *politically savvy*. For our purposes here, I define being political as pushing your agenda to the exclusion of others and often for personal benefit or gain. We tend to see this kind of political as negative. In contrast, being politically savvy is knowing how to navigate within your organizational system in service to something larger than ourselves—for the good of the client, the organization, the family, the community. I strongly encourage you to develop your political savviness.

In doing so, you want to understand the four typical characters of organizational life: decision-maker(s), ally, adversary, and gatekeeper. I purposely offered a plural when identifying decision-makers. For most highly visible, high-risk, high-stakes decisions to be made, there are multiple layers or levels of **decision-makers**. For example, your boss has to say yes and then you take it to your boss's boss. You may use different influencing styles with different hierarchical levels. A program participant once offered, "Don't take no for an answer if the person stating no is not the final decision-maker." In other words, be prepared to escalate if you feel strongly that what you are proposing is for the larger good.

The second character is your **ally**. Allies will likely differ depending on what you are proposing. One can be an ally in one scenario and an adversary in a different scenario. I encourage you to have a "meeting before the meeting" to determine if someone, indeed, is an ally. If they are, make sure you ask them to publicly voice their support of your proposal (ask for what you want).

The third character is your **adversary**. This is a person who has a different proposal or simply doesn't support your proposal. Again, I strongly encourage you to have a "meeting before the meeting" to determine objections or alternative views. Knowing this information ahead of time allows you to develop your points to negate or neutralize those objections.

The fourth character is the **gatekeeper**. Gatekeepers are people who can give you access (open the gate) to information and/or people you need to build your business case, or not (close the gate). Gatekeepers can range from business intelligence analysts, financial analysts, human resources personnel, or executive assistants. Maintaining a good relationship with these gatekeepers can help you when you need such access to information or time on someone's calendar.

DEVELOPING SYSTEMS & CRITICAL THINKING

Another related area of influence is to help broaden another person's perspective and even develop better systems and critical thinking skills. Let me preface what I am about to offer by sharing that I believe that having perspective is one of the most important competencies that an effective leader has. According to the *Britannica Dictionary*, *perspective* is defined as "a way of thinking about and understanding something" and "a condition in which a person knows which things are important and does not worry or think about unimportant things."[9] The broader and deeper your perspective, the more credible and influential you will be.

I further believe that in order to develop a broader and deeper perspective, you need to think systemically and critically. I was working with a coaching client recently that was lamenting that their direct reports often brought ideas, proposals, recommendations, and solutions that reflected a very narrow and shallow perspective. They did not look beyond their own function or scope of responsibility when bringing their ideas forward. In other words, they were not thinking critically or systemically. After that call, I challenged myself with creating a tool that my clients could use for themselves to encourage more systemic thinking. The result of my efforts produced a set of questions (the tool) that you can use to make sure that your ideas and solutions have considered the broader impact in the organization. You will see that some of these questions have been included in other parts of this chapter. This tool/list is intended to support better systemic thinking. Before we get to the questions I developed, let me lay a bit of the foundation as further context.

CRITICAL THINKING SKILLS

In both my personal and professional lives I have found it extremely valuable to develop critical thinking skills. This does *not* mean learning how to be critical of others. Most of us are quite skilled in that area if we allow ourselves to go down that path. I like the definition that is shared by the University of Louisville: "Critical thinking is the intellectually disciplined process of actively and skillfully conceptualizing, applying, analyzing, synthesizing, and/or evaluating information gathered from or generated by, observation, experience, reflection, reasoning, or communication, as a guide to belief and action."[10] As I was thinking about developing a tool for critical thinking, I remembered something that I learned in my master's degree program, and that is Bloom's taxonomy.[11] Developed by Benjamin Bloom, the taxonomy is a set of three hierarchical models used for classification of educational learning into levels of complexity and specificity. The three levels are cognitive, affective, and psychomotor domains. I am going to focus on the first one: cognitive. (I worry that I am getting a bit too academic. I hope you will stay with me as I try to simplify and make this practical. Having and teaching critical thinking skills is very important for leadership thinking.)

The cognitive domain is broken into six levels of objectives:

1. Knowledge
2. Comprehension
3. Application
4. Analysis
5. Synthesis
6. Evaluation

Knowledge—Includes remembering or memorizing information. Note that it does not necessarily include that you know what the information means. This reminds me of all the things I had to memorize when I was in school, such as the dates of certain wars, the location of certain events, principles, and even reciting poems. For example, we might know the theory of relativity is $E = mc^2$ without having any idea at all what this equation actually means.

Comprehension—Includes an understanding of the information you have recognized or memorized—you have the ability to state the core ideas that the information represents. For example, we might understand that $E = mc^2$ actually refers to a formula that represents the concept of mass-energy equivalence and is considered a fundamental principle in Albert Einstein's theory of special relativity.

Application—Includes using the information you have remembered, memorized, and understand in levels one and two above in order to solve problems in new situations. In other words, to what use can we put Einstein's theory of relativity? What other ideas does it help us to understand?

Analysis—Includes breaking down the information into more granular parts to better determine how these different parts relate to one another. Returning to Einstein's theory, we need to understand energy, mass, and the speed of light, *and* how they all work together before we can understand precisely how and if the theory works.

Synthesis—Includes taking those granular parts from various elements and putting them together to form new meaning. For example, how can we understand the theory of relativity in relation to other theories?

Evaluation—Includes presenting and offering your point of view about the information, as well as the validity and quality of the information based on a set of validity and quality criteria. Is information good or bad . . . sound or unsound . . . effective or ineffective? We might ask these questions of the theory of relativity, its applications, and so on. Evaluation is also to be able to judge: Is the theory of relativity a good theory (meaning a "sound" theory)? Have its applications been good?

The following summary is what I think of as the "tool." I can relate to it in a practical way. I hope you can too.

TOOL: DEVELOPING SYSTEMS & CRITICAL THINKING

- What problem are you trying to solve?
- Do key stakeholders/others share your thoughts about this being a problem?
- How will solving this problem help the organization, for example by increasing revenue and improving profitability, productivity, quality, and customer satisfaction?
- What have you done to determine the root cause of the problem?
- What is the root cause?
- Who is impacted by this problem—customers, employees, vendors, shareholders?
- What is your recommendation for solving this problem?
- Where does this recommendation fit related to our current priorities? Does the organization have the "capacity" to take on this recommendation in light of other priorities?
- Is this an individual, interpersonal, team, or organizational problem? Is this a process, policy, technology, communication, or other problem?
- How did you go about developing your recommendation, for example, research, best practices, conversations with subject matter experts?
- What timeline do you recommend for implementing this recommendation?
- What staffing will be required to implement and support this recommendation?

- What is the cost-benefit analysis for implementing this recommendation?
- Are there ongoing costs required to support this recommendation year-over-year?
- Is there a capital investment to implement this recommendation? What is the amount?
- What assumptions did you make arriving at this recommendation?
- What other options did you consider arriving at this recommendation?
- What were your decision criteria for arriving at this recommendation?
- How did you consider the impact on related teams, downstream processes, and so on?
- What obstacles or challenges do you anticipate with this recommendation?
- How will you handle those obstacles or challenges?
- Who are your allies supporting this recommendation? What is the best way they can show their support?
- Who are your adversaries as it relates to your recommendation? Have you talked to them to truly understand their position? How will you mitigate their opposition or resistance?
- Who are the decision-makers as it relates to your recommendation?
- Who do you need to inform and get their "buy-in" as it relates to your recommendation?

continued

- What do you propose as next steps?

- What do you need from me to move this forward?

And one more thing that is important to note: You must master one level of thinking before you can move to the next level. You can't expect someone to evaluate information if you haven't first been able to understand it, comprehend it, apply it, and so on. Also note that it takes time to build these critical thinking skills. When I developed the systems thinking questions, I was bringing my anecdotal experiences together with my critical thinking skills, by taking accountability for my own breadth and depth of thinking, in critical and systematic ways. If I could learn that, you can too.

An abbreviated version of introducing critical thinking skills are my favorite learning agility questions:

1. What did I do?
2. What did I learn?
3. How will that help me going forward?

Feel free to modify, add, or customize these questions for yourself, your team, your organization, and even your industry. Once you have mastered this kind of thinking, you can apply it in almost any situation. Your breadth and depth of thinking will enable you to be seen as a credible influencer at all levels.

As we wrap up this chapter, I hope you have gained some new ways of thinking about influence. Once you get to the place where decisions are made, you want to be able to influence those decisions. Effective influencing skills reflect your ability to bring others to a way of thinking about a certain topic without force or coercion while also acknowledging their thoughts and opinions.

REFLECTION

Describe a time when you have used each of these influencing styles:

- Partnering
- Coaching
- Negotiating
- Captivating
- Selling
- Directing
- Which one is your strongest style?
- Which style would you like to work on, and what will you do to work on it?
- What upcoming opportunity do you have that would enable you to impact the outcome? Which style(s) will you use?

CHAPTER 12

BELONGING

"Diversity is a fact. Equity is a choice.
Inclusion is an action. Belonging is an outcome."

—Arthur Chan

The world continues to make efforts to rearrange spaces to feel safe, aware, educated, oriented, curious, and passionate about the value and impact of diversity within our communities, our schools, our places of worship, and our workplaces. We strive to not only make room for the stories of others, but more importantly, to make room for the humans who share those stories. Through education, ownership, and accountability, there is a slowly evolving and acute understanding of the vital necessity of creating a seat at the table that invites an *informed* voice to represent and educate on that which is dismissed or unknown, by allowing others to be seen, heard, and valued in a way that enhances the entire value of an organization or community. Stepping intentionally into the call of truly listening, we will hear the sounds of effective, impactful, and psychological leadership that make equitable room for all. That is my desired goal: making equitable room for all.

As you begin this chapter, I invite you to reflect on the following questions:

REFLECTION

- When was the first time you had a conversation regarding differences (race, age, education, religion, geography, socioeconomic status, accent, ethnicity, etc.)? Describe the conversation.
- Were you allowed to play or interact with people who were different than you?
- When have you felt like an outsider?
- What messages or beliefs did you take away from your stories and experiences?
- How have those messages or beliefs influenced you as a human being? As a leader?

I offer these questions early in this chapter for you to get in touch with that part of you that has experienced being different or feeling like an outsider. The stories I've heard have ranged from "I was the only woman in the room" (the most common) to "I wasn't wearing a tie and everyone else was." I share these two examples to show that answers will cover the spectrum. Discussing these questions with a group—your family, your team, your book club—will be interesting and maybe even enlightening.

My own story and my answer to the first question is from something that happened when I was five years old. I had two older brothers, and as a tomboy, I loved to play the games the boys played. One summer night, several of the neighborhood boys were going to camp out in our backyard. Well, of course, I wanted to do that too, but my mother said, "Absolutely not!" I was so mad—it wasn't fair! As an adult woman, I understand and appreciate my mother's decision, and I'm pretty sure a seed was sown that has prompted me to do the work I do, which leads to my answer to the last reflection question.

I encourage you to share your stories. The world needs to hear your story. It adds to the world's understanding of the human experience, the human condition. I hope your story provides empathy for another person's story. One of my favorite books is *Cassandra Speaks: When Women Are the Storytellers, the Human Story Changes* by Elizabeth Lesser. Don't you love and relate to that subtitle? Tell your stories and invite others to do the same.

So now, let's examine each line of Arthur Chan's quote from the opening of this chapter.[1]

"DIVERSITY IS A FACT"

I want to recognize and share the work of Michelle Bogan.[2] She has provided a visual that I find very helpful in describing the many facets of diversity. In Image 12.1, the inner circle of age, gender, race, and so on shows the dimensions that most regularly come to mind in discussions about diversity. The outer circle of work experience, political ideology, education, and so on represents the things we often find in common (or not) with people who are not like us in the inner circle dimensions.

As you review the graphic and consider the many dimensions, it's easier to accept and understand that diversity is a fact. With more than eight billion people in the world, imagine all the combinations.

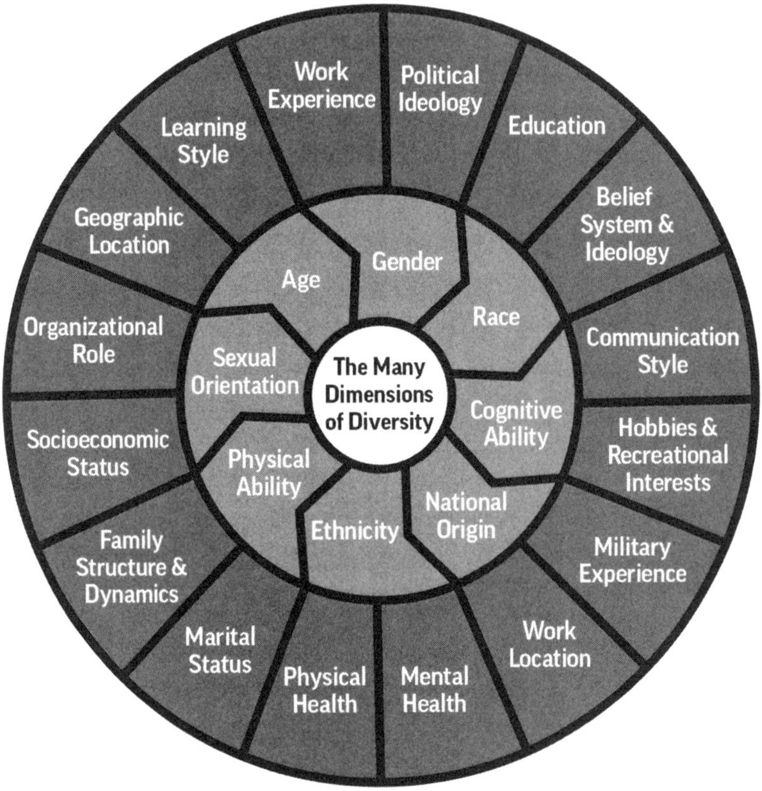

Image 12.1: The Many Dimensions of Diversity. Image courtesy of Michelle Bogan

ACTIVITY

In a group, ask each person to find three to five dimensions that define who they are. Each person shares their three to five dimensions and how those dimensions show up in their life. You can also do this with a partner.

Remember:

- It's their story, their truth.
- Listen with your head *and* your heart.

"EQUITY IS A CHOICE"

According to *Random House Unabridged Dictionary*, *equity* is defined as "the quality of being fair and impartial."[3] This is so easily written and so hard to do. I'm pretty sure that if you're reading this book, you know that there are all kinds of inequality and partiality around us. In a 2019 study, "Economic Inequality by Gender" by Our World in Data,[4] the researchers summarized the most predominant qualities:

- All over the world, men tend to earn more than women.
- Women are often underrepresented in senior positions within firms.
- Women are often overrepresented in low-paying jobs.
- In many countries, men are more likely to own land and control productive assets than women.
- Women often have limited influence over important household decisions, including how their own personal income is spent.

When you read this, you have to look beyond your own experience, your own world. These are macro, bell-shaped research findings. I offer this information in lieu of the masses of statistics to understand the big picture and not get lost in the numbers. (In my humble opinion, I think arguing about whether a finding is 32 percent versus 44 percent, for example, is merely a distraction. Okay, off my soapbox.)

In this same report, there is also some good news.[5]

- In most countries, the gender pay gap has decreased in the last couple of decades.
- Gender-equal inheritance systems, which were rare until recently, are now common across the world.
- Composite indices that cover multiple dimensions show that on the whole, gender inequalities have been shrinking substantially over the last century.

While I've dedicated all of chapter 10 to the topic of asking for what you want, in general, I want to spend time on stereotypes and biases and how they impact our thinking, our beliefs, and our decisions.

As always, let's start with definitions. According to *Oxford Reference*, *stereotype* is defined as "a preconceived and oversimplified idea of the characteristics which typify a person, race, or community which may lead to treating them in a particular way."[6] I offer this characterization: When I walk into a room in this physical representation of an older woman and no one there knows me, there will be assumptions made about how I will (or *should*) act, behave, and speak—just because I am a woman. That's the oversimplified image of me. Now, let's look at the definition of *bias*, which *Oxford Learner's Dictionaries* defines as "a strong feeling in favor of or against one group of people, or one side in an argument, often not based on fair judgment."[7] I see stereotyping and bias walking hand in hand. For example, a woman will be too emotional when making decisions; therefore, I won't invite her in or listen to her perspective or recommendations because they are rooted in emotion rather than fact (stereotype) . . . therefore, I will not hire or promote her because she (all women) is too emotional (bias). According to Dr. Sandra Bem's research, if a woman acts outside of the woman stereotype and succeeds, she is considered the exception. If a woman acts outside of the woman stereotype and fails, the comment is often, "I told you women couldn't do it [whatever 'it' might be]."[8] This merely reinforces one's stereotypes and biases.

The point I want to make here is not that we shouldn't have stereotypes; we are going to have them—we do have them—all of us. The point is whether we are going to hold on to them and not be open to persons being human, being themselves, and not being placed into some limited category of bias. When you acknowledge your stereotypes and choose to move beyond them through curiosity and learning, new relationships will open up.

REFLECTION

What stereotypes do you have?

____

____

____

Here are some commonly held stereotypes to get you thinking:

- Girls are good with language; boys are good at math.
- Women are not risk-takers; men take more risks.
- Women are too emotional; men take nothing personally.
- Millennials are an entitled generation.
- Women from the north, south, east, or west are . . .

STEREOTYPES

Let's deepen our understanding of stereotypes. Chris Drew, PhD, offers these nine types of stereotypes:[9]

1. **Gender Stereotypes**—This involves making assumptions about what a man or woman can and can't (or *should* and *shouldn't* do). The dominant gender stereotypes today are dominant masculinity and dominant femininity.

   With dominant masculinity, a man is expected to be assertive, take a leadership role, and take on dangerous or physical tasks in service of women. Men who do not fit this stereotypical norm are often looked down upon by others in society. With dominant femininity, a woman is expected to be passive, sweet, shy, and soft-spoken. Some people think she should "act like a lady" and take a more active role in household chores than men.

   Here is a recent example of this stereotype at play. Jacinda Ardern, prime minister of New Zealand, and Sanna Marin, prime minister of Finland, met in November 2022 to discuss trade relations and opportunities for economic relations between their two countries. A male journalist from a New Zealand radio network asked about the reason for the talks, saying, "A lot of people will be wondering are you two meeting just because you're similar in age and got a lot of common stuff there." To her credit, Ms. Ardern interrupted the question to say that she wondered "whether or not anyone ever asked Barack Obama and John Key (her predecessor) if they met because they were of similar age?" (Obama and Key were born within days of each other).[10] Yes, this happened in 2022—and at the highest of political positions. Let's not pretend this doesn't happen.

2. **Race and Ethnicity Stereotypes**—This is a prejudgment about people based on their race (Black, White, Asian) or ethnicity (e.g., Hispanic, Native American, Pashtun). Societies create

archetypes about people based on their race and ethnicity, and these can follow them throughout their lives.

3. **Sexuality Stereotypes**—Many people continue to hold prejudices against people based on their sexual orientation. This can lead to harsh discrimination against those whose sexual orientation is different than yours.
4. **Social-Class Stereotypes**—Stereotypes about working-class people have followed them through the centuries, which can prevent them from getting a good job or access to education and housing. These stereotypes work both ways. The working class has long been seen by wealthier classes as uneducated and narrow-minded. On the flip side, wealthier people can be seen as pompous, arrogant, and uncaring by working-class people. These stereotypes can certainly make it hard to build or strengthen relationships.
5. **(Dis)Ability Stereotypes**—People with disabilities were long excluded from social participation. For example, someone with speaking difficulties might be considered unable to do a job that, in reality, they are perfectly capable of doing. As the older sister and frequent caregiver of a special needs sibling, I personally witnessed and experienced the cruelty of others when faced with the realities of a special needs person.
6. **Age Stereotypes**—Ageism is another stereotype that can go in either direction. This stereotype assumes older people are incapable and losing intellect, or similarly, that a young person is incapable purely due to their younger age. My personal experience is that there are different standards for men and women inherent in this stereotype. For example, if a man's hair starts to gray, he looks distinguished. If a woman's hair starts to gray, she is often encouraged to color her hair and may even be replaced by a younger woman.
7. **Nationality Stereotypes**—When you make a statement like "people from England are . . . ," you are probably perpetuating a

stereotype. In this case, you are making an assumption about all people from a nation that can be damaging to individuals from that nation who don't fit the stereotypical mold. Again, from my personal experience, this can come from knowing *one person* from England and then applying that stereotype to the millions of people from England.

8. **Religious Stereotypes**—A religious stereotype can create fear of religious groups you don't belong to. It can involve "othering" people of certain religions, such as Islam or Judaism. Our history as well as current world events demonstrate that these stereotypes literally kill people.
9. **Political Stereotypes**—A political stereotype is created when we retreat into our political tribes and paint people with different political views in the worst possible light.

REFLECTION

Now that I have provided additional information regarding common stereotypes, think further about the following questions.

- What stereotypes do you hold about each of the nine stereotypes presented here?
  - Gender stereotypes

    ____

  - Race and ethnicity stereotypes

    ____

  - Sexuality stereotypes

    ____

  - Social-class stereotypes

    ____

- Disability stereotypes
- Age stereotypes
- Nationality stereotypes
- Religious stereotypes
- Political stereotypes

- What do I get from holding on to these stereotypes? What do I give up from holding on to these stereotypes?

Please continue with a deeper set of questions from Martha Beck's blog entitled "Seeing Your Emotional Blind Spots":[11]

- What am I afraid to know?
- What's the one thing I least want to accept?
- What actions will I take to get beyond these stereotypes?

Stereotypes can be harmful to everyone. They rely on prejudices and biases that see people not as unique and complex individuals but instead as the worst version of a social trope about a group of people. The nine stereotypes I have shared here have persisted for many generations. Dare I say, they are an easy way out. Don't be taken in by the stereotype. Do your homework. Take the time and make the effort to get to know the unique and complex human being instead.

BIAS

Now let's think about bias. I want to focus on how bias shows up in the workplace, including how bias impacts our hiring decisions, delegating tasks or assignments, and promotions. You likely have heard about unconscious bias. I want to also offer some thoughts on conscious bias.

Conscious bias is an active, understood, and calculated choice to act in a certain way. With conscious bias, you are aware of the decisions you are making and know what is motivating you to make such a decision. With unconscious bias (also referred to as implicit bias), your behaviors, actions, inactions, and decisions come from an unconscious place. In contrast to conscious bias, people who are operating unconsciously have no idea they are acting in a way that includes some people and excludes others. Since unconscious bias is often undetected or an automatic default, it can be very challenging. In the spirit of learning (when you know better, you can do better), I hope to raise your awareness (consciousness) and deepen your understanding so you can make more conscious and intentional choices. Your choices are tied to your values. Indeed.com offers valuable information on bias in the workplace.[12]

As you read about the following eleven types of bias that are ever present in our workplaces, keep your values in mind.

1. **Conformity Bias**—This usually occurs when you are encouraged or even pressured into going along with the group. You likely will second-guess your own thoughts, ideas, or decisions based on the feedback—both verbal and nonverbal—from others. A way to make conformity bias more visible is to keep track of this in

your group or organizational meetings. Make two columns on a notepad. In one column, document your thoughts and feelings about a certain person (e.g., when making hiring, promoting, compensating, and succession planning choices). In the other column, document how others are thinking and feeling about the person being discussed. This will help you determine if you are thinking and feeling similarly to the group or not. You can then choose to speak up and ensure that your perspective will be heard and considered in the decisions being made. Always make sure you are speaking in support of what is in the best interest of the organization or the team and not from a place of ego or an overwhelming need to be right or to win.

2. **Beauty Bias**—Many people are biased toward those that society traditionally reflects as beautiful or attractive people. Plenty of research reflects that those who meet societal standards of beauty are more likely to be hired, offered desirable assignments, and given promotions than those deemed less attractive. To combat this type of bias, consider holding blind interviews, particularly early on in the hiring process. This will help ensure that the most qualified people get far enough into the hiring process before being disqualified based on societal beauty standards. Obviously, this is much harder when you know the person and are looking for someone to promote, compensate, or give that desirable assignment. In those situations, you will have to challenge the basis of your decision. Having specific decision-making criteria can help you get past this bias.
3. **Affinity or Similarity Bias**—This bias occurs when another person thinks like you, has similar interests, or behaves like you. It's easier to form a deeper connection with someone who is like you. This bias is sometimes expressed as having chemistry with another person. When you are considering another person for

hiring, promoting, and so on, ask yourself if you are deciding based on your affinity bias. Again, having decision-making criteria can help you neutralize this bias.

4. **Halo Effect Bias**—This bias occurs when you consider one outstanding quality or accomplishment, and it outweighs or takes precedence over any or all negative attributes of the person being considered. For example, if a person went to a prestigious school, you may be immediately prompted to see how smart they are and ignore their poor communication skills. To manage this bias, keep your decision-making criteria on a notepad and objectively note the plus and minus behaviors and responses the person gives related to each criteria.
5. **Horns Effect Bias**—As you might surmise, this bias is the opposite of the halo effect bias. Instead of focusing on that one positive quality, you focus on a negative quality or experience. You may have only heard about this negative quality or experience from another person; you have not personally observed or experienced it for yourself. Again, go back to your decision-making criteria and objectively note the plus and minus behaviors and responses the person gives related to each criteria.
6. **Contrast Effect Bias**—This particular bias is often viewed as the most detrimental in the hiring process. As the person making the hiring decision, you will likely compare resumes or interviews with other candidates instead of using decision-making criteria.

Take the time before even posting the job to:

- Have a current and accurate job description.
- Have relevant interview questions. Document criteria of what you are looking for in the candidate's responses to each interview question.

- Have a method for assessing a resume.
- Have a qualified slate of people who will conduct the interviews.

7. **Attribution Bias**—Often we attribute a candidate's success or failure to different factors. This is when you may make assumptions and subsequently a decision based on inaccurate factors. For example, if someone shares a success story, you may think this is an anomaly or the person just got lucky. (Remember what I shared earlier in this chapter about women acting out of stereotype and how we interpret their success and failure.) If a person fails at something, we might assume they are incompetent. I recommend you interpret their responses regarding failure as an authentic and mature response. True leaders—in the context of leadership as a mindset—are willing to be vulnerable and share their less-than-favorable experiences. As an interviewer, your follow-up question is targeted at what they learned from the failure and how they applied that learning in subsequent assignments. Let's face it, we're all going to have some failures and less-than-stellar performances. If a candidate declares that they have had no failures, you might question their self-awareness, learning agility, and their trustworthiness.

8. **Confirmation Bias**—I often think about this one as the Ego or Arrogance Bias. This bias is operating when you assume you are right regardless of the facts. I'm a big believer in holding our thoughts, feelings, and even our decisions lightly. I learned this principle about fifty years ago when I heard Arthur Hays Sulzberger's quote: "A [wo]man's judgment cannot be better than the information on which [s]he bases it."[13] What that means to me is that you should a) know the facts before you decide, and b) if new facts emerge, be open to making a new and potentially different decision.

9. **Affect Heuristics Bias**—This bias prompts you to make decisions based on superficial or unimportant details rather than facts or evidence. For example, if a candidate wears a purple blouse, and you don't like the color purple, you are less likely to invite them to the next round of interviews. Yes, really! Make sure you check those gut feelings before making these important decisions. Return to your decision-making criteria (and I hope "doesn't wear purple clothing" is not on there—ha-ha!).
10. **Illusory Correlation Bias**—This bias occurs when you make connections between unrelated concepts and then make assumptions based on those unsubstantiated relationships. For example, the candidate is wearing a piece of clothing similar to something you wore in your interview. It's almost as though you are confirming your own choice of what to wear for an interview by giving the candidate unconscious credit for making a similar choice. Make sure you find compelling and concrete evidence that supports your conclusions and decisions.
11. **Intuition Bias**—This bias reflects the practice of relying on an emotional response rather than facts when making a decision. Now, let me be clear: I'm a fan of paying attention to your intuition. In this scenario, you have to dig deep and challenge yourself to discern whether it's an unconscious bias that is driving your decision or a feeling that keeps tugging at you and you can't quite put your finger on it. Only you can know the answer to that.

I encourage everyone reading this material who makes hiring, promotion, compensation, and assignment decisions to keep this list of unconscious biases handy. Making hiring decisions is really hard, and you have a fifty-fifty chance of getting it right. The reality is that some people interview well and perform poorly and vice versa. By acknowledging and understanding these biases, you will improve your odds of making a good decision.

One more note to remember—if you are using behavioral interviewing as your methodology for interviewing and making your hiring decisions, it's very important to know and document what you are listening for in the candidate's responses. For example, if you are assessing whether or not the candidate is a good team player, you might ask: "What is the best team you worked on and what are your criteria for determining it as a best team?" You would then be listening for a spirit of unity, mutual respect and trustworthiness, being open to each other's ideas and recommendations, sharing knowledge, shared learning, and the ability to give and receive constructive feedback.

As we wrap up our topic of bias, consider these negative outcomes when biases are driving our decisions:

- **Turnover**—When you make biased decisions, you may find out the person you hired is not performing at the level you expected. If you find yourself in this situation, set clear expectations and provide timely and constructive feedback. If performance continues to fall short, be a leader and take action. This might mean transferring them to a role that is better suited to their skills and capabilities. It might also mean exiting them from the organization.

Two additional leadership principles:

1. *Bad news doesn't improve with age.* Decide and act sooner rather than later. I've never heard anyone say, "I wish I would have waited longer." In fact, the opposite is true. I almost always hear, "What took me so long?"
2. *A Players hire A Players, and B Players hire C Players.* Don't be afraid to hire people who are or who have the potential to

be better than you. That is a jewel in your crown and *not* a threat to your leadership.

- **Colleague Loss of Trust**—Often the people working with the candidate you chose, both as peers and direct reports, will likely know before you do that this person is not performing well. This can lead to loss of trust in your ability to make good hiring decisions. These same peers and direct reports are also waiting for you to address the poor performance. If too much time passes before you act, they will lose further trust in you as a leader in the organization.
- **Legal Issues**—If someone accuses you of making a biased decision or accuses the organization of having biased practices, you can face lawsuits, fines, and court hearings regarding workplace discrimination.
- **Homogeny**—When you make biased decisions, you can often find yourself in an echo chamber, leading a group of people who often think and act alike. Research tells us that not much innovation or creative thinking surfaces when this is the case. It has been proven many times that diversity and equity improve business outcomes.

REFLECTION

- When have these biases shown up for you?

____

____

- When have you seen them show up in others?

____

____

- When might you have been on the receiving end of someone else's biases?

- How will you better recognize and manage your own biases?

- How will you help your team and organization recognize and manage these biases?

- What will your first steps be?

Having stereotypes and biases is being human. This is an inevitable and unavoidable part of your personal and professional life. My hope is that with this information you can manage your stereotypes and biases. *You can no longer operate from a default place.* From this point forward, decide to make conscious and intentional choices. Choose wisely and in support of your values.

"INCLUSION IS AN ACTION"

In a volatile and complex world, predicting the future with any precision is risky business. That said, according to a 2016 Deloitte study by Dr. Juliet Bourke and Bernadette Dillon, "The Six Signature Traits of Inclusive Leadership,"[14] there are four megatrends that are shaping and will continue to shape the marketplace. Knowing these megatrends will definitely influence business and institutional priorities. I refer to Dr. Bourke's article throughout this section.

1. **Diversity of Markets**—Demand is shifting to emerging markets. With their growing middle classes, these new markets represent the biggest growth opportunity in the portfolio of many companies around the world.

2. **Diversity of Customers**—Customer demographics and attitudes are changing. Empowered through technology and with greater choice, an increasingly diverse customer base expects better personalization of products and services.

3. **Diversity of Ideas**—Digital technology, hyperconnectivity, and deregulation are disrupting business value chains and the nature of consumption and competition. Few would argue against the need for rapid innovation.

4. **Diversity of Talent**—Shifts in age profiles, education, and migration flows, along with expectations of equality and opportunity and work-life balance, are all impacting employee populations.

These simultaneous and parallel shifts are the new context. The fundamental aspects of being an effective leader, such as setting direction and influencing others, will always be required. With this new context, however, some necessary and additional skills will be required. Deloitte's study identified six traits of inclusive leadership that characterize an inclusive mindset and inclusive behavior. Before I share these six traits, I want to emphasize that what I offer from the research is with the foundation of authentic leadership. These traits can be displayed in different ways. Elements of inclusive leadership are echoed in transformational, servant, and authentic leadership. The six traits offered here are amplified and built on these known attributes to define a powerful new capability uniquely adapted to a diverse environment.

INCLUSIVE LEADERSHIP TRAITS

When people feel that they are treated fairly, their uniqueness is appreciated, and they have a voice in decision-making, they will feel included. Putting this into the context of inclusive leadership, these aims enable leaders to operate more effectively.

- Treating people and groups fairly—that is, based on their unique characteristics, rather than on stereotypes
- Personalizing individuals—understanding and valuing the uniqueness of diverse others while also accepting them as members of the group
- Leveraging the thinking of diverse groups for smarter ideation and decision-making that reduces the risk of being blindsided

The six traits that follow are tangible and can be developed.

Trait 1: Visible Commitment

"Highly inclusive leaders are committed to diversity and inclusion because these objectives align with their personal values and because they believe in the business case."[15]

This is an interesting one, and also one I strongly agree is a necessary trait. If either conditions of personal values alignment or belief in the business case is absent, you might get what I call malicious compliance, which is typically short-lived. This is in contrast to true commitment and engagement, which are sustainable over the long haul. They're the combination of head (business case) and heart (personal values). If both are present, you will move beyond talking about it. You will give priority, focus, energy, and resources to ensure inclusive leadership and an inclusive culture.

The bravery to challenge the status quo is a fundamental behavior of an inclusive leader, and it occurs at three levels—with the organizational system, with others, and with yourself. Bravery also comes into play in a willingness to challenge entrenched organizational attitudes and practices that promote homogeneity.

Trait 2: Humility (to be humble and vulnerable)

"Highly inclusive leaders are . . . humble about their strengths and weaknesses."[16]

There is a vulnerability to being an inclusive leader because confronting others and challenging the status quo immediately invites the spotlight to shine on you. Being an agent of change will often be met with cynicism, challenges, and resistance from others. It takes courage to stay the course. Humility is also required when admitting you don't have all the answers. According to the Catalyst organization's research, humility also encompasses learning from criticism and different points of view, as well as seeking contributions from others to overcome your own limitations. In addition, "Leaders who are humble acknowledge their vulnerability to bias and ask for feedback on their blind spots and habits. Our research shows that when cognizance of bias is combined with high levels of humility it can increase feelings of inclusion by up to 25%."[17]

Trait 3: Cognizance of Bias

"Highly inclusive leaders are mindful of personal and organizational blind spots, and self-regulate to ensure 'fair play.'"[18]

Dr. Rohini Anand, senior vice president and global chief diversity officer at Sodexo, describes this well: "The leaders that are inclusive do a couple of things. At the individual level, they are very self-aware, and they act on that self-awareness. And they acknowledge that their organizations, despite best intentions, have unconscious bias, and they put in place policies, processes, and structures in order to mitigate the unconscious bias that exists."[19]

Inclusive leaders think about these three features of fairness with the aim of creating an environment of "fair play":

1. **Outcomes**—Are outcomes such as pay and performance ratings, as well as developmental and promotion opportunities, allocated on the basis of capability and effort, or does their distribution reflect bias?
2. **Processes**—Are the processes applied in deciding these outcomes transparent, applied consistently, based on accurate information, free from bias, and inclusive of the views of individuals affected by the decisions, or are they tinged with bias, thus leading to undeserved success for some and failure for others?
3. **Communication**—Are the reasons for decisions made, and processes applied, explained to those affected, and are people treated respectfully in the process?

Trait 4: Curiosity

"Highly inclusive leaders have an open mindset, a desire to understand how others view and experience the world, and a tolerance for ambiguity."[20]

This thirst for continual learning helps drive attributes associated with curiosity—open-mindedness, inquiry, and empathy. Such behaviors do not come easily to everyone. These behaviors result in loyalty from others who feel valued along with access to a richer set of information that enables better decision-making. Asking curious questions and actively listening are core skills that are key to deepening your understanding of perspectives from diverse individuals. Openness involves withholding fast judgment that can stifle the flow of ideas.

Trait 5: Culturally Intelligent

"Highly inclusive leaders are confident and effective in cross-cultural interactions."[21]

While an understanding of cultural similarities and differences is important, inclusive leaders also recognize how their own culture impacts their personal worldview, as well as how cultural stereotypes can influence their expectations of others. At a deeper level, an inclusive leader's thirst for learning means they are also motivated to deepen their cultural understanding and to learn from the experience of working in an unfamiliar environment. This curiosity leads them to value cultural differences, defying ethnocentric tendencies that cause people to judge other cultures as inferior to their own, and enabling them to build stronger connections with people from different backgrounds. Inclusive leaders are tolerant of ambiguity, and this enables them to manage the stress imposed by new or different cultural environments as well as situations where familiar or behavioral cues are lacking. Finally, inclusive leaders understand that the ability to adapt does not mean "going native," which can cause leaders to lose sight of what they want to achieve by overcompensating for new cultural demands.

Many of the above capabilities are encapsulated in a model known as "cultural intelligence" (CQ), which comprises four elements:

1. **Motivational**—The leader's energy and interest toward learning about and engaging in cross-cultural interactions
2. **Cognitive**—The leader's knowledge of relevant cultural norms, practices, and conventions
3. **Metacognitive**—The leader's level of conscious cultural awareness during interactions
4. **Behavioral**—The use of appropriate verbal and nonverbal actions in cross-cultural interactions

Research has demonstrated the positive relationship between CQ and a range of important business outcomes, including expatriate job performance, intercultural negotiation effectiveness, and team process effectiveness in multicultural teams.

Trait 6: Collaborative

"Highly inclusive leaders empower individuals as well as create and leverage the thinking of diverse groups."[22]

Dr. Bruce Stewart has said that the old intelligence quotient (IQ) is about how smart *you* are, and the new IQ is about how smart you make your *team*. If you take this to heart, instead of leading from the top of the pyramid, you will lead from the middle of the circle. At its core, collaboration is about individuals working together, building on each other's ideas to produce something new or solve something complex. It is also an effective strategy when you need the team's psychological buy-in and you need the team to make it happen. While collaboration among similar people is comfortable and maybe even easier, you may lose out on the innovation and creativity of a more diverse team. Inclusive leaders understand that for collaboration to be successful, individuals must first be willing to share their diverse perspectives.

You might want to review the material in chapter 2 on creating psychological safety, which encourages and supports individuals to share their thoughts, ideas, and recommendations. For inclusive leaders, diversity of thinking is a critical ingredient for effective collaboration. Far from being guided by stereotypes or biases, inclusive leaders adopt a disciplined approach to diversity of thinking, paying close attention to team composition and the decision-making process.

A special thanks to Dr. Juliet Bourke. I consider her work to be the gold standard for identifying the attributes of an inclusive leader.

ACTIVITY

How would you describe your effectiveness in deploying these traits in your day-in and day-out responsibilities?

Score yourself on each trait on a 1-5 scale (1 = low; 5 = high).

Trait	Family	Workplace	Community	Other
Visible Commitment				
Humility				
Cognizance of Bias				
Curiosity				
Culturally Intelligent				
Collaborative				

- Which trait would you like to develop further? What will your first steps be?

- How can you share this information with your team? Your family? Your organization? Other groups?

Now that you have gotten clear about your own personal effectiveness as an inclusive leader, let's evaluate your organization's effectiveness as it relates to policies, procedures, practices, and metrics for success.

REFLECTION

- Can you acknowledge that there are inequities? If yes, what are you willing to do? (Know that you will be asked to do more and more.)

- Will it take you longer than expected? How will you support yourself in going the distance?

- What do you believe are the biggest challenges for organizations (of all kinds) to create diverse, equitable, and inclusive (DEI) cultures?

- What practical and impactful policies and practices have you identified thus far in your professional and personal life that positively impact and further DEI cultures?

- Does your organization want a Disrupter (someone who will *challenge* the status quo) or a Carrier of the Culture (someone who will protect the status quo)? Which do you want to be?

- What accountability systems have you observed or experienced to be effective and impactful in supporting DEI cultures?

continued

- What is the most critical lever to pull in order to advance DEI in organizations? In your organization?

A note of heartfelt thanks to Tina Bowers, DEI consultant and coach, and Raquel Daniels, DEI consultant and coach. I have adapted these questions from their work and what I have learned from them.

What I cover in this chapter is complex and hard. If it were simple and easy, I wouldn't need to write this chapter. I hope I have provided some clarity along with actionable steps that you can take to be an inclusive leader and help create an inclusive culture.

Yet we haven't covered that final line in the Arthur Chan quote . . .

"BELONGING IS AN OUTCOME"

According to *Oxford Reference*, *belonging* is "a person's sense of attachment to, and rootedness in, a specific community, neighborhood, place, region, or country."[23] Cornell University provides additional texture with their definition: "Belonging is the feeling of security and support when there is a sense of acceptance, inclusion, and identity for a member of a certain group."[24] These "certain groups" can be family, friends, workplaces, clubs, places of worship, and communities. Belonging is a sense of fitting in and feeling valued. Ah! Here we are again. What every human being wants is to be seen, heard, and valued. Belonging is fundamental to our sense of happiness and well-being. Research has shown that loss of belonging is associated with stress, illness, decreased well-being, and depression.[25] Just think about all the stories, articles, and personal experiences regarding today's mental health challenges.

If belonging is an outcome, what is the input? Here is my summary:

- Acknowledge that **diversity is a fact,** and understand the many facets or dimensions of diversity. Value the perspectives diversity offers.
- Understand that the **choice of equity** means each person or group is given the same resources or opportunity—beyond stereotypes and beyond biases.
- Take **action to be an inclusive leader**. Display the six inclusive leadership traits, and bring others along with you as you continuously work on being an authentic, inclusive leader. Create psychological safety that encourages *everyone* to contribute their best thinking, ideas, solutions, perspectives, experience, and recommendations. Give weight and consideration to those contributions.

None of us get it right every time. Give yourself and others grace as you travel the path of continuous learning and improved effectiveness. Each and every one of us deserves a sense of belonging. I hope you will join me by doing your part to provide that sense of belonging in your personal and professional life.

I would like to add a "PS" or postscript here. As this book is being published, Diversity, Equity, and Inclusion (DEI) laws, policies, and programs are under attack in the United States. I am unsure how this attack will play out. I see this as a critical moment for all human beings. For any human being who is considered "other," there are risks. Will the discrimination of the old return? Will hiring, promoting, and compensating be done fairly? Will biases and stereotypes be defended or not seen as a problem by those who make these hiring, promoting, and compensating decisions? Only time will tell. I know that I choose to continue to fight the good fight to make my contributions to a world that values women and girls. I invite every person who reads this book to join me. Here's to women (and men) supporting women and girls!!

PART 3

DISCUSSION QUESTIONS

Some of you will be reading this book on your own. Others may be reading and reviewing the book as a book club or a women's group. At the end of each chapter, I've included some reflection questions that focus on what you've learned from the chapter and how you plan to apply it in your life.

If you are reading the book as a group, I encourage you to answer the questions individually before discussing them as a group. You want to do your own personal work. Once you hear others' responses, you can add, change, or even delete items in your own responses. Remember, women learn through stories. Share yours freely and deeply, and listen as others do the same.

PART 3 REFLECTION QUESTIONS

- What did you learn about yourself while reading this section?

- What stands out for you about organizational systems, influencing organizations, and leading in a way that creates a sense of belonging?

- What are three things you'll do differently going forward based on what you've learned?

EPILOGUE

As this book comes to a close, I offer this poem as a provocative invitation to be your best self and to live your best life.

"The Invitation"
By Oriah "Mountain Dreamer"

It doesn't interest me what you do for a living. I want to know what you ache for, and if you dare to dream of meeting your heart's longing.

It doesn't interest me how old you are. I want to know if you will risk looking like a fool for love, for your dream, for the adventure of being alive.

It doesn't interest me what planets are squaring your moon. I want to know if you have touched the center of your own sorrow, if you have been opened by life's betrayals or have become shriveled and closed from fear of further pain. I want to know if you can sit with pain, mine or your own, without moving to hide it or fade it or fix it.

I want to know if you can be with joy, mine or your own, if you can dance with wildness and let the ecstasy fill you to the tips of your fingers and toes without cautioning us to be careful, to be realistic, to remember the limitations of being human.

It doesn't interest me if the story you are telling me is true. I want to know if you can disappoint another to be true to yourself; if you can bear the accusation of betrayal and not betray your own soul; if you can be faithless and therefore trustworthy.

I want to know if you can see Beauty, even when it's not pretty, everyday, and if you can source your own life from its presence.

I want to know if you can live with failure, yours and mine, and still stand on the edge of the lake and shout to the silver of the full moon, "Yes!"

It doesn't interest me to know where you live or how much money you have. I want to know if you can get up, after the night of grief and despair, weary and bruised to the bone and do what needs to be done to feed the children. It doesn't interest me who you know or how you came to be here. I want to know if you will stand in the center of the fire with me and not shrink back.

It doesn't interest me where or what or with whom you have studied. I want to know what sustains you, from the inside, when all else falls away.

I want to know if you can be alone with yourself and if you truly like the company you keep in the empty moments.[1]

As you finish reading this book, I hope I have helped you expand your power—in your family, your professional life, among your friends, and in your community—always in service to something larger than yourself. You are more powerful than you know. Use your power to leave every place you visit better than you found it.

APPENDIX

LIST OF TOOLS

Many of my clients share with me that one of the things that differentiates my work is that I don't just teach "what" people can do to be better leaders, I also teach "how" to be better leaders. Tools are an important part of that "how." One of my foundational beliefs about leadership is that "good leaders know what tool to use when." You can now enrich your leadership tool kit with the following tools found in each chapter of this book.

PART 1

CHAPTER 1

1. "Embrace Your Own Greatness" Poem
2. Self-Awareness Insight List
3. Pity-Sympathy-Empathy-Compassion Framework

CHAPTER 2

1. What Is Trauma?
2. Trauma vs. trauma
3. Unhealed Trauma
4. Signs of Lingering Trauma in Adults

5. Handle with Care (Poem)
6. How We Respond to Stress: The Four F's: Fight, Flight, Freeze, and Flock
7. Safe Spaces: Group Trust & Creating a Safe Space

PART 2

CHAPTER 3

1. Tuckman-Jensen Model: Forming, Storming, Norming, Performing
2. Build It Exercise
3. New Team Checklist
4. Responsibility Charting: Establishing RASIN

CHAPTER 4

1. High-Performance Team Framework
2. Expectations Menu
3. Checks and Balances
4. Seven-Step Feedback Model
5. Love Languages and the Language of Appreciation
6. KYP: Know Your People
7. Run the Company So the Best People Love it!

CHAPTER 5

1. Inclusion, Control, and Openness Framework
2. Definition of:
    - Self-awareness
    - Self-concept
    - Self-esteem
3. Eight Principles Behind the Human Element
4. Inclusion
    - In or Out
    - Underlying Feeling of Significance

5. Control
    - Top or Bottom
    - Underlying Feeling of Competence
6. Openness
    - Public or Private
    - Underlying Feeling of Likability, Lovability

CHAPTER 6

1. Change Exercise: Identify Three Changes
2. Productivity Curve
3. Grief Cycle: Betrayal, Denial, Identity Crisis, Renewal
4. Quantity, Quality, Effort Exercise
5. Change Readiness Assessment
6. Timing Matters
7. Supporting Others Through the Change Cycle
8. BMW (Bitch, Moan, Whine) Sessions
9. Communicating Rules of Thumb
10. Change Tips
11. Operationalizing "The Serenity Prayer"

CHAPTER 7

1. Ending Well: Goodbye/Thank You Spreadsheet
    - Update and Retention Spreadsheet
    - Tool: Ending Well: The Handoff
2. First Sixty Days Tools
    - Know Your Mandate
    - Conduct Stakeholder Interviews
    - Communicate Interview Results with Priorities
    - Assess Existing Talent Framework
    - Develop a Communication Plan
    - Review Your Calendar
    - Create and Execute Your Plan

PART 3

CHAPTER 8

1. Concept of Tops, Middles, Bottoms, and Customers
2. The Side Show and Center Ring
3. Predictable Conditions and Responses, and Familiar Disempowering Scenarios
4. Top, Bottom, Middle, and Customer Principles
5. Top, Bottom, Middle, and Customer Empowerment Strategies

CHAPTER 9

1. Disintegration of the Middles
2. Middle Integration Process
3. Levels of Integration
4. Empowering Middles

CHAPTER 10

1. Asking Propensity
2. Likability Factor, Assertive Behaviors, and Communal Behaviors
3. Self-Schema
4. Childhood Socialization
5. Accumulation of Disadvantage
6. Tool: Preparation Worksheet

CHAPTER 11

1. Influencing Framework: Advocacy, Inquiry, and Integration
2. Partnering
3. Coaching
4. Negotiating
5. Captivating
6. Selling
7. Directing
8. Being Politically Savvy

CHAPTER 12

EPILOGUE

RECOMMENDED READING LIST AND RESOURCES

EMBRACING YOUR POWER

1. Clark, Marsha L. *Embracing Your Power*. Greenleaf Book Group, 2021.
2. Gandy, Dottie Bruce, and Marsha L. Clark, *Choose: The Role That Choice Plays in Shaping Women's Lives.* Brown Books, 2004.

TRAUMA

1. Chiuzi, Rafael. "The Case for Psychological Safety and Better Teams." TEDxMcMasterU, March 2022, 16:00, https://www.ted.com/talks/rafael_chiuzi_the_case_for_psychological_safety_and_better_teams.
2. Lee, David. "*The Hidden Cost of Workplace Trauma.*" Human Nature at Work. *EAPA Exchange* (January 1996): 18–21.

LEADING AND BUILDING TEAMS

1. Climer, Amy. "The Power of Deliberate Creative Teams." TEDxAsheville, September 2018, 16:40, https://www.ted.com/talks/amy_climer_the_power_of_deliberate_creative_teams.

2. Pink, Dan. "The Puzzle of Motivation." TEDGlobal 2009, July 2009, 18:22, https://www.ted.com/talks/dan_pink_the_puzzle_of_motivation/transcript.

GROUP DYNAMICS

1. Hammer, Allen, and Eugene R. Schnell. *FIRO-B: Technical Guide.* Consulting Psychologists Press, 2000.
2. Schnell, Eugene R., and Allen Hammer. *Introduction to the FIRO-B Instrument in Organizations.* Consulting Psychologists Press, 2003.
3. Schutz, Will. *FIRO: A Three-Dimensional Theory of Interpersonal Behavior.* 3rd ed. Will Schutz Associates, 1994.
4. Schutz, Will. *The Human Element: Productivity, Self-Esteem, and the Bottom Line.* Jossey-Bass, 1994.

CHANGE MANAGEMENT

1. Kegan, Robert, and Lisa Laskow Lahey. *Immunity to Change: How to Overcome It and Unlock the Potential in Yourself and Your Organization.* Harvard Business Review Press, 2009.

ORGANIZATIONAL SYSTEMS

1. Oshry, Barry. *The Possibilities of Organization.* Power & Systems Training, 1986.
2. Oshry, Barry. *Seeing Systems: Unlocking the Mysteries of Organizational Life.* Berrett-Koehler, 2007.

INFLUENCING AND NEGOTIATIONS

1. Babcock, Linda, and Sara Laschever. *Women Don't Ask: Negotiation and the Gender Divide.* Princeton University Press, 2021.
2. Fisher, Roger, and William Ury. *Getting to Yes: Negotiating Agreement Without Giving In.* Penguin, 2011.
3. Hauser, Robin. *The Likability Dilemma for Women Leaders,* TEDx video, 9:45.
4. Kolb, Deborah, and Judith Williams. *The Shadow Negotiation: How Women Can Master the Hidden Agendas That Determine Bargaining Success.* Simon & Schuster, 2001.

5. Pinkley, Robin L., and Gregory B. Northcraft. *Get Paid What You're Worth: The Expert Negotiators' Guide to Salary and Compensation*. St. Martin's, 2000.

DIVERSITY, EQUITY, AND INCLUSION

1. Johnson Sirleaf, H. E. Ellen. "How Women Will Lead Us to Freedom, Justice, and Peace." TEDWomen 2019, December 2019, 14:02, https://www.ted.com/talks/h_e_ellen_johnson_sirleaf_how_women_will_lead_us_to_freedom_justice_and_peace?language=en.
2. Ngozi Adichie, Chimamanda. "The Danger of a Single Story." TEDGlobal 2009, July 2009, 18:32, https://www.ted.com/talks/chimamanda_ngozi_adichie_the_danger_of_a_single_story?language=en.
3. Simon Psihoterapeut, Diana. "Brené Brown on Empathy vs Sympathy." YouTube, April 1, 2016, 2:53, https://www.youtube.com/watch?v=KZBTYViDPlQ.
4. Additional resources regarding trauma are available at https://marshaclarkandassociates.com/.

NOTES

CHAPTER 1

1. "Marsha," The Bump, https://www.thebump.com/b/marsha-baby-name.
2. Rasmus Hougaard, Jacqueline Carter, and Marissa Afton, "Connect with Empathy, but Lead with Compassion," *Harvard Business Review*, December 23, 2021, https://hbr.org/2021/12/connect-with-empathy-but-lead-with-compassion.

CHAPTER 2

1. Nicole Lewis-Keeber, "Big T Trauma vs. little t trauma: The Continued Effect of Adverse Childhood Experiences," *Medium*, May 31, 2021, https://nicolelewiskeeber1.medium.com/big-tr-trauma-vs-little-t-trauma-the-continued-effect-of-adverse-childhood-experiences-a19b6466853c.
2. Lewis-Keeber, "Big T Trauma vs. little t trauma."
3. Dakota King-White, "Childhood Trauma: Types, Causes, Signs, & Treatments," Choosing Therapy, March 21, 2024, https://www.choosingtherapy.com/childhood-trauma/.
4. Clare Rolquin, "Unhealed Trauma: Signs, Impacts, & How to Heal," Choosing Therapy, January 14, 2024, https://www.choosingtherapy.com/unhealed-trauma/.

5. Wendy Rose Gould, "How to Spot the Signs of Codependency," VerywellMind, updated May 21, 2024, https://www.verywellmind.com/what-is-codependency-5072124.
6. Rolquin, "Unhealed Trauma."
7. Carl Blanz, "The Inside Story of Conflict," Growing Edge, https://www.growing-edge.com/post/the-inside-story-of-conflict.
8. Rolquin, "Unhealed Trauma."
9. Rolquin, "Unhealed Trauma."
10. Shelley E. Taylor, Laura Cousino Klein, Brian P. Lewis, Tara L. Gruenewald, Regan A. R. Gurung, and John A. Updegraff, "Biobehavioral Responses to Stress in Females: Tend-and-Befriend, Not Fight-or-Flight," *Psychological Review* 107, no. 3 (2000): 411–429, https://taylorlab.psych.ucla.edu/wp-content/uploads/sites/5/2014/10/2000_Biobehavioral-responses-to-stress-in-females_tend-and-befriend.pdf.
11. Pat Heim, Tammy Hughes, and Susan Golant, *Hardball for Women: Winning at the Game of Business* (Plume, 2015).
12. Brené Brown, *Rising Strong: How the Ability to Reset Transforms the Way We Live, Love, Parent, and Lead* (Random House, 2017).
13. "KAHRMM Newsletter Articles: Assuming the Best in Your Co-Workers," Kansas Hospital Association, August 2021, https://www.kha-net.org/AlliedOrganizations/KAHRMM/kahrmm-newsletter-articles/Assuming-the-Best-in-Your-Co-Workers_162114.aspx.
14. Courtney E. Ackerman, "What Is Flourishing in Positive Psychology? (+8 Tips & PDF)," PositivePsychology.com, May 9, 2018, https://positivepsychology.com/flourishing/.

CHAPTER 3

1. "Bruce Tuckman's Forming, Storming, Norming & Performing Team Development Model," Culture at Work, https://www.coachingcultureatwork.com/wp-content/uploads/Bruce-Tuckmans-Forming-Storming-Norming-Performing-Team-Development-Model.pdf.
2. Source: © 2021 Reina Trust Building®, reinatrustbuilding.com.

CHAPTER 4

1. Jim Harter, "World's Largest Ongoing Study of the Employee Experience," Gallup Workplace, September 4, 2024, https://www.gallup.com/workplace/649487/world-largest-ongoing-study-employee-experience.aspx.
2. Dennis Reina and Michelle Reina, *Trust and Betrayal in the Workplace* (Berrett-Koehler, 2015).
3. *OED (Oxford English Dictionary)*, "obstacle," accessed February 17, 2025, https://www.oed.com/dictionary/obstacle_n?tab=meaning_and_use.
4. "How Frequent Should Employee Recognition Be?," Ovation Incentives, https://www.ovationincentives.com/articles/how-frequent-should-employee-recognition-be#:~:text=We%20would%20always%20recommend%20taking,an%20employee%20does%20recognisable%20work.
5. Gary Chapman, *The 5 Love Languages: The Secret to Love That Lasts*, reprint ed. (Northfield Publishing, 2024).
6. Gary Chapman and Paul White, *The 5 Languages of Appreciation in the Workplace: Empowering Organizations by Encouraging People* (Northfield Publishing, 2019).

CHAPTER 5

1. Schutz, *The Human Element: Productivity, Self-Esteem and the Bottom Line* (Jossey-Bass, 1994), xv.
2. Patrick Lencioni, *The Five Dysfunctions of a Team: A Leadership Fable* (Jossey-Bass, 2002).
3. Will Schutz, *The Human Element.*
4. Schutz, *The Human Element*, xv.
5. Schutz, *The Human Element*, 71.
6. Schutz, *The Human Element*, 56.
7. Schutz, *The Human Element*, 71.
8. Schutz, *The Human Element*, 71.
9. Schutz, *The Human Element*, 71.
10. *Merriam-Webster Dictionary*, "self-acceptance," accessed February 16, 2025, https://www.merriam-webster.com/dictionary/self-acceptance.

11. Schutz, *The Human Element*, jacket cover.
12. Schutz, *The Human Element*, 21.
13. Ethan Schutz, "Wants, Not Needs: A Key Part of the Evolution of FIRO Theory," The Human Element, 2009, https://thehumanelement.com/wp-content/uploads/2020/01/Wants_Not_Needs.pdf.
14. *Oxford English Dictionary*, "want," accessed February 16, 2025, https://www.oed.com/dictionary/want_v; *Merriam-Webster Dictionary*, "want," accessed February 16, 2025, https://www.merriam-webster.com/dictionary/want; Vocabulary.com, "want," accessed February 16, 2025, https://www.vocabulary.com/dictionary/want.
15. Schutz, "Wants, Not Needs."
16. Schutz, *The Human Element*, 35.
17. *Merriam-Webster Dictionary*, "dominant," accessed February 1, 2025, https://www.merriam-webster.com/dictionary/dominant.
18. *Merriam-Webster Dictionary*, "dominate," accessed February 16, 2025, https://www.merriam-webster.com/dictionary/dominate.
19. Schutz, *The Human Element*, 40.
20. Schutz, *The Human Element*, 41.
21. Schutz, *The Human Element*, 43.
22. Schutz, *The Human Element*, 43.
23. Schutz, *The Human Element*, 47.
24. You can find my video on Foundational Elements here: Marsha Clark, "Marsha Clark's Foundational Elements," May 30, 2018, by Marsha Clark & Associates, YouTube, 18:05, https://www.youtube.com/watch?v=DQuV72fCM6o.
25. *The Power Dead-Even Rule*, Heim Group, 46:00, https://heimgroup.com/product/the-power-dead-even-rule/.
26. Schutz, *The Human Element*, 47.
27. Schutz, *The Human Element*, 50.
28. Schutz, *The Human Element*, 50–51.
29. Schutz, *The Human Element*, 53.

30. *Oxford Languages*, "pretending," accessed February 17, 2025, https://www.google.com/search?q=pretending+definition.
31. Schutz, *The Human Element*, 69.
32. Schutz, *The Human Element*, 58.

CHAPTER 6

1. *American Heritage Dictionary*, "change," accessed February 17, 2025, https://ahdictionary.com/word/search.html?q=change.
2. "Serenity Prayer," Psalm 91, https://psalm91.com/2021/01/02/serenity-prayer/.

CHAPTER 8

1. Barry Oshry, *Seeing Systems: Unlocking the Mysteries of Organizational Life* (Berrett-Koehler, 2007), "Seeing the Big Picture, Act I."
2. *OED (Oxford English Dictionary),* "facilitator," accessed February 17, 2025, https://www.oed.com/dictionary/facilitator_n?tab=meaning_and_use.
3. Barry Oshry, Organization Workshop Certification training, used with permission.

CHAPTER 9

1. Barry Oshry is the founder of Power + Systems, Inc. of Boston. Power + System's network of Training Associates teaches the principles of total system empowerment to organizations and institutions throughout the world. Prior to founding Power + Systems in 1975, Barry served as chairman of the Organization Behavior Department at Boston University. He is a pioneer in the study of power and empowerment and in the development of educational programs addressing these and other social system issues. Power + Systems' high-impact educational programs have been hailed as major breakthroughs in illuminating the possibilities and challenges of organizational and community life. See www.powerandsystems.com.

CHAPTER 10

1. Linda Babcock and Sara Laschever, *Women Don't Ask: Negotiation and the Gender Divide* (Princeton University Press, 2021), introduction, page 1.
2. Babcock and Laschever, Women Don't Ask, introduction, page 3.
3. "Negotiating on Behalf of Others; Are Women Better Agents," *Harvard Law School Daily Blog*, April 6, 2009, https://www.pon.harvard.edu/daily/business-negotiations/negotiating-on-behalf-of-others-are-women-better-agents/.
4. Laura J. Kray, Jessica A. Kennedy, and Margaret Lee, "Now, Women Do Ask: A Call to Update Beliefs about the Gender Pay Gap," *Academy of Management Discoveries* 10, no. 1 (2024): 49, https://doi.org/10.5465/amd.2022.0021.
5. Kray et al., "Now, Women Do Ask," 13.
6. Kray et al., "Now, Women Do Ask," 31.
7. Babcock and Laschever, *Women Don't Ask*, 87.
8. Babcock and Laschever, *Women Don't Ask*, 106.
9. Anna B. Orlowska, Eva G Krumhuber, Magdalena Rychlowska, and Piotr Szarota, "Dynamics Matter: Recognition of Reward, Affiliative, and Dominance Smiles From Dynamic vs. Static Displays," *Frontiers in Psychology* 9 (2018): 938, https://www.ncbi.nlm.nih.gov/pmc/articles/PMC6004382/.
10. Orlowska et al., "Dynamics Matter."
11. "Healthy vs Abusive," A Better Way, https://abetterwaymuncie.org/resources/types-of-relationships/.
12. Oxford Languages, "Nonconfrontational," accessed February 21, 2025, https://www.google.com/search?q=non+confrontational+definition&sca_esv=044f2881569159f1&rlz=1C1SQJL_enUS876US879&sxsrf=AHTn8zo-ueUcYNd-dNdeWXU3v88vl2810A%3A1740171806992&ei=Huq4Z-KWPLbdwN4PiNO9yA4&oq=non-confrontational+defin&gs_l=Egxnd3Mtd2l6LXNlcnAiGW5vbi1jb25mcm9udGF0aW9uYWwgZGVmaW4qAggAMgYQABg WGB4yBhAAGBYYHjIGEAAYFhgeMgYQABgWGB4y

BhAAGBYYHjIGEAAYFhgeMgYQABgWGB4yBhAAGBYYHjIGEAAYFhge
MgYQABgWGB5IsaQBUJpgWIGaAXABeACQAQCYAY0
BoAGxBaoBBDEwLjG4AQHIAQD4AQH4AQKYAgyg
Au8FqAIUwgIHECMYJxjqAsICEBAuGMcBGCcY6gIYjgUYrwHCAg0QLhjR
AxjHARgnGOoCwgIQEAAYAxi0AhjqAhiPAdgBAcICEBAuGAMYtAIY6g
IYjwHYAQHCAgUQABiABMICCBAuGIAEGNQCwg
IEEAAYHsICChAAGIAEGEYY-QHCAiQQABiABBh
GGPkBGJcFGIwFGN0EGEYY-QEY9AMY9QMY9gPYAQHCAg
YQABgHGB7CAgsQABiABBiGAxiKBcICCBAAGIAEGKIEmAMM8QVT_
pz6pm7cdboGBggBEAEYCpIHBDExLjGgB5Ni&sclient=gws-wiz-serp.

13. "self-schema," *APA Dictionary of Psychology*, https://dictionary.apa.org/self-schema.
14. Babcock and Laschever, *Women Don't Ask*, 120.
15. Babcock and Laschever, *Women Don't Ask*, 120.
16. Babcock and Laschever, *Women Don't Ask*, 120.
17. Babcock and Laschever, *Women Don't Ask*, 120.
18. Babcock and Laschever, *Women Don't Ask*, 120.
19. Babcock and Laschever, *Women Don't Ask*, 131.
20. Rakesh Kochhar, "The Enduring Grip of the Gender Pay Gap," Pew Research Center, March 1, 2023, https://www.pewresearch.org/social-trends/2023/03/01/the-enduring-grip-of-the-gender-pay-gap/.
21. Nancy M. Carter and Christine Silva, *The Myth of the Ideal Worker: Does Doing All the Right Things Really Get Women Ahead?* (Catalyst, 2011), 10, https://www.catalyst.org/wp-content/uploads/2019/02/The_Myth_of_the_Ideal_Worker_Does_Doing_All_the_Right_Things_Really_Get_Women_Ahead.pdf.

CHAPTER 11

1. *The Cambridge Dictionary*, "Influence," accessed February 1, 2025, https://dictionary.cambridge.org/us/dictionary/english/influence.
2. Andrew Sobel and Jerold Panas, *Power Questions: Build New Relationships, Win New Business, and Influence Others* (Wiley Publishing, 2012), various pages.
3. Sobel and Panas, *Power Questions*, 3.
4. "Advocacy with Inquiry," The Complete Medic, https://thecompletemedic.com/communication/advocacy-with-inquiry.

5. Oshry, *Seeing Systems*, 85.
6. John F. Kennedy, "We Choose to Go to the Moon," Rice University, September 12, 1962, https://www.rice.edu/jfk-speech.
7. Martin Luther King Jr., "I Have a Dream," August 28, 1963, Lincoln Memorial, Washington, DC, Transcript, The Avalon Project, Yale Law School: Lillian Goldman Law Library, https://avalon.law.yale.edu/20th_century/mlk01.asp.
8. Francesca Gino and Bradley R. Staats, "Why Organizations Don't Learn," *Harvard Business Review*, November 2015, https://hbr.org/2015/11/why-organizations-dont-learn.
9. *Britannica Dictionary*, "perspective," accessed February 17, 2025, https://www.britannica.com/dictionary/perspective#:~:text=Britannica%20Dictionary%20definition%20of%20PERSPECTIVE,problem%20from%20a%20new%20perspective.
10. "What Is Critical Thinking," University of Louisville, https://louisville.edu/ideastoaction/about/criticalthinking/what#:~:text=Critical%20thinking%20is%20the%20intellectually%20disciplined%20process,as%20a%20guide%20to%20belief%20and%20action.
11. Bloom's Taxonomy, Utica.edu, https://www.utica.edu/academic/Assessment/new/Blooms%20Taxonomy%20-%20Best.pdf.

CHAPTER 12

1. Arthur Chan, LinkedIn, https://www.linkedin.com/posts/arthurpchan_diversity-is-a-fact-equity-is-a-choice-activity-6709122719918755840-WU76/.
2. Michelle Bogan, founder and CEO, Equity at Work; The Many Dimensions of Diversity. Graphic used with permission.
3. *Random House Unabridged Dictionary*, "equity," accessed February 17, 2025, https://www.infoplease.com/dictionary/equity.
4. Esteban Ortiz-Ospina, Joe Hasell, and Max Roser, "Economic Inequality by Gender," Our World in Data, March 2018 (revised March 2024), https://ourworldindata.org/economic-inequality-by-gender.
5. Ortiz-Ospina et al., "Economic Inequality by Gender."
6. Oxford Reference, "stereotype," accessed February 1, 2025, https://www.oxfordreference.com/display/10.1093/oi/authority.20110803100530532.

7. *Oxford Learner's Dictionaries,* "bias," accessed February 1, 2025, https://www.oxfordlearnersdictionaries.com/us/definition/english/bias_1.
8. Dr. Sandra Bem, an American psychologist, is best known for her pioneering research into gender roles and stereotypes. Her work had a direct impact on employment opportunities for women; Cynthia Vinney, "Gender Schema Theory Explained," ThoughtCo., updated August 22, 2019, https://www.thoughtco.com/gender-schema-4707892.
9. Chris Drew, "The 9 Types Of Stereotypes (A Guide for Students)," Helpful Professor.com, October 18, 2023, https://helpfulprofessor.com/types-of-stereotypes/.
10. Elsa Maishman, "Jacinda Ardern and Sanna Marin Dismiss Claim They Met Due to 'Similar Age,'" *BBC News*, November 30, 2022, https://www.bbc.com/news/world-63803342.
11. Martha Beck, "Seeing Your Emotional Blind Spots," *Martha's Blog*, https://marthabeck.com/2011/11/seeing-your-emotional-blind-spots/#:~:text=If%20the%20evidence%20suggests%20that,able%20to%20tolerate%20more%20awareness.
12. "5 Types of Unconscious Bias in the Workplace & How to Eliminate Them," Indeed.com, updated January 30, 2025, https://www.indeed.com/hire/c/info/unconscious-bias; "How to Address 11 Types of Bias in the Workplace," Indeed.com, updated November 20, 2024, https://www.indeed.com/hire/c/info/types-of-bias.
13. Arthur Hays Sulzberger, https://quotefancy.com/quote/1434794/Arthur-Hays-Sulzberger-Obviously-a-man-s-judgement-cannot-be-better-than-the-information.
14. Juliet Bourke, "The Six Signature Traits of Inclusive Leadership," *Deloitte Insights*, April 14, 2016, https://www2.deloitte.com/us/en/insights/topics/talent/six-signature-traits-of-inclusive-leadership.html.
15. Bourke, "The Six Signature Traits."
16. Bourke, "The Six Signature Traits."
17. Juliet Bourke and Andrea Titus, "The Key to Inclusive Leadership," *Harvard Business Review*, March 6, 2020, https://hbr.org/2020/03/the-key-to-inclusive-leadership.

18. Bourke, "The Six Signature Traits."
19. Quoted in Bourke, "The Six Signature Traits of Inclusive Leadership."
20. Bourke, "The Six Signature Traits."
21. Bourke, "The Six Signature Traits."
22. Bourke, "The Six Signature Traits."
23. *Oxford Reference*, "belonging," https://www.oxfordreference.com/display/10.1093/acref/9780199599868.001.0001/acref-9780199599868-e-113?rskey=AGkPIm&result=1.
24. "Sense of Belonging," Cornell University Diversity and Inclusion, https://diversity.cornell.edu/belonging/sense-belonging.
25. Angela Theisen, "Is Having a Sense of Belonging Important?," Mayo Clinic Health System, December 8, 2021, https://www.mayoclinichealthsystem.org/hometown-health/speaking-of-health/is-having-a-sense-of-belonging-important.

EPILOGUE

1. Oriah "Mountain Dreamer" House, *THE INVITATION* (HarperONE, 1999), presented with permission of the author, www.oriah.org.

ABOUT THE AUTHOR

Marsha Clark is an independent consultant who started her entrepreneurial journey in 2000, establishing her own company. With her rich background at EDS, where she ascended from secretary to corporate officer during her twenty-one-year tenure, Marsha brings a wealth of corporate experience to her consulting practice.

Over the past two decades, Marsha has become a driving force in the realm of leadership development, change management, strategic planning, performance management, team development, and executive coaching. A visionary leader, she has dedicated over twenty years specifically to crafting and delivering leadership development programs tailored for women. Marsha's unique approach revolves around a comprehensive four-stage developmental framework, progressing from the personal to the interpersonal, extending to teams, and ultimately impacting entire organizations. This holistic methodology ensures nuanced growth and development, fostering the emergence of dynamic leaders.

Marsha's global leadership and executive development programs have garnered worldwide recognition, solidifying her reputation as a prominent figure in the field.

Marsha is not only a seasoned consultant but also an Amazon Best Selling Author in two categories for her book *Embracing Your Power: A Woman's Path to Authentic Leadership & Meaningful Relationships.*

Complementing her literary success, she hosts a weekly podcast, *Your Authentic Path to Powerful Leadership*, accessible on marshaclarkandassociates.com.

In 2025 Marsha received the Women in Play Award recognizing her outstanding success and leadership in family, business, and philanthropy from the Volunteers of American Organization. Marsha's dedication and groundbreaking work in the field of women's leadership development continues to garner attention. Texas Women's Foundation celebrated Marsha in 2024 as a recipient of the Maura Women Helping Women Award. In 2021 Marsha received SMU Women's Symposium, Profiles in Leadership Award and was voted an Honoree of Women in Business by the *Dallas Business Journal*. She received the Accenture Plaque of Appreciation (Manila, The Philippines) in years 2013–2018. In 2015 Marsha received the EY Culture Coin, which represents the program she created for women that supported and reinforced their culture of diversity and inclusion. She is the only vendor to ever be awarded this Culture Coin. Marsha received the DFW Alliance of Technology & Women—Inaugural Lifetime Achievement Award in 2014. She is also a recipient of the Champion of Diversity award from UT Dallas. Marsha has received Honors from Women in Technology International (WITI)—Nominee for WITI Hall of Fame, 1999, and Dallas Women's Foundation—Circle of Honor, 1998.

Marsha supports numerous nonprofit organizations in many different ways. She is active in the community and has served on several nonprofit boards, especially those supporting women, girls, and children. She is currently the incoming Board President of the Children's Advocacy Center of Collin County. She provides pro-bono consulting services, volunteering, as well as financial support. Board memberships include Children's Advocacy Center of Collin County, Empowering Women as Leaders, Journey of Hope, Novus Academy, Power & Systems, and SPARK!